Spaniards in the Colonial Empire

Viewpoints/Puntos de Vista

Themes and Interpretations in Latin American History

Series editor: Jürgen Buchenau

The books in this series will introduce students to the most significant themes and topics in Latin American history. They represent a novel approach to designing supplementary texts for this growing market. Intended as supplementary textbooks, the books will also discuss the ways in which historians have interpreted these themes and topics, thus demonstrating to students that our understanding of our past is constantly changing, through the emergence of new sources, methodologies, and historical theories. Unlike monographs, the books in this series will be broad in scope and written in a style accessible to undergraduates.

Published

A History of the Cuban Revolution
Aviva Chomsky

Bartolomé de las Casas and the Conquest of the Americas
Lawrence A. Clayton

Beyond Borders: A History of Mexican Migration to the United States
Timothy J. Henderson

The Last Caudillo: Alvaro Obregón and the Mexican Revolution
Jürgen Buchenau

A Concise History of the Haitian Revolution
Jeremy Popkin

Spaniards in the Colonial Empire: Creoles vs. Peninsulars?
Mark A. Burkholder

In preparation

Dictatorship in South America
Jerry Davila

Mexico Since 1940: The Unscripted Revolution
Stephen E. Lewis

Spaniards in the Colonial Empire

Creoles vs. Peninsulars?

Mark A. Burkholder

WILEY-BLACKWELL

A John Wiley & Sons, Ltd., Publication

This edition first published 2013

Blackwell Publishing was acquired by John Wiley & Sons in February 2007. Blackwell's publishing program has been merged with Wiley's global Scientific, Technical, and Medical business to form Wiley-Blackwell.

Registered Office
John Wiley & Sons Ltd, The Atrium, Southern Gate, Chichester, West Sussex, PO19 8SQ, UK

Editorial Offices
350 Main Street, Malden, MA 02148-5020, USA
9600 Garsington Road, Oxford, OX4 2DQ, UK
The Atrium, Southern Gate, Chichester, West Sussex, PO19 8SQ, UK

For details of our global editorial offices, for customer services, and for information about how to apply for permission to reuse the copyright material in this book please see our website at www.wiley.com/wiley-blackwell.

Library of Congress Cataloging-in-Publication Data

Burkholder, Mark A., 1943-
Spaniards in the colonial empire : creoles vs. peninsulars? / Mark A. Burkholder.
p. cm. – (Viewpoints / Puntos de vista)
Includes bibliographical references and index.
ISBN 978-1-4051-9642-0 (hardback : alk. paper) – ISBN 978-1-4051-9641-3 (pbk.)
1. Creoles–Latin America–History. 2. Creoles–Legal status, laws, etc–Latin America–History. 3. Spaniards–Latin America–History. 4. Spaniards–Legal status, laws, etc.–Latin America–History. 5. Latin America–History–To 1830.
6. Spain–Colonies–Administration. I. Title.
F1419.C74B85 2013
980'.01–dc23

2012025033

A catalogue record for this book is available from the British Library.

Cover image: *A Spaniard and His Mexican Indian Wife and Their Child*, by Miguel Cabrera (1763) © The Gallery Collection / Corbis
Cover design by Richard Boxhall Design Associates

Set in 10 on 12.5 pt Minion by Toppan Best-set Premedia Limited

Printed in Malaysia by Ho Printing (M) Sdn Bhd

1 2013

For

Sue Burkholder, D. S. Chandler, and James S. Saeger

Contents

Illustrations

Maps

Figures

Series Editor's Preface

Each book in the *Viewpoints/Puntos de Vista* series introduces students to a significant theme or topic in Latin American history. In an age in which student and faculty interest in the Global South increasingly challenges the old focus on the history of Europe and North America, Latin American history has assumed an increasingly prominent position in undergraduate curricula.

Some of these books discuss the ways in which historians have interpreted these themes and topics, thus demonstrating that our understanding of our past is constantly changing, through the emergence of new sources, methodologies, and historical theories. Others offer an introduction to a particular theme by means of a case study or biography in a manner easily understood by the contemporary, nonspecialist reader. Yet others give an overview of a major theme that might serve as the foundation of an upper-level course.

What is common to all of these books is their goal of historical synthesis. They draw on the insights of generations of scholarship on the most enduring and fascinating issues in Latin American history, and through the use of primary sources as appropriate. Each book is written by a specialist in Latin American history who is concerned with undergraduate teaching, yet has also made his or her mark as a first-rate scholar.

The books in this series can be used in a variety of ways, recognizing the differences in teaching conditions at small liberal arts colleges, large public universities, and research-oriented institutions with doctoral programs. Faculty have particular needs depending on whether they teach large lectures with discussion sections, small lecture or discussion-oriented classes, or large lectures with no discussion sections, and whether they teach on a semester or trimester system. The format adopted for this series fits all of these different parameters.

In this sixth volume in the *Viewpoints/Puntos de Vista* series, Professor Mark Burkholder analyzes Spanish colonialism in the Americas from the vantage point of the "Spaniards" themselves, a group that included peninsulars, recent arrivals born in Spain, and creoles, people born of Spanish descent in the New World. *Spaniards in the Colonial Empire: Creoles vs. Peninsulars?* discusses the relationship between these groups, and particularly the growing conflict over the Crown's favoring of peninsulars for political office, which helped predicate the devastating Wars of Independence and, ultimately, the emergence of Latin American nations in the 1820s.

Burkholder skillfully disaggregates the terms "creole" and "peninsular," both of which included a wide variety of individuals from different social strata. He also examines the many similarities between the groups, including shared social, legal, and economic privileges that placed them atop colonial society. He pays close attention to intermarriages and other forms of union and cooperation between peninsulars and creoles, concluding that open conflict was rare before the Spanish empire in the Americas entered its decline following Napoleon's invasion of Spain in 1807. Ambitious in scope yet concise and accessible to undergraduate students, this is the only current work that brings the Spaniards in their vast colonial empire to life.

Jurgen Buchenau
University of North Carolina, Charlotte

Preface

This short book for undergraduates focuses on a large topic – creoles (Spaniards born in the "Indies," as they termed the New World), and their relationships, rivalries, and ultimately open conflict with peninsulars (Spaniards born in Spain). It pays particular attention to "native sons" and "native daughters," terms used as synonyms for "creoles" *within the region of their birth*, two issues, and an offensive attitude. The first issue is the rewards that native sons and daughters and other creole descendants of conquistadors and early settlers claimed they should receive in recognition of their ancestors' service to the Crown. The second issue concerns appointments to ecclesiastical and royal offices that native sons believed were legally theirs by virtue of their birthplace. The offensive attitude is the smug superiority that numerous peninsulars displayed in their relations with the rest of society, including native sons and daughters and other creoles, by reason of their birth in Spain and claims of unsullied Spanish ancestry. Portuguese born in Brazil similarly objected to immigrants from Portugal because of their arrogant attitude.

Spaniards in the Indies were either immigrants or born there. While place of birth affected their view of themselves and each other as well as their position in colonial society, all Spaniards in America enjoyed benefits denied to indigenous peoples and others of non-Spanish descent. This was also true in Brazil where Portuguese distinguished between compatriots from Iberia or *reinois* and native sons known as *mazombos* or *brasileiros*. Besides being peninsulars or creoles, Spaniards had other identities: all were natives of (*natural de*) a specific municipality and a larger administrative region. For example, creoles born in Arequipa, Peru, were native sons and daughters of that city as well as the region under the jurisdiction of the high court or *Audiencia* of Lima. Regions became their homelands or *patrias*; municipalities were their hometowns or *patrias chicas*. Both provided compatriots (*paisanos*) who frequently supported each other.

The collective term "creoles" is useful when applied broadly to Spaniards born in different jurisdictions. Whenever possible, however, this book employs "native sons" and "native daughters" and distinguishes them from "other creoles" born in different administrative and ecclesiastical units. The Crown made the same distinction. Importantly, it drew upon early Castilian legislation to justify a general policy of excluding native sons from royal offices with judicial responsibilities in their home jurisdiction because of family and economic ties. Native sons and daughters, of course, were not homogeneous. Disputes arose among them as well as with other groups in society. Differences in social "quality" (*calidad*), occupation and financial status also divided them from other creoles and peninsulars regardless of location or birthplace.

Conflict among Spaniards contesting the rewards of conquest in the New World pitted "old hands" – the first conquistadors and settlers – against later arrivals from Spain – the "newcomers" or "greenhorns." Antagonism also emerged between native sons, including the legitimate American-born descendants of old hands, and outsiders, whether peninsulars or creoles living away from their homelands. Repeatedly, native sons focused attention on institutions in which they faced discrimination. Initially this included admission to religious orders; subsequently it expanded to elective positions within these orders' provinces or territorial units. The Crown's appointment of peninsulars to ecclesiastical and royal offices to which native sons asserted a legal right provoked repeated and outspoken protest.

Despite internal rivalries, all whites in the Indies shared identifiable cultural characteristics. Originally they referred to themselves as "Christians" and "Spaniards" regardless of place of birth. Most arrived in the Indies speaking Castilian Spanish. They shared a belief in Christianity and allegiance to a single monarch; emphasized honor and marital, family, local, and regional bonds; pursued economic interests; and displayed an attitude of superiority toward the rest of society. These commonalities helped to unite them regardless of place of birth.

By the early 1560s, the word *criollo* or "creole" designated a Spaniard born in the Indies. *Criollo* is derived from the Portuguese *crioulo*, a word that imported Africans (*bozales*) used to refer derogatorily to American-born descendants of earlier slaves. This connection to slavery gave "creole" a pejorative connotation, although by the late seventeenth century, some native sons proudly adopted it. Other synonyms for creole included *indiano, hijo de la tierra, benemérito* and, especially in the eighteenth century, *español americano* (American Spaniard) or simply *americano* (American). From the seventeenth century onward, *gachupín* (one who wear spurs) in New Spain and *chapetón* (tenderfoot or greenhorn) elsewhere became widespread although somewhat deprecating terms for recently arrived Spanish immigrants in particular. "Peninsular" as a synonym for a person born in Spain entered frequent usage in the early nineteenth century as an outgrowth of the "Peninsular War," as the British dubbed the conflict fought against Napoleon's armies in Iberia from 1808 to 1814. Because of its convenience, historians continue to apply the term when identifying Spaniards born in Spain. Far from their birthplace, these immigrants quickly realized that their identity had to encompass more than the village, town, or even city and bishopric from which they came. Thus, they identified themselves by their "nation" or region in Spain, for example, as Andalusians, Extremadurans, Basques (conflating the Basque Provinces of Vizcaya, Guipúzcoa, and Alava, plus sometimes Navarre), and *Montañeses* (as persons from the mountains of Burgos north into Cantabria or Santander were known). At times, language separated the immigrants. The majority shared the Castilian dialect, but Basques, Galicians, and Catalans often had to learn that language in America.

Creoles frequently asserted that recent immigrants only sought to get rich quickly and return wealthy to Spain, but probably less than 10% ever did so. Most found work in the Indies, established a residence, and embedded themselves in their new locale. This book uses "radicados" as a collective term for "rooted" Spaniards or Portuguese who settled outside of their homeland (*patria*) and often married in their new place of residence; developed local economic, family, and political interests; and became heads of citizen households (*vecinos*) in their new municipality.[1]

Contemporaries writing about the wars of independence in the early nineteenth century emphasized the importance of peninsular discrimination against creoles and claimed superiority over them as a cause of the conflicts. Independence itself brought the expulsion or execution of peninsulars either during the conflict or soon afterward in every former mainland colony. Native sons and other political and military leaders repeatedly made their Old World rivals scapegoats as well as a source of funds. The Liberator Simón Bolívar's infamous proclamation of "war to the death" was the most extreme example of anti-peninsular policy. But patriots also hurled phrases like "300 years of servitude" as political slogans and to draw attention to creoles' claim during and immediately after the wars of sharing centuries of oppression with the indigenous population.

But how widespread was discrimination against creoles? How deep was their antipathy toward peninsulars? It is impossible to know for certain, but after the age of conquest, a relatively small number of immigrants arrived with enviable positions or achieved remarkable financial success. In contrast, examples of poor whites – of both genders and regardless of place of birth – abound.

Enviable peninsulars were those who gained wealth and honors. They included very successful wholesale merchants and a much smaller number of miners; high-ranking officeholders and clerics; and retainers who accompanied viceroys and bishops to their posts, especially in the Habsburg centuries, and received benefits as a result. Aside from clerics, many of these immigrants married native daughters who thus created ties that rooted their husbands in their district of residence and distinguished them from unmarried Spaniards. These *radicados* were probably as likely to take a "native son" position, or one of several positions, on most issues of the day as were local creoles.

This book is one of the few scholarly efforts to examine the relationship between creoles in general and native sons and daughters in particular with peninsulars from the sixteenth century through independence. It goes beyond claimed discrimination to pay special attention to the extent to which native sons and other creoles actually secured offices. Among its points are the following: (i) all persons recognized as Spaniards in the Indies, regardless of gender or place of birth, enjoyed privileges that set them apart from the rest of the population; (ii) the native son heirs of conquistadors and early settlers could document royal promises of preference for certain appointments; (iii) conflicts between peninsulars and creoles were most vehement in the male religious orders, but occurred in the nunneries as well; (iv) American-born lawyers, especially those educated in Lima, both advocated for native son and other creole preference and were among the beneficiaries of royal patronage; (v) recently arrived peninsulars ignited more opposition than those of longer residence; (vi) cooperation, mutual interest, and native daughter incorporation of peninsulars into local elites through marriage characterized most creole–peninsular relations at the apex of local society throughout the empire; (vii) despite repeated allegations to the contrary, the number of elite creoles genuinely hostile toward peninsulars was rarely large prior to

1808–1810, but increased over the next 10–15 years; and (viii) during the wars of independence and formation of independent states, leaders spawned an unprecedented level of opposition to peninsulars that resulted in confiscation of their property, expulsion, and sometimes death.

Acknowledgments

This book would not have been possible without the work of other historians. While its format and student audience preclude a lengthy multi-language bibliography, I want to single out the contributions of the following scholars: Lucrecia Raquel Enríquez Agrazar; Javier Barrientos Grandon, Michel Bertrand, Paulino Castañeda Delgado, Jorge Comadrán Ruiz, Paul Ganster, Bernard Lavallé, Guillermo Lohmann Villena, Juan Marchena Fernández, Oscar Mazín Gómez, Angel Sanz Tapia, Ernst Schäfer, John Frederick Schwaller, Stuart B. Schwartz, Renan Silva, and Susan M. Socolow. Their publications, materials that D. S. Chandler and I gathered long ago, and subsequent information I have collected provide the core of the book's discussion of royal officials and clerics.

I thank Jürgen Buchenau and Peter Coveney for supporting the proposal that led to this book and Allison Medoff for shepherding the manuscript through the publication process. Douglas Catterall encouraged me to think of the project as a contribution to the history of the Atlantic World. Conversations and coauthored publications with D. S. Chandler many years ago laid the basis for the book's emphasis on native sons and *radicados*. Mary Zettwoch and Erica Marks at the Thomas Jefferson Library of the University of Missouri-St. Louis consistently provided outstanding interlibrary loan service. I greatly appreciate the anonymous readers who offered thoughtful and at times trenchant critiques of the manuscript. Additionally, I am grateful to Kristen M. Burkholder for carefully reading a late draft of the manuscript despite the constraints on her time. The result is a much better book for which I alone remain responsible for errors and foibles. With grace and charm, Carol D. Burkholder endured my seemingly endless hours at the computer. I thank her for her love and support.

Mark A. Burkholder
St. Louis, Missouri

Map 1 Bishoprics in the Americas, 1620.

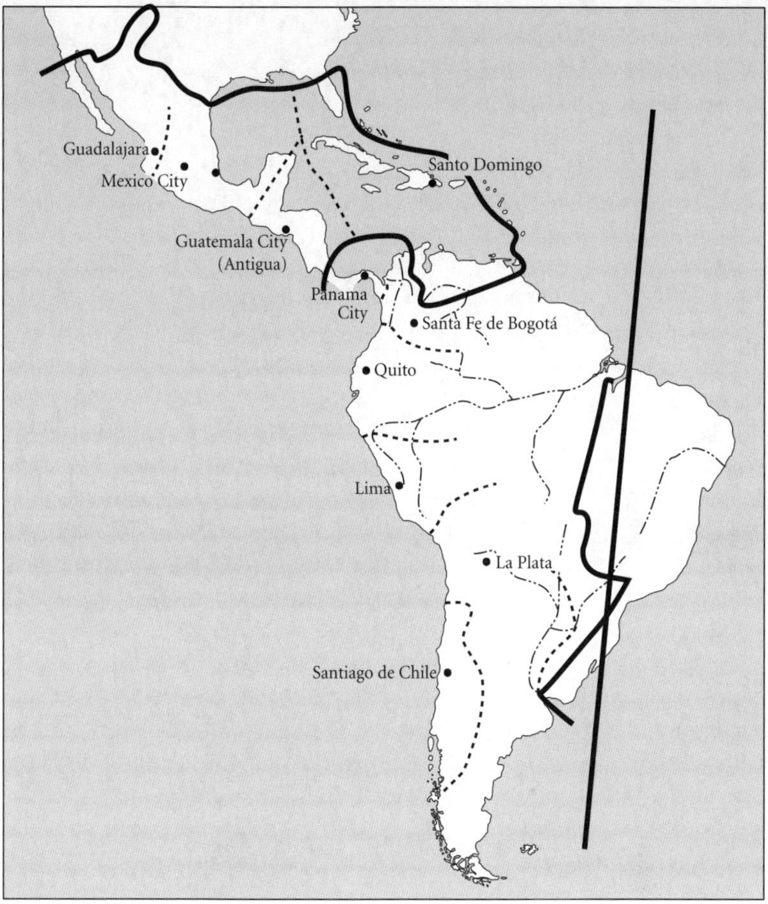

Map 2 *Audiencia* Capitals, 1750.

1

Spain and Its Early Empire in America

On the eve of Europeans' first sustained contact with the Americas, Castile was the largest, most prosperous, and most populous kingdom of the Iberian Peninsula. Victory over the Muslims in Granada in 1492 confirmed Castilians' belief that they enjoyed their God's favor. Simultaneously it demonstrated that military success led grateful monarchs to reward service on their behalf by enriching aristocrats, elevating commoners into the nobility, and providing poor soldiers with land.

Conquistadors, settlers, officials, merchants, clerics, and a growing stream of Spanish women followed Columbus and other explorers, founded municipalities, expanded royal dominion, and sought corresponding recompense. As settlement followed conquest, the immigrants replicated insofar as possible the social organization they had left behind, with the important difference that many assumed more elevated social status. Their leaders awarded the most fortunate grants of native labor and tribute (*encomiendas*). These *encomenderos* became a new but insecure nobility, for the Crown initially recognized the grants for only one lifetime rather than making them hereditary. Thus, it denied recipients a key attribute in the perpetuation of aristocratic families in Spain while making them dependent on royal favor. Charles I (1516–1556) introduced royal officials to oversee the tribute and labor that reverted to the Crown as the original recipients died. At the same time, he indicated that he would name unrewarded conquistadors and their heirs to these new positions. The installation of government offices, the erection of bishoprics, an increase in missionaries, and the foundation of nunneries

Spaniards in the Colonial Empire: Creoles vs. Peninsulars?, First Edition. Mark A. Burkholder.

accompanied the continued arrival of peninsular immigrants and the growing number of their predecessors' native son and other creole descendants. By 1580, the institutions of Church and state as well as a transatlantic trading system were in place, and rising silver production was enriching the treasury of Philip II. By this date as well, descendants of the conquistadors and early settlers recognized that the prosperity based on *encomiendas* had largely disappeared and their pursuit of positions in the Church and state intensified.

Spain on the Eve of Empire

Marked by mountains, few navigable rivers, and an extensive coastline, the Iberian Peninsula in 1492 contained five kingdoms. Castile, Aragon, Granada, and Navarre would later comprise the country known as Spain; Portugal was joined to the Crown of Castile from 1580 to 1640. Conquered by Muslim invaders that first arrived from North Africa in 711, Iberia was the site of intermittent warfare for centuries as Christians emerged from modest mountain bases in the north and commenced what became known as the Reconquest. Toledo fell to the Christians in 1085 and in the thirteenth century Ferdinand III of Castile and León conquered Córdoba, Murcia, Seville, and Cádiz. The advance southward brought booty, land, and upward social mobility, especially for mounted warriors. As a legendary hero in a thirteenth-century epic declared, "I gain more in war than I do in peace, for the poor knight lives better in times of war than in times of peace."[1] By the mid-eleventh century, the expanding nobility sought to limit this status to their children, but intermittent warfare on the moving frontier impelled monarchs to reward the military contributions of particularly valorous commoners with ennoblement.

As the frontier advanced, the Crown encouraged repopulation through the creation of chartered Christian municipalities and land grants. Settlers in new and refounded towns received urban and rural plots and access to the community's land. Nobles gained and later expanded large estates, as did the military orders of Alcántara, Calatrava, and Santiago. The fall in 1492 of Granada, the last independent Muslim kingdom, reinforced the booty mentality of the Reconquest and reaffirmed commoners' awareness that conquest on behalf of the Castilian Crown could yield noble rank among other rewards. Some 35 000–40 000 Christian colonists arrived to repopulate the kingdom between 1485 and 1499, and by 1530, about 100 000 were present. Leaving one's home for an anticipated better life remained attractive.

Inheritance shaped ruling families and their patrimony as well as those of nobles and commoners. The Spanish monarch Charles I (1516–1556) inherited through his Castilian mother the kingdoms of Castile, Aragon, and Navarre, the Basque Provinces, Sicily and Naples, and the Indies; from his Habsburg father he received the provinces of the Netherlands, Franche Comté, and Austrian and German lands. He ruled each of these territorial units as if it were his only realm, confirming its laws and privileges or *fueros* as the latter were known in Spain. As sovereign of a vast composite monarchy, Charles united his extensive inheritance through his person rather than by common laws, customs, taxes, institutions, or languages.

Nearly all Iberians in the late fifteenth century were commoners. In cities and towns they included merchants and international traders, professionals in law and medicine, officials, clerics, retailers, artisans, tradesmen, and domestics. Most commoners – over 80% of them – lived in villages, farmed, raised livestock, and worked as artisans, tradesmen, and weavers. They walked to their fields, grazed animals, and gathered wood from their town's municipal lands.

Villages provided residents with a sense of identity, a focus of loyalty, and kinship ties. Villagers were citizens and local office holders. Prejudiced regarding outsiders, they would occasionally resort to violence against men from other villages over such things as boundary disputes and use of municipal woodlands and pastures. Nevertheless, they needed those outsiders. Itinerant peddlers often sold the items not available in local shops. Rural craftsmen and artisans including shoemakers, blacksmiths, and carpenters similarly took to the road to expand their market. Migration and mobility were frequent and not simply a response to economic woes or other problems.

At the base of Iberian society were slaves. Slavery was common during the Reconquest as victors enslaved prisoners of war; the conquest of Granada (1482–1492) yielded thousands. African slaves entered Iberia from trans-Saharan trade by at least the fourteenth century, and starting in 1479, the Portuguese became major suppliers of sub-Saharan slaves.

Everywhere in Iberia, the Church with its clerics, saints, relics, and bells affected inhabitants' lives. Like the nobility and municipalities, the Church as a corporate body had its own *fuero*. Numerous clerics ministered in urban churches and monasteries, but every village had a parish church, celebrated a patron saint, and enjoyed religious festivals. The presence of a cleric on even an occasional basis emphasized the centrality of religion in village life. So, too, did the requirement to pay the tithe, a tax on agricultural production, and the increase in livestock that went to the Church.

Place of Birth and Identity

Iberians' greatest loyalty was to their family and the municipality within which they were born and lived. This allegiance diminished as the municipality was included in a larger jurisdiction. Thus, a man born in Seville would identify himself first by his family, then as a *sevillano* (native or *natural de* Seville), next as an Andalusian, and finally as a Castilian or Spaniard. Each Castilian was a subject or vassal of the monarch as well as a citizen of a municipality, the foundational building block of the kingdom's territorial organization. Although cities were self-governing and initially exempt from royal jurisdiction in their internal affairs, in the many towns and their villages under the jurisdiction of an ecclesiastical or noble lord or a military order, citizens were also vassals of their lord. Castilians' identity thus expanded from family to municipality to lord to Crown.

By birthright free individuals in Castile became citizens (*vecinos*) of their home village, town, or city. This status typically began when marriage transformed a new husband into a family head. As a citizen he fell under his municipality's judicial system, normally paid its taxes, and could be counted on to display solidarity with neighbors against outsiders from another village. Outsiders were initially suspect even (or perhaps especially) when born in an adjacent town. After taking up residency in a new locale, it required time for them to become citizens themselves, a status that often followed marriage to a local woman and the payment of local taxes.

Monarchs of Castile in the sixteenth and seventeenth centuries confirmed villages' right of self-government, generally acknowledged that local citizens should hold local offices, and accepted that those born in them enjoyed preference. Accordingly, a native (*natural de*) and citizen (*vecino*) of a village enjoyed specific privileges that originated in charters granted during the Reconquest. Place of birth also restricted royal appointments and ecclesiastical positions. Within Castile and Aragon, men native to each kingdom filled its posts. When the Crown of Castile annexed the southern portion of Navarre in 1513, the terms of its incorporation limited to a handful the number of Castilian officials in the kingdom. Clerics similarly benefited by appointments to ecclesiastical positions in the diocese of their birth.

Opposition to outsiders could be intense. The Comuneros' Rebellion of municipalities and some lower nobles against Charles I in 1520 occurred in part because the monarch, an outsider born in the Flemish city of Ghent and initially unable to speak Castilian, arrived with numerous Flemish advisors. These quickly acquired prominent positions and devoted themselves to self-enrichment. Although the rebellion failed, Castilians long remembered its defense of native sons' right to offices.

The Model of the Castilian Nobility

Legislation divided Castilian society into distinct estates (noble, clerical, and commoner) and corporate bodies based on function, for example, merchants' and artisans' guilds, each with its own judicial status. Villages frequently included nobles as well as commoners who were peasant-farmers (*labradores*). Their offices might be divided between the two estates or selected without distinction. In general, the percentage of nobles in Castile declined from north to south. Most Andalusian aristocrats made Seville their urban residence. Although only 15 of its nobles held the titles of count, marquis, or duke at the end of the sixteenth century, they included several of great opulence, enormous rural properties, and jurisdiction over numerous villages. Their princely and ornately decorated palaces, abundant retainers and servants, costly clothing, horses, and other signs of riches and status provided a model observed by the thousands of emigrants who left for the Indies via this port city on the Guadalquivir River. Of course all emigrants recognized the affluence, power, and privileges of members of aristocratic families located closest to their homes, but most nobles were of lower rank. These *hidalgos* tenaciously claimed the benefits of their estate, but typically lacked the wealth of the urban and titled nobility.

Nobility initially rested on leadership and notably valorous military deeds, but lineage was its usual source in the fifteenth century. Nonetheless, Ferdinand of Aragon and Isabel of Castile distributed hundreds of grants of nobility (*hidalguía*) as compensation for personal and military contributions, especially in the years before, during, and immediately after the fall of Granada. By explicitly identifying the reciprocity between service and tangible rewards on the eve of empire, the Crown ensured that the conquistadors in America would expect royal remuneration proportional to their achievements.

Nobility conveyed legal benefits that included exemptions from imprisonment for debt; seizure of one's house, horse, or weaponry for debt; torture; and certain types of punishment. Of particular symbolic importance was exemption from the direct taxation (*pecho*) paid by commoners. Indeed, documenting if one owned arms and horses, lived a military lifestyle, and was a descendant of a family that had not paid the direct tax for three years or more was often sufficient to demonstrate *hidalgo* status. In addition, noblemen alone were eligible for knighthoods in the military orders.

The number of nobles created by Ferdinand and Isabel and their successors paled in comparison to nobles by heredity. Nobility was a family rather than an individual quality, and noble lineage, especially through the male line, was its most important qualification. The titled nobility of dukes, marquises, and counts numbered fewer than a dozen in 1400, and Castile had but 62 in 1520 and about 120 as late as 1600. As a sign of their rank, titled nobles and their legitimate offspring were addressed as "don" ("lord") or "doña" ("lady"), honorifics whose usage spread to the lower nobility starting in the early sixteenth century. In the late sixteenth century, some 10% of the population of Castile claimed nobility, the highest percentage in a western European country.

Early in his reign, Charles I, established grandees as the highest nobility of Castile. This additional honor confirmed the preeminence of a small number of families, most with titles of nobility awarded after 1450, that owned enormous, entailed estates (*mayorazgos*) over whose residents they exercised jurisdiction and collected fees (*señorío*). The privileges of the nobility in general and the ability of grandees and other nobles to transfer wealth and seigneurial rights to their heirs constituted a model that conquistadors and first settlers in America soon sought to emulate.

Religion

For centuries religion divided the Castilian population into Christians, Jews, and Muslims. The substantial majority was composed of "Old

Christians," those whose families were Christian before the forced conversion of many Jews in 1391 created "New Christians" or *conversos.* Spain's religious diversity ended when Ferdinand and Isabel expelled the Jews in 1492 and the Muslims in 1502. Their actions simultaneously increased the number of *conversos* and made emigration attractive. Despite legislative prohibitions, some New Christians would sail to the Indies and settle there.

In the mid-fifteenth century, statutes began to require proof of *limpieza de sangre* ("purity of blood"). Designed to exclude New Christians from civil and ecclesiastical positions, entry into a knighthood, and even some educational opportunities, they forced aspirants to prove their eligibility through documenting a lineage without Jewish or Muslim ancestors. The military orders became renowned for their detailed reviews of ancestry; obtaining a knighthood "proved" *limpieza de sangre* and frequently noble ancestry as well.

With few exceptions, early Castilian emigrants to America took with them a shared belief in Christianity as well as loyalty to their monarch, extended family, and others from their hometown. They left a social environment marked by hierarchy and corporate bodies as well as widespread prejudice against outsiders and newcomers. They also carried an understanding of the characteristics and significance of nobility in Castilian society and a conviction that conquest and the establishment of permanent municipalities would bring royal recompense that could include noble status and income. Immigrants in the Indies drew upon these values as they sought the upward social mobility and economic status beyond their reach in Iberia. Thus, they worked to create a living environment complete with the Iberian food, drink, and amenities they enjoyed. Of particular importance, they believed, like nobles in Castile, that they would be able to bequeath rewards they had earned to their descendants.

Peninsulars Create Their New World

Iberians first arrived in the western hemisphere or "the Indies," as Christopher Columbus christened it, in 1492. Soon, Spanish ships were annually depositing European Spaniards, almost exclusively Castilians, in America. African slaves brought from Seville first reached the New World in 1501, and their regular importation from Africa began in 1518, the eve of Fernando Cortés' expedition to the mainland that includes today's Mexico. By 1580, the institutional and geographical frameworks of both state and Church extended from New Spain in the north to Chile in the south and from the coast of the Pacific Ocean in the west to the Atlantic coast in the east. Cities were the lifeblood of Spanish civilization and, throughout this vast area, Spanish and Portuguese explorers and settlers had established more than 225 municipalities. As chronicler Francisco López de Gómara noted: "Without settlement there is no good conquest, and if the land is not conquered, the people will not be converted."[2] With the permanent founding of Buenos Aires in 1580, the contours of regional societies built around a small number of administrative and commercial cities and mining centers were firmly in place, and Brazil's sugar production was underway in the region around Bahia.

Crossing the Atlantic

Iberian emigrants, like the French, English, and Dutch who followed them to America, shared the common experience of crossing the Atlantic Ocean. Sailing from Andalusia to Española averaged a little over seven weeks; reaching Vera Cruz or the Isthmus of Panama frequently required another three to four weeks. Lisbon to Bahia could take up to two months, depending on the season. No transatlantic voyage was for the faint hearted. Before sailing, Spaniards were to document their *limpieza de sangre* and to obtain a royal license specifying a destination and reason for traveling. Private citizens often noted their poverty and a relative in the Indies who had offered to pay for the trip. By 1600, Portuguese emigrants also had to secure a license to sail to Brazil.

Ships in the early sixteenth century often accommodated between 100 and 120 people who had on average less than 17 ft^2 each for luggage, a sea chest, and food. Also on board were pigs, sheep, goats, chickens, cockroaches, lice, and bedbugs. Only the wealthiest travelers could obtain privacy in small wooden chambers constructed in the castle of the ship. Other voyagers made do with hanging curtains. Another cost was travel to Seville. Since it took some 80 days to walk from Asturias or a still long 30 days from Madrid, reaching Seville could require a significant sum. The total expenses meant that licensed passengers were persons who had some means, had access to credit, had passage paid by the Crown or a relative already in the Indies, or were in the employ of another traveler.

Not uncommonly, emigrants liquidated their assets to pay for the trip. Notwithstanding examples of stowaways and forged licenses, the best way to get to the Indies for young men without means was to join a prominent official's retinue or to sign on as a sailor. More ships departed for America than returned and to jump ship at a New World port was usually relatively easy.

Spanish Emigrants to the Indies: Males

Men were the first Europeans to reach the Indies. Columbus transported no women on either his initial voyage or, although accompanied by 1500 males, on the second in 1493. The growing presence of abusive and exploitive Spaniards and the ravages of epidemic disease nearly eliminated the indigenous population on the island of Española in less than 30 years. Rapidly publicized conquests, led most notably by Fernando Cortés in Mexico and Francisco Pizarro in Peru, attracted additional immigrants. Bernal Díaz del Castillo, a foot soldier with Cortés, summarized their objectives: "[T]o serve God and His Majesty, to give light to those who were in darkness, and to grow rich, as all men desire to do."[3] Between 1560 and 1600, males accounted for over 70% of the arrivals from Iberia and comprised an even larger majority for the remainder of Spanish rule.

High mortality and disappointment plagued the early newcomers. Many returned to Spain and others perished prematurely, including two-thirds of all Spaniards in Española within the first decade of settlement. Overall mortality among the conquistadors on the mainland of America was also high. Despite exaggeration and self-promoting claims, survivors and descendants of deceased conquistadors had a solid factual foundation when referring to the suffering and death of their companions, fathers, and other relatives. The expedition to Castilla del Oro in 1514 led by Pedrarias de Avila left Seville with 1500 men or more; soon after landing at Darien two-thirds of them died. More than half of 2100 Spanish conquistadors of the Aztec capital of Tenochtitlan were killed. An even worse disaster was the expedition led by Pánfilo de Narváez to Florida in 1527; only four of approximately 600 men survived. Some 1600 men led by Pedro de Mendoza arrived at the River Plate in early 1536. Two-thirds of them died by late 1537 and, according to a German chronicler, some survivors succumbed to cannibalism.

Like gamblers unable to leave the table, many Spanish conquistadors repeatedly joined expeditions in their search for greater and sometimes any rewards. Among the conquistadors of Tenochtitlan, almost a quarter reached the Indies by the end of 1513, and nearly 20% were remnants of the large, disastrous expedition led by Pedrarias Dávila. Many would-be or actual conquistadors perished, leaving neither wife nor legitimate children behind. High mortality underscored a widespread belief among survivors throughout the Indies that, as one of them expressed: "[T]he least of the conquistadors merited great reward, for at his own expense . . . he gave the king so great a world as this."[4] In 1519, Europeans in the Indies totaled fewer than 5000 spread among a small number of municipalities and the Cortés expedition.

Length of time in the Indies influenced a conquistador's opportunities and rewards. Fernando Cortés probably arrived in 1506 and his chief lieutenant, Pedro de Alvarado did so in 1510. About half of the 168 "Men of Cajamarca" who captured the Inca Atahuallpa and shared his ransom had spent five years or more in the Indies. Approximately half of the identified conquistadors of New Granada boasted five to nine years of prior New World experience. The difference in an expedition led by an "old hand" like Cortés or Francisco Pizarro or by a "greenhorn" like Pedrarias could determine success or death.

Claims of nobility by conquistadors and first settlers in New Spain, Peru, and elsewhere increased over time. In fact, probably more than 90% were commoners. Only 16 *hidalgos* were present with Cortés at the founding of Vera Cruz in 1519, and just 69 have been confirmed among over 1200 identified conquistadors of Tenochtitlan. Nobles among the "Men of Cajamarca" numbered an unusually high 23%. Other than royal officials, subsequent immigrants were also mostly commoners, but, aside from some sailors, generally above the dregs of society. Early arrivals included a few professionals, merchants, artisans ranging from cobblers and tanners to blacksmiths and silversmiths, and varied laborers. The missing category was peasant-farmer, by far the dominant occupation in Spain. New arrivals of this background had no intention of engaging in agricultural labor again. Notably, Spanish immigrants in the Indies included neither numerous criminals sent into exile, as was the case in Brazil, nor indentured servants as comprised 75–85% of English immigrants in the Chesapeake in the seventeenth century.

By the mid-sixteenth century, single, vagabond Spanish males of unspecified birthplace were causing problems. The instructions for viceroy of New Spain Luis de Velasco in 1550 identified these men as settling in native villages where they abused the indigenous people, raped wives and daughters, and created other difficulties. Velasco was to remove them from the villages and order them to find gainful employment. He was also to watch the peninsular secular clerics and friars, a majority of whose behavior allegedly set bad examples.

Nearly 70% of over 55 000 identified immigrants between 1493 and 1600 came from Andalusia, Extremadura, and New Castile. Their origins gave them first-hand knowledge of nobles owning and controlling large estates and villages populated by impoverished laborers. Although small in number, Basques were the most distinctive group to arrive. They participated in the expansion and administration of Castile's possessions in the Indies as captains and sailors, merchants and miners, clerics and officials. They brought skills in deep-sea fishing, iron production, shipbuilding, agriculture, herding, and international commerce. Additionally, they enjoyed historic privileges confirmed by Charles I. These included juridical equality and "universal nobility," the latter endowing them with a unique and favored legal status that, added to their frequent success and prominence, fueled resentment among other peninsulars, notably those from Andalusia and Extremadura.

Basque inheritance practices accustomed families to their sons leaving home. They favored a single heir, whether male or female, and sons passed over worked either outside of the farmstead on their community's common lands or beyond their native locale in mines, foundries, commerce, or other activities. Extending their destination to the Indies remained within the traditional practice. Although some learned to speak Castilian, all spoke Euskara, their native tongue. When residing outside of their native locale, they had a history of creating mutually advantageous networks that, like their universal nobility and distinctive language, often set them apart from other emigrants.

In sum, Spanish emigrants to the Indies ranged from the small numbers of grandees who sailed as viceroys in the sixteenth and seventeenth centuries to stowaways and single-trip sailors unable to pay their passage. They included the fully literate, persons able only to sign their names, and many complete illiterates. Although entire families made the voyage, a majority of travelers were young men eager for a better life in the more open societies and economies of the Indies. Wealthy or poor, literate or not, Europeans arrived with a skin color that marked them as "white" and a spoken language that underlined their distinctiveness. At least in their own eyes, pale skin placed them above persons of indigenous, African, or mixed ancestry.

Relatively few Europeans realized the dream of returning to Spain. The men present at Cajamarca were unique in receiving substantial shares of gold and silver, a form of riches that, along with precious jewels, could be transported to Spain. Nonetheless, more than half of them remained in the Indies. As part of an extraordinarily fortunate conquest, they could usually obtain an *encomienda* and remain in Peru as part of a new, self-styled aristocracy. But even very successful men discovered that the economic and social advantages they had gained in America were place bound. One could neither transfer Indian laborers, land, nor office to Spain nor safely leave them with an overseer or manager charged with forwarding profits via Seville. Probably more than 90% of the immigrants remained in the Indies, although some tried multiple locations.

Spanish Emigrants to the Indies: Females

Few Spanish women sailed to the Americas before 1560. Columbus conveyed the first ones, a total of 30, on his third voyage in 1498. Nearly 10% of the identified females reached the Caribbean by 1519; these early arrivals sailed primarily to already settled Española. A small number subsequently accompanied campaigns of conquest. At least 15 *conquistadoras* followed Cortés; at most two remained single. In contrast, only men were present at Pizarro's celebrated capture of the Inca, although two presumably immigrant women joined them at Cajamarca and accompanied them to Cuzco. The percentage of females increased between the 1520s and 1550s and exceeded 25% of the newcomers for the remainder of the sixteenth century. About 60% of those arriving from 1560 to 1599 were unmarried.

The number of Spanish women in Peru rose from maybe 200 at the time of Pizarro's assassination in 1541 to perhaps 1000 of about 8000 Spaniards in 1555. High male mortality in the Indies left numerous widows. Those with a handsome inheritance from their first husband often remarried a second, third, or even fourth time. The creation of female convents that began in 1540 only modestly reduced the number of Spanish women eligible for marriage.

The Crown recognized the potential damage to families resulting from husbands leaving their wives thousands of miles away and for extended periods of time. Already before Cortés initiated the Conquest of Mexico, the Crown exhorted and even threatened married Spaniards living in the Indies without their wives. Husbands were either to return to their wives in Spain or to send for them; the order clearly sidestepped the reality that some married men undoubtedly had fled to the Indies to get away from their spouses.

The desire to encourage stable families in America led sixteenth-century monarchs to extend benefits to husbands living with their wives. These included continuation of an *encomienda*, land grants near a desirable Spanish settlement, offices, and tax breaks. The incentives worked, especially since early *encomiendas* supported an *encomendero* and his extended family, retainers, and servants. Their recipients were willing to marry for the sake of their households as well as the desire to father a legitimate heir with a Spanish wife. Typically, both spouses wed for practical reasons rather than love. At a reception in Mexico for several young female immigrants in 1528, the guests of honor entertained each other at the expense of their host and his friends. Some women remarked that they would never marry "those rotten old men." One observed, however, that the men would die soon and leave their assets behind. Then, she added, "[W]e will be able to choose a young man of our liking to take the place of the old one, as one changes an old, broken pot for a new one in good condition." Although the conversation angered the conquistadors that overheard it, the women almost certainly found husbands in a marriage market that for several decades overwhelmingly favored females from Spain.[5] Only 32 of nearly 500 *encomenderos* in Peru were single in 1563.

By 1600, over 10 000 identified Spanish females had reached the Indies. During the two previous decades, Peru attracted more than New Spain, and New Granada was a distant third. Female Portuguese immigrants in Brazil were always fewer in number than their Spanish counterparts in the Indies. Female Spaniards usually reached America either as wives accompanying their husbands or as daughters or nieces journeying with parents or another relative. Many husbands established themselves and then called for their wives and other relatives, both male and female, to join them. Licensing officials considered this an acceptable reason for travel when accompanied by a promise of necessary financial support.

After the mid-sixteenth century, families sailing together were more common than earlier. Nonetheless, even then, Spanish families were only about half as likely to emigrate as a group as were English families that arrived in New England in the seventeenth century.

The Spanish Crown's policy toward single women journeying to the Indies varied over time. In 1539 it tried to prevent such travel, but the restriction proved ineffective. Faced with a surfeit of women in Spain and a shortage in the Americas, it subsequently encouraged their passage. While single women did emigrate as servants and retainers of officials' wives, only eight unwed females were among more than 50 retainers and servants licensed to accompany a viceroy and his wife to New Spain in 1566. With unmarried Spanish women at a premium, these few did not change the balance. Philip II changed policy in 1575 after the viceroy of Peru complained about the arrivals' dissolute character. Nonetheless, the Spanish Crown sent neither groups of women of dubious background to become wives of soldiers and colonists as the French practiced later in Canada, nor orphans and prostitutes as did the Portuguese in Brazil.

The paucity of peninsular women barred most male immigrants from marrying females from home. Until the native daughters of Spanish families were of age, some conquistadors and early settlers married indigenous women, especially those from the nobility, and fathered legitimate children. Nonetheless, most offspring of Spaniards and native women resulted from less formal unions. If reared in their father's home, these illegitimate children were culturally Spaniards and routinely accepted as such. If reared in their mother's home, they were considered indigenous. When unwanted by either parent, they joined the growing number of *mestizos*, a term applied to these racially mixed offspring in Mexico starting in the late 1530s. *Mestizos* joined the mulatto offspring of (almost always) Spanish males and African females, and other persons of mixed ancestry to constitute the *castas*, a collective noun applied to the entire racially mixed population marked by illegitimacy or the suspicion of it due to African ancestry. By 1580, multiracial hierarchies were in place in Spanish cities throughout the Indies as the initial distinction between "Christians" and the indigenous yielded to lineage and legitimacy.

The white population in America expanded from several thousand by 1520 to some 120 000–150 000 in 1570 as a result of continued peninsular immigration, natural reproduction, and the acceptance of some persons as whites despite only partially Spanish ancestry. In early seventeenth-century Lima, females and males of Spanish descent in Lima were roughly equal in number. Native daughters of well-to-do families were brought up to become wives and mothers. While some entered the nearly 50 convents available by 1600, a substantial majority wed (Figure 1.1), and large families were not unusual, especially among the more well-to-do.

Figure 1.1 A lady of Lima wearing her wedding dress. Successful peninsular merchants and officials in Lima often married young native daughters of the city's elite families.
Source: John Constanse Davie, *Letters from Buenos Ayres and Chile* (London: R. Ackermann, 1819), 64. Reproduced by permission of the Mercantile Library at the University of Missouri-St. Louis.

Native daughters and sons born of successful conquistadors and early settlers continued to pay homage to these ancestors, for they had established the fundamental social division between Spaniards at the top and all others below them.

Seeking the Familiar, Identifying the New

Spaniards in the Indies aspired to live like titled nobles of Castile with themselves at the apex of the new societies they were creating. During decades of exploration and conquest, they encountered lands and peoples previously unknown to Europeans. They paid their expenses, left behind dead comrades, and shed blood on behalf of their monarch. Survivors assiduously sought what they considered just rewards: permanent grants of native labor and tribute, wealth, higher social status, a Spanish wife, a municipal office, a palatial urban residence, and land for livestock and crops.

The Indies offered both the familiar and the exotic. Explorers, conquistadors, and settlers sought and found items, notably gold and silver, they knew from experience in Europe. But they also came across much that was new: peoples and languages, religious practices and monumental buildings, plants and animals, food and drink, jungles and hurricanes, illnesses and cures. All forced Spaniards to come to terms with previously unsuspected cultures and environments. They needed labels to identify both what they found and what resulted from their presence. Thus, they homogenized and mislabeled peoples born in the Americas as "Indians" (*indios*), a consequence of Columbus's erroneous geographical knowledge, and soon began to import Africans. To identify groups in the emerging social order, they invented and adapted terms of varied origins.

The Spaniards' presence and persistence was evident in old vocabulary used in unprecedented ways as well as new words. "Spaniard" antedated the creation of an American empire and applied to everyone with Spanish ancestry. Used without modification, both "Spaniards" and "whites" or *blancos* referred to all persons of Spanish descent, but only "European Spaniards" were also called *gachupines* and *chapetones*, disparaging terms that emphasized their recent arrival. Because their place of origin was the Iberian Peninsula, contemporaries starting in the early nineteenth century and subsequently historians have designated these Europeans "peninsulars."

By the early 1560s, the term "criollo" or "creole" identified the American-born offspring of Spaniards as well as others of New World birth accepted as such. The word was already being used to distinguish black slaves born in the Indies from those imported from Africa. Thus, the earliest known usages simply meant place of birth – the Indies – for both Spaniards and African slaves. Licenses to return to the Americas from Spain often referred to a slave born in the Americas as a creole, and at times the word appeared in the name, for example, Juan Criollo. In contrast, the American-born masters were identified as Spaniards from a specific city or region of birth and thus its native son (*natural de*).

The ongoing existence of a peninsular population in the western hemisphere depended upon the continued arrival of Spanish immigrants. In contrast, the creole population reproduced and expanded from within and increased further as a result of marriage between creoles (usually native daughters) and peninsulars (usually males). Although both groups descended from Spaniards, a substantial minority of whites born in the Indies had at least one increasingly distant indigenous ancestor as well. Coupling among Spaniards, Indians, and Africans engendered offspring identified as mestizos, mulattoes, and *zambos*, among other terms.

Although divided by place of birth, both European and American Spaniards could be found in the sixteenth century among landowners, miners, professionals, wholesalers, retailers, artisans, and, occasionally, day laborers, as well as in other income-producing activities. They ranged from the wealthy to the impoverished. While occupational, social, and educational differences resulted in diverse perspectives and concerns, they shared one overriding belief: ancestry, religion, and conquest made them superior to all non-Spaniards.

Spaniards in Early Municipalities

Spanish settlers as well as the Crown believed that civilized life required communities, and thus the creation of municipalities was indispensable for implanting Spanish culture. Encouraged by Ferdinand, Isabel, and later monarchs, settlers clustered together to establish towns and cities on Caribbean islands and the American mainland. These included rechristened preconquest cities located within a large, sedentary indigenous population: for example, Cuzco in Andean Peru. In other cases, such as Puebla de los Angeles in Mexico, the Spaniards founded new communities. Most followed a grid pattern extending from a large, central plaza flanked by a church, a municipal building, a royal office, and merchants' stalls. By 1580, they included administrative centers, regional market centers, ports, and mining camps, some of which evolved into full-fledged municipalities. Spaniards dominated all of them even when a minority of the population.

Founders included conquistadors and first settlers (*pobladores*) who held or soon obtained grants of indigenous labor and tribute (*encomiendas*). They erected a municipal government, became aldermen, and granted themselves choice residential lots close to the central plaza. They also filled local offices overseeing basic services that included the administration of justice and the use of honest measures for meat, bread, and other products sold in shops and markets. If living conditions proved tolerable, most founders planned to settle down. The initial shortage of Spanish women meant, of course, that a number of settlers lived with and in some cases married non-white women. Their legitimate and illegitimate offspring contributed to the racial diversity that quickly marked Spanish cities and towns.

Immigration from Spain and migration from elsewhere in the Indies contributed to the creation and growth of municipalities. The island of Española in 1514 had 14 towns with 392 *vecinos*, 92 married to Castilian women and 54 to indigenous. Founded on the ruins of Tenochtitlan, the city of Mexico in 1526 had some 600–750 peninsulars, a number that rose to about 2000 Spanish *vecinos* by 1550. With 15 000–18 000 white residents in 1574, it held about 30% of New Spain's total. African slaves in the capital numbered some 8000 and mulattoes another thousand. Antequera (Oaxaca) in 1525 had about 125 Europeans and was only modestly larger in 1544. Puebla increased from 42 adult peninsulars in 1531 to 205 in 1534; between 1531 and 1560, female immigrants comprised just over a quarter of its population.

The white population in South America also expanded rapidly. Spanish immigrants reached Peru quickly after word spread of Atahuallpa's treasure and at least 2000 were present by 1536. In the 1590s, an estimate of Lima's population revealed that blacks and mulattoes outnumbered all other residents combined. Among Spaniards, females outnumbered males by 1636, but their combined total was less than the black population. In Chile, Europeans and their legitimate descendants increased from about 150 in 1540 to some 7000 in 1570.

Their growing numbers accentuated for Spaniards the critical importance of controlling the native population's labor, services, and tribute.

Initial Spanish Control of Labor, Services, and Tribute

In his first two voyages, Columbus obtained a little gold and some curiosities, but not the wealth he had promised Ferdinand and Isabel. Foreshadowing later expeditions to Mexico and South America, however, during his second stay on Española he defeated the native Tainos (Arawaks) in battle, enslaved captives, and inaugurated a tribute system. When he returned to the island again in 1498, he found a faction of Spaniards in rebellion. To mollify them, he inaugurated *repartimiento*, the division and assignment of the Tainos into grants that typically included a chief (*señor*) and a village or villages of "his" Indians, to labor for specific Spanish settlers. Formalized in 1503 under Governor Nicolás de Ovando, this distribution of indigenous labor to Spaniards known as *encomenderos* quickly split the conquerors into an elite with access to ample labor and a larger group without it. The latter's antipathy toward Columbus reflected an antiforeign, in his case specifically anti-Genoese, sentiment as well.

Conquistadors carried the expectation of *repartimiento* to the mainland and demanded the grants after every successful campaign. *Encomiendas* and native slaves were the most valuable rewards Cortés distributed following victory over the Aztec. Initially without authorization, he awarded thousands of tributaries to about 300 conquistadors and a few other old hands. Francisco Pizarro followed suit after taking Cuzco, and later frontier governors (*adelantados*) allotted labor and tribute after each new conquest. Factional disputes often followed over who received the grants, the reasons for their selection, and the number of natives assigned. *Encomenderos* did agree, however, on one issue – inheritance. All wanted the legal right to bequeath their grants.

Encomenderos were never numerous. In Mexico there were fewer than 600; in Peru, Quito, and Charcas, under 500; and in New Granada, only 280. These modest totals left most conquistadors and first settlers empty-handed. While recipients anticipated supporting a family with an *encomienda*, the grants varied substantially in size and value. *Encomenderos*, moreover, sought to wring all possible value from "their Indians." Forced to provide manual labor; to transport goods; to pay tribute; to have their wives and daughters seized and their lands usurped; in short, to put up with unlimited abuse and exploitation, natives in *encomiendas* during the 1520s and 1530s suffered a living hell. Population decline resulting from disease, abuse, overwork, changed and inadequate diet, and other causes soon reduced *encomiendas*' worth.

Although *encomenderos* valued tribute, access to labor was more critical for economic success. They wanted workers to transport goods, construct houses and other buildings, work in mines, tend animals, and plant, weed, water, and harvest crops, among other assignments. Access to labor, moreover, was necessary to make land grants valuable. Those who diversified their investments through their use of native labor and tribute were able to survive economically as the indigenous population plummeted. Those who failed to do so were even more anxious to bequeath what remained of their grants, partly because *encomendero* status was still the Indies' most prestigious social rank. But the signs were ominous; by 1555, more than half of the *encomenderos* in New Spain had failed to retain their awards in their immediate families.

An Alternative to Encomienda

The Crown viewed *encomienda* warily and in 1530 introduced in New Spain the Castilian office of *corregidor* to oversee the collection of tribute from *encomiendas* that reverted to its control. To fill the position, it recommended that the *Audiencia* of Mexico name former *encomenderos* and other worthy conquistadors and first settlers. The New Laws issued in 1542 contained three provisions to benefit conquistadors and their heirs:

1. "In the distribution of *corregimientos* the first conquerors are to be preferred."
2. "Those first conquerors and their heirs who have no Indians in *encomienda* are to be provided for out of the tributes of the Indians removed from *encomiendas*."
3. "*Corregimientos* are to be assigned preferably to those conquerors who were not provided for [in the distribution of *encomiendas*], and to their sons."[6]

In early 1543, the Crown clarified for New Spain that it considered "the first conquistadors" to be those who served with Cortés when he arrived in New Spain and were present at the surrender of Tenochtitlan. These men had earned the title and were to be preferred in royal grants (*mercedes*). *Corregimientos* thus were an alternative to *encomiendas* through which, in essence, the Crown was moving toward becoming the sole *encomendero*.

Besides expanding the number of *corregidores* in New Spain, the Crown established them in other parts of the Americas and increased their authority. By the 1550s, these provincial officials enjoyed civil and criminal jurisdiction over both Indians and Spaniards in their districts. Because it linked viceregal government in the capital to native municipalities and provided a salaried position with ample opportunity for illegal gain, the new provincial post, at least in populous districts, became highly desirable. Not surprisingly, appointments to serve as *corregidor* became a major source of contention between peninsulars and frustrated conquistadors, early settlers, and their heirs.

In 1561, Philip II responded to a charge that a viceroy in Peru had ignored meritorious candidates who had served the king there in order to name his peninsular retainers as *corregidores* and other officials. He ordered that the viceroy's appointees be removed and replaced by *personas beneméritas*, that is, by conquistadors, first settlers, and their heirs. Several years later, the king noted that the municipal council of the city of Mexico had appointed outsiders as municipal magistrates and admonished it to prefer and appoint qualified "first conquistadors" and then married settlers. In 1570, he reminded the *Audiencia* of New Galicia that it should name conquistadors and their sons for positions of provincial administration (*alcaldes mayores* and *corregidores*). The Crown seldom consistently followed a strict policy, however, and in the previous year, Philip had forbidden viceroy of Peru Francisco de Toledo to appoint to any *corregimiento* a person who was an *encomendero*, citizen, or native of the jurisdiction's capital and to remove those who were serving.

Nonetheless, in general, the Crown recognized its moral obligations. In 1586, Doña María del Alcazar, widow of a first conqueror with Cortés and recipient of low-yield *encomiendas* inherited by her son, successfully sought annuities for five surviving daughters and two sons from royal tribute income dedicated to descendants of the "first explorers, pacifiers, settlers, and most senior citizens." Not long afterward, Philip II reaffirmed an earlier law of 1568 favoring similar descendants. Although considerable legislation by that time gave preference to the *beneméritos*, as the locally born heirs of the conquistadors and settlers were known, *encomenderos*' failure to secure inheritable property rights over their grants was manifest.

Encomienda and Inheritance

The overriding issue in the Indies in the mid-sixteenth century was succession to *encomiendas*. *Encomenderos* considered the grants an indisputable mark of high noble status and desperately wanted the Crown to designate them as inheritable property. The Crown objected even more strongly to the idea of a powerful, hereditary nobility with jurisdiction over vassals taking root in the Indies. In the New Laws of 1542, it seemed to end decades of ambivalence toward the inheritance of *encomiendas* when it outlawed the practice and prohibited new grants. The recently named founding viceroy of Peru Blasco Núñez Vela's intention to implement this provision led to rebellion and his death by its opponents. In New Spain, Viceroy Antonio de Mendoza cooperated with the visitor Francisco Tello de Sandoval to delay implementation and requested the Council of the Indies to review its mandate. Upon reflection, the Council allowed grants of *encomienda* to continue for a "second life" and thus retained the loyalty of New Spain's *encomenderos*. Soon afterward it separated labor and tribute in New Spain, assuming direct control over the former in 1549. Although it had backed down over succession for another generation, the Crown refused to recognize *encomiendas* as real property, Instead, it kept *encomenderos* anxiously waiting to see if subsequent "lives" would be allowed. In this netherworld in which they valued hope over experience, financial failure was not uncommon for grantees and their heirs who had neglected to diversify their investments and faced the consequences of their *encomiendas*' falling value as a result of the decreasing indigenous population. In 1549, Extremaduran Juan de la Torre, one of 13 men ennobled for having remained with Francisco Pizarro on Gallo Island in 1527, received an *encomienda* not far from Arequipa, Peru, and proceeded to live well until his death in 1580. Native son Hernando, born in Arequipa to his father's third wife, a woman from Granada, succeeded to his father's grant as well as substantial agricultural land. His heir was less fortunate. Following Hernando's passing in 1610, the native son heir pleaded that his father had left him both enormous debts and a mother and several sisters to support. Left with an *encomienda* inadequate to sustain his family, he solicited an appointment to office.

In contrast to the De la Torre family's financial travail, *encomenderos* who had wisely invested in land and livestock, agriculture, trade, and sometimes mining and textile production had accumulated significant estates. Officeholders and other peninsulars successful in varied economic activities had become wealthy as well. *Sevillano* Francisco Pérez de Lezcano settled in Trujillo, Peru, in 1551, after a successful military career. The city council granted him an office and some land that he used to build a house and a flourmill. Soon he was exporting flour and had become an alderman. Already independently wealthy, he married a young native daughter whose substantial dowry included a house on the central plaza, more than 25 slaves, numerous cows and swine, and several flour mills. Their daughter Graciana later shared an *encomienda* with her mother and married a captain from Spain who had arrived in Peru in 1534. In this case, as in many others, the female line was central to the incorporation of successful peninsulars in a locally prominent family. Not all Spanish immigrants, however, received such treatment, for earlier arrivals often deprecated those who followed.

From Old Hands versus Greenhorns to Creoles versus Peninsulars

On the "sorrowful night" in June 1520, Cortés, other conquistadors, and native allies suffered heavy casualties as they fled Tenochtitlan. Remembering the flight years later, foot soldier Bernal Díaz del Castillo wrote contemptuously that "many" of the men who had arrived in Mexico with Pánfilo de Narváez in 1520 "had loaded themselves" with gold and, as a result of their greed, "the greater number were left at the bridges weighed down with gold."[7] The implication was obvious: experience and wisdom had saved many old hands, but innumerable greenhorns perished because of their greed. The old conquistador's disdain for newcomers (*advenedizos*) persisted throughout the colonial period as revealed in the widespread use of the terms *chapetón* and *gachupín*. The passage of time, of course, resulted in immigrants becoming old hands themselves and, in turn, often viewing more recent arrivals with hostility. This antipathy increased when such men brought appointments to civil or ecclesiastical office or simply delivered copies of new royal directives that threatened the interests of existing Spanish residents. As native sons succeeded the initial waves of conquistadors and settlers, they and their descendants represented the old hands. The continued arrival of greenhorns who intended to create an enviable life in America as well as peninsulars who hoped to get rich quick and return to their homeland perpetuated competition and rancor with native sons whose birthplace and ancestry linked them more to America than Spain.

The Variety of Peninsulars

Europeans that reached Spanish America were overwhelmingly male. A very few came from Castile's highest noble families, as was apparent in the mid-1530s when Antonio de Mendoza, son of the Count of Tendilla, reached New Spain as its first viceroy. The preeminent administrators in the Indies, viceroys were the personal representatives, the alter egos, of Spain's Habsburg monarchs (1516–1700), and thus vested with the power of patronage and the obligation to use it. They confirmed their status by arriving with large retinues and immediately finding these greenhorns positions, incomes, and sometimes spouses. While some of the clients expected to return to Spain with riches, others accepted that enhanced circumstances in the Indies would lead to permanent residence. These men, and to a lesser degree the retainers of bishops, *audiencia* ministers, and other high-ranking officials, thus represented direct competition to earlier arrivals, native sons, and other creoles in the pursuit of office and economic gain. Despite the high visibility associated with their status and personal connections, these favored peninsulars counted for few of the Castilian immigrants.

Merchants comprised a second significant group of peninsulars. The earliest ones often represented wholesalers in Seville, expected to return to Spain, and refrained from purchasing land or marrying locally. This approach was short-lived. Within several decades, successful merchants frequently married descendants of conquistadors and first settlers who had a claim to an *encomienda*, still the most important designation of elite social standing despite its declining economic value.

Professional men, retailers, and artisans were also immigrants. Many of the initially small number of professionals – notaries, lawyers and procurators, physicians – prospered and their ranks expanded.

Retailers ranged from itinerant merchants to established businessmen with stores adjoining a municipality's central plaza. Indigenous and *casta* women offered competition as ambulatory vendors and shopkeepers at the low end of retail trade. Indeed at times they dominated the sale of a particular product, for example, coca leaves in the mining center of Potosí.

In the early decades after conquest, artisans probably constituted the largest single occupational category of legal immigrants. Whatever their dreams of laborless prosperity, artisans often turned to their trade as a source of income. By the mid-sixteenth century, they had established in major cities guilds that, among others, organized masons and carpenters in Lima and silk weavers, painters, and shoemakers in the city of Mexico. They trained indigenous, *casta*, and black apprentices in the use of Spanish technology to make products that appealed to Spanish tastes. Guilds also founded religious brotherhoods or *cofradías* that provided social interaction and arranged for funeral services and burial of members. Although respectable, peninsular artisans were unable to join the colonial elite, and it was unthinkable that they would order an *hidalgo* to do anything. They belonged to the ranks of commoners and could lay no claim to nobility.

Sailors who jumped ship may have comprised the most numerous group of peninsulars. Many were previously unemployed in Seville or elsewhere and became sailors of occasion who planned to labor during a single outbound trip because they lacked the money to sail as passengers. Reprisals for desertion could be serious, but fugitives had a reasonable chance of escaping. Burdened with a miserable reputation, sailors' major asset in many cases was probably peninsular birth. If able to contact a relative or *paisano* and willing to work, their fortune could improve. Such was the case of Alonso de Bello.

Born into an Asturian *hidalgo* family in 1552, Bello received some schooling and even studied law, at least briefly. A realistic younger son, he recognized that his modest inheritance would not support him and followed many earlier Asturians to the Indies. In 1575, he signed on as one of nearly 20 Asturians on the crew of a ship captained by another countryman. After landing at several other ports, he jumped ship in 1576 at Nombre de Dios in Panama and disappeared from view until the 1580s. He surfaced in the Kingdom of Quito as a muleteer and merchant involved in conveying and selling salt and collecting tribute for some *encomenderos*. Entering a partnership with a textile merchant of Quito, he transported to the great mining center of Potosí a large quantity of cloth that he sold profitably. Wrapping up his affairs, he returned to Asturias in 1605. There he invested his savings in land and annuities and married a young, wealthy heiress of good family. He died in 1632 without children, a pious and prosperous peninsular whose career demonstrated that with connections, hard work, and luck, not all sailors were lower class failures. A friend of both native sons and Asturians in Quito, his departure with his earnings supported the popular creole argument that peninsulars went to the Indies only to make their fortunes and retire to Spain.

By 1580, peninsulars in the Indies had established an expanding urban world. Most native sons were born and reared in the empire's cities, the heart of Spain's imperial project. In these urban centers, one could find powerful royal and ecclesiastical institutions as well as markets for merchants who specialized in importing European and Asiatic goods. Viceroys, captains-general, *audiencias*, treasury offices, merchant and artisan guilds, owners of haciendas, religious orders, convents, diocesan hierarchies, tribunals or agents of the Inquisition, lawyers, licensed physicians, unlicensed curers, servants, slaves, and the homeless were intimately connected to city life. Organized as hierarchical societies with *encomenderos* and a few officials in the elite, cities also had numerous other Spaniards, the indigenous, and increasing numbers of *castas* and African slaves. Epidemic disease had reduced and in some cases nearly eliminated the indigenous in regions of contact, stripped *encomiendas* of their original worth, and created a labor shortage in many locations. Rich lodes of silver discovered in Peru and Mexico were providing increased revenue for Charles I in his final years as monarch and, more importantly, for his heir Philip II during his long reign (1556–1598). While the era of conquest had not ended – especially on the northern frontier of New Spain and the southern frontier of Chile where warfare continued – the most spectacular triumphs were ever more distant memories for the few remaining conquistadors and early settlers.

Peninsulars continued to sail to the Indies, but increasingly after mid-century, they encountered both earlier emigrants and their descendants. Native sons and daughters soon outnumbered the European Spaniards and reduced their initial preeminence. A royal administrative structure attracted candidates from both sides of the Atlantic for its positions. The expansion of the regular clergy and the creation of an ecclesiastical hierarchy offered even more opportunities. As part of the growing Church, convents in Mexico, Peru, and other locations provided native daughters with an alternative to marriage. Growth, however, provoked conflict as native sons sought first to enter religious orders and the secular clergy and then to lead them.

2

Native Sons and Daughters in the Church

Serious and ongoing contention between peninsulars and native sons started first in the Church. At stake in the secular or diocesan clergy alone were urban and rural parishes, prebends in cathedral chapters, and ultimately several dozen bishoprics. The religious orders, also called the "regular clergy" because they followed a "rule" (Latin *regula*), offered extensive opportunities as well. Major mendicant orders – Franciscans, Dominicans, and Augustinians – made available programs for novices and a series of elective positions in each province. Conflict emerged first over whether to admit native sons and other creoles to the orders, and then over their participation in offices. The rotational system imposed to resolve the latter angered them for the remainder of Spanish rule. The creation of convents starting in 1540 enabled native daughters to embrace the religious life, but their heated elections for abbess were often among factions in which place of birth was not at issue. Consequently, they were spared a mandated rotation.

Patronage and the Preparation of Clerics

Royal Patronage

Pope Alexander VI granted the Crown of Castile sovereignty over the yet undefined lands of the Indies by the "papal donation" of 1493. In exchange, Ferdinand and Isabel agreed to undertake the conversion of the indigenous peoples to Christianity. Over the next 15 years, additional

Spaniards in the Colonial Empire: Creoles vs. Peninsulars?, First Edition. Mark A. Burkholder.

papal bulls clarified this relationship, outlined the royal patronage (*Patronato Real*) or authority held by the monarch over the Church in the Indies, and identified resources, notably the tithe, to support it. The Crown, in turn, assigned almost all tithe income to the Church so it could execute its responsibilities. The remainder it employed in education, hospitals, and charitable institutions. Extending a precedent awarded to Queen Isabel during the conquest of Granada, royal patronage also included the "rights of presentation," effectively the authority to name all secular clergy from parish clergy to archbishops. The Portuguese Crown also enjoyed royal patronage in Brazil and supported the natives' Christianization. In contrast, the English monarchs showed little concern for the spiritual welfare of indigenous in their American colonies.

The Spanish Crown embraced the obligation to support Christianization and its corollary of Hispanicizing the indigenous population. The first friars sailed with Columbus on his second voyage, the initial response to Alexander VI's charge. Scarcely a decade later, Pope Julius II acceded to Ferdinand's request and erected an archbishopric and two bishoprics on Española, an action that ensured that diocesan clergy would minister in America. Over time, thousands of clerics would find employment there.

Clerics regularly accompanied major expeditions of exploration and conquest. Groups of mendicants sailed to the Indies in the early years of Spanish settlement, took the lead in converting the indigenous peoples, and established churches and friaries. The Jesuits initiated missionary activities in Brazil in 1549 and reached Peru in 1568 and New Spain in 1572. By 1560, some 800 regulars were located in New Spain alone. Elsewhere in the empire, living communities of one or more orders frequently could be found where Spaniards had settled and indigenous villages were located. The papal bull *Omnimoda* issued in 1522 granted unusually broad rights to religious orders in the Indies. It authorized friars to perform marriages, administer sacraments, grant absolution, and engage in other priestly functions. In addition, the bull allowed those residing in friaries more than two days' travel from the nearest bishop to assume many episcopal functions. In contrast to the papal grant of authority to friars, royal dictates specified the rights and responsibilities of diocesan clergy in nondoctrinal matters.

Peninsulars in the secular clergy arrived as individuals and, like lay immigrants, some used America for personal and familial gain that would enable them to return to Spain wealthy. Many more remained in the Indies, pursued advancement within the Church, and established themselves in their region of ministry. Juan de Figueroa Farfán exemplified the first group. After his arrival in New Spain, he served as a notary, secretary, and local magistrate. He then received ordination, rose to canon of the cathedral chapter of Michoacán, and served there for three years before returning to Spain permanently. In contrast, Sancho Sánchez de Muñón, born in Spain in 1528, arrived in Mexico in 1560 to assume a position as schoolmaster (*maestrescuela*) of the capital's cathedral chapter. Soon afterward he enticed his brother Hernán and his family to join him. Despite a visit to Spain, Sancho returned to Mexico City in 1575 and remained on its cathedral chapter until his death early in the next century.

While many early friars focused on converting the indigenous peoples, secular clerics often dedicated their attention to the growing Spanish population. The bishopric of Tlaxcala (later Puebla) was erected in 1526 and in the 1530s, the secular clergy in the new see of Mexico assumed the traditional hierarchical structure that included a bishop (later archbishop), cathedral chapter, and parish priests. Lima followed suit a decade later and Bogotá was erected in 1553. Brazil's first bishopric, Salvador da Bahia, was created in 1551. Although many early bishops in the Indies belonged to a religious order, in general the regulars had little use for the diocesan clergy whether born in Spain or the Indies, belittled their education, and denounced their efforts at evangelization.

Added to their initial numerical advantage, the regular clergy's claims of superiority and higher moral character poisoned relations with secular clerics. At last the Crown intervened. In 1574, Philip II issued the Ordinance of Patronage (*Ordenanza del Patronazgo*), a major policy statement that placed all clerics under royal ecclesiastical authority. Seculars were to replace regulars in missions, and their appointments to new rural benefices (*beneficios*) were to be based on competitions known as *oposiciones*, although as patron the monarch or his representative could appoint these clerics directly. Part of the selection process was to evaluate the candidates' ability to speak relevant native languages; for example, Nahuatl and Otomí in central Mexico, or Quechua in Peru. This provision obviously benefited native sons for they often grew up with indigenous nursemaids and other servants and learned their language. But the Ordinance provided another advantage by specifying that, in filling benefices, preference be given to "the sons of Spaniards who have served us" in the Indies. This explicit mandate gave native sons an unequivocal legal advantage over both peninsulars and priests known as *domiciliarios*, immigrants who frequently had reached the Indies as boys, entered the Church in America, and generally had more in common with native sons than clerics from Spain.

Both religious orders and the diocesan clergy provided opportunities for native sons and other creoles seeking a religious vocation or simply a respectable livelihood. The creation of benefices made the position of parish priest attractive because it provided the recipients a guaranteed salary and life-long appointment. Policies adopted by the Council of Trent (1545–1563) underscored the importance of an educated clergy and called for a seminary in every diocese. Philip II ordered that graduates from the universities in Lima and Mexico and approved universities of Castile receive preference for positions in the cathedral chapters of the Indies. The Ordinance of Patronage laid out how candidates could translate their education into an occupation. As their fathers' *encomiendas* lost value and their inheritance was uncertain, even some sons of *encomenderos* readied themselves for a life in the Church.

Preparation for the Secular Clergy

While *encomenderos* could be illiterate – as many early ones were – clerics needed to be able to read, write, and apply mathematical skills. Having emigrated to find a better life, conquistadors and early settlers sought to provide additional benefits for their sons. The desire to make them eligible for benefices, prebends, and prelatures underlined the immediate need for readily available formal education. Until it was available, however, *encomenderos* and other early settlers arranged as best they could for their sons to learn the basic skills. Initially they hired private tutors or clerics to teach their sons Latin because of its use in administering the sacraments, its role as the academic skill requirement for university admission, and its importance as the common language of intellectuals and many authors. While a few wealthy peninsulars sent sons to Spain for their education, most fathers considered the cost prohibitive and supported the establishment of colleges (*colegios*) and universities where they resided.

Aspirants for the secular clergy needed to meet specific social, moral, and educational requirements prior to ordination. These included legitimate birth and Old Christian ancestors, virtuous personal habits, literacy in Latin, and an education. Increasingly, candidates completed a baccalaureate degree and studied theology for four years. These credentials enabled them to pass a public examination in moral theology. A few priests also boasted advanced degrees, an asset when seeking a position on a cathedral chapter or as bishop.

Usually a candidate progressed from minor orders through the major orders of subdeacon, deacon, and presbyter or priest, the last allowing him to say mass. Licenses to hear confession, to administer baptism, last rights, and other sacraments, and to preach qualified the candidate for the priesthood. Ordination followed, usually when the candidate was in his early to mid-twenties, but did not guarantee that the cleric would become a parish priest. Without the income of a benefice, many ordained priests served as assistant and temporary replacements for beneficed parish clergy and others became chaplaincy priests saying memorial masses.

Formal Education

Implementation of the Council of Trent's more stringent requirements for clerical schooling spurred higher education to new heights in sixteenth-century Castile. Before Trent, a young male could enter the lowest level of priesthood with only literacy in Spanish and knowledge of basic prayers. Advancement required demonstrated knowledge of Latin and the liturgy.

The regular orders took the lead in establishing novitiates with studies in Latin grammar, philosophy, and theology for the preparation of new friars. In New Spain, the Franciscans founded the first novitiate in the city of Mexico by 1527 and created a second in Puebla several decades later. Although the Dominicans had created some early *colegios* or secondary schools and even a university in Santo Domingo, it was the Jesuits who established educational institutions of exceptional importance for the formation and continuation of native son elites. While bishops and archbishops founded cathedral schools, the Jesuits created *colegios* in viceregal capitals, lesser cities, and Brazil as well. The students in these primary and secondary schools included a few creoles who continued their education at universities in Spain, or, much more frequently, at new universities established in America. While a Portuguese colony, Brazil had no university, and its elite youth had no option except the University of Coimbra in Portugal. In the English colonies, the foundation of Harvard in 1636 and the College of William and Mary in 1693 made higher education available for a few youth.

The municipal councils of Mexico City and Lima lobbied successfully for universities. Mexico City sought one in the 1530s and Viceroy Mendoza supported its request. In January 1550, Lima's city council asked that the recently created Dominican *colegio* be turned into a university. The Crown acceded and in 1551 authorized universities in both capitals to benefit "the sons of the citizens"; females had no opportunity for higher education anywhere in the Americas. The Royal and Pontifical University of Mexico (Figure 2.1) held its first classes in 1553, and the Royal and Pontifical University of San Marcos replaced its Dominican predecessor in the 1570s. Both offered degrees in the five faculties that characterized a "major" university: arts or philosophy, medicine, theology, and civil and canon (Church) law. Admission required proficiency in Latin – the ability

Figure 2.1 Interior courtyard of the University of Mexico. The University of Mexico was the first university of mainland North America. Its alumni included many native sons who became clerics and officeholders.
Source: Vicente Riva Palacio, *Mexico a través de los siglos*, Vol. 2 (Mexico: Ballescá y Compañía, 1888), 521. Reproduced by permission of the Mercantile Library at the University of Missouri-St. Louis.

to read, write, and understand it – for lectures and assignments were in that language. The bachelor of arts degree was somewhat akin to a modern high school degree and required for subsequent study in every faculty.

The Society of Jesus specialized in the provision of high-quality education without cost to the students. Soon after arriving in a major city, the Jesuits would establish one or more schools. In Lima, for example, they founded the College of San Pablo in 1568. By the end of the sixteenth century, civil authorities awarded them a monopoly over instruction in the humanities, making San Pablo the official preparatory institution for the University of San Marcos. They taught the same curriculum in Lima and elsewhere in America that they used in Iberia and throughout much of Europe, thus insuring a comparable education. In addition, they offered studies in Quechua in Lima. San Pablo grew to some 500 students in the early seventeenth century and served 1000 or more boys annually between the 1660s and the 1760s.

After completing the course of study at San Pablo, students by 1592 could proceed to one of several other educational institutions in Lima. The *Royal Colegio Mayor* of San Martín established in 1582 was the Jesuits' most important facility in the City of Kings for the study of arts, grammar, and Latin. Students (*colegiales*) could enter at the age of 12 and remain until they were 24; some resided at the college and a few scholarships were available. *Limeños*, other creoles, and peninsular students unavoidably knew each other as they shared classes and extracurricular activities. Student matriculation at San Martín demonstrated, not surprisingly, that starting in the late sixteenth century, native sons and other creoles always outnumbered peninsular students. The increased identification over time of the American-born students as nobles (*dons*) documented an attributed higher social status that accompanied the declining number of peninsulars enrolled.

The *Royal Colegio Mayor* of San Felipe, established in 1592, was a residential facility that housed 16 students pursuing work in arts or philosophy, canon law, or theology. San Felipe was created under royal patronage specifically for "sons, grandsons and descendants of conquistadors and settlers" of Peru and others of appropriate merit and service. Its first constitution stipulated that students were to be well behaved sons of honorable fathers and could not be descended from persons from the lower class, those punished by the Inquisition, or mulattoes or *zambos*, the offspring of indigenous people and blacks.

Students pursuing a religious vocation could enroll in the Royal College-Seminary of Nobles founded in 1590 by Lima's second archbishop and future saint Toribio de Mogrovejo and later named after him. There they would study theology and sacred scripture, although lay students could also study civil and canon law. At the peak of Lima's educational institutions stood the University of San Marcos. Unlike their counterparts in sixteenth-century Spain, many of whom were from poor *hidalgo* backgrounds, creole students often came from well-to-do families of local oligarchies composed of *encomenderos*, owners of substantial properties, high-ranking officials, and merchants. Earning a degree in civil or canon law required five years for the baccalaureate and four years of postbaccalaureate training (*pasantía*) with an approved attorney. A relatively small number of students with a baccalaureate in civil or canon law subsequently secured a higher degree.

Within a year or two of opening, San Marcos conferred its first law degree to *limeño* Doctor Diego de Salinas. Subsequently, other native sons, creoles from outside of the jurisdiction of the *Audiencia* of Lima, and the occasional peninsular received law degrees and obtained the tribunal's approval to practice law. By the 1580s, native sons and other creoles started to form a recognizable cohort advancing into positions of Church, local posts, and offices as royal magistrates and administrators.

Besides those in Mexico City and Lima, subsequent universities were ultimately established, some under royal auspices and others by religious orders. As a result, native sons ultimately enjoyed educational opportunity in most major cities of the Indies. In Guatemala, for example, Dominican, Franciscan, and Mercedarian friaries (Figure 2.2) were teaching philosophy by the 1570s and at least the Franciscans were making scholastic theology available by the early 1580s. The diocesan seminary to educate secular clergy opened in 1597, and the long-desired University of San Carlos de Guatemala was at last founded in 1676.

An earned baccalaureate degree separated native son and other creole recipients from nearly all peninsulars in both Castile and the Indies. Americans with the higher licentiate and doctorate degrees stood out even more, as numerous peninsulars serving as *audiencia* ministers, archbishops, bishops, and members of cathedral chapters lacked them. Higher education thus enabled native sons to compete with peninsulars as well as among themselves. Graduates in theology, scripture, and canon law quickly availed themselves of employment opportunities in the Church.

Figure 2.2 Mercedarian convent. One of many convents for friars in Mexico. *Source*: Vicente Riva Palacio, *Mexico a través de los siglos*, Vol. 2 (Mexico: Ballescá y Compañía, 1888), 316. Reproduced by permission of the Mercantile Library at the University of Missouri-St. Louis.

The Regular Clergy

The Church never had enough friars and priests to serve the entire population of the Indies. Although the Spanish Crown sent more than 5400 missionaries to America in the 1500s, it was apparent by mid-century that peninsular regular clergy were too few to meet the demands placed on them. After an initial effort to educate the sons of indigenous nobles in Mexico foundered on opposition to their ordination, native sons and other creoles remained as obvious sources of the additional clerics needed. Their admission, however, provoked serious struggles within most orders. The dilemma was as follows: missionary work required able-bodied, educated friars knowledgeable in one or more indigenous languages, a need that local creoles could meet; the ordination of native sons in substantial numbers, however, would transform the internal dynamics of individual friaries as well as provincial chapter meetings when elections were held. In the absence of an ongoing supply of peninsulars, every native son ordained would reduce the immigrants' majority in the order's province, its administrative and geographical unit. By the seventeenth century, the numbers were stark. Both the Dominicans and Augustinians received less than a tenth of the friars who had arrived in the previous century; their combined total of peninsulars plummeted by more than 90%, from over 1900 to just 169. The need for American-born friars was imperative.

Antipathy between native sons and peninsulars in the orders began when the former sought admission to novitiates. The reasons were several. First, as old hands, the regulars enjoyed seniority and initially dominated institutions with clearly defined levels of authority. They could determine whom they would admit and at times used this power to deny admission to native sons and other creoles. Later they required them to be older than peninsulars for ordination. Thus, from the outset, they insulted Spaniards born in America. In addition, peninsulars accepted and employed European arguments declaring the inferiority of people born in the New World. This extended beyond the indigenous and mixed races to include descendants of Spaniards. Examination of admission policies and practices by the Franciscans, Dominicans, and Augustinians will demonstrate their importance.

Franciscans

The Order of Friars Minor or Franciscans reached New Spain in 1523 and Peru in the early 1530s. Already in 1527, they were admitting novices in their friary in the city of Mexico and in the late 1560s were doing so in their community in Puebla. This occurred despite some internal resistance. For example, Fray Gerónimo de Mendieta in 1562 expressed his opposition to creoles or mestizos being admitted to the priesthood, alleging that they shared the vices of Indians. Nonetheless, after 1570, the Franciscans promoted an increase in creole friars and in 1574, the Franciscan commissary general for New Spain informed the president of the Council of the Indies that the Crown did not need to send more friars. These statements initiated a decline in the arrival of regular clergy ordained in Spain. Although the 1583 General Statutes of the Order made admission much more difficult for creoles than peninsulars, native sons continued to seek ordination. Throughout the Indies as a whole, 1825 Franciscans resided in nearly 300 friaries in 1595. In 1600, New

Spain had more than 1000 of them divided among four provinces. The Province of the Holy Gospel, which included the city of Mexico, had 600 friars, about a third of them creoles, most of whom were undoubtedly native sons. By that date, nearly as many Franciscans had been educated in Mexico as the more than 600 peninsular friars that had arrived from Spain.

As was the case for secular clergy, admission to the Order of Friars Minor required meeting specific qualifications. These included being faithful Catholics untainted by suspicion of heresy or any scandal; free men of legitimate birth and at least 16 years of age; single, healthy, and without debt; and literate. Although Franciscans prohibited the admission of indigenous men into the Order before 1540, only in 1569 did the Province of Mexico formally decree:

> No Indian or mestizo may be received to the habit of our Order, nor may those born in this country [i.e., native sons] be received, except it be by the unanimous joint action of the Father Provincial and the Definitorium [advisory body] of the Province. Any investiture made contrary to this provision is invalid.[1]

Reflecting earlier practice of asking candidates whether they were of Indian or mestizo descent, a statute of *limpieza de sangre* adopted by the Province in 1614 limited admission to candidates of pure Spanish ancestry for four generations.

The Franciscans in Peru barred mestizos by 1580 but actively encouraged creoles to become friars. Indeed, the provincial of Lima from 1601 to 1604 pursued a vigorous recruitment program that enabled him to attract native sons from Lima's most eminent families as well as creoles from beyond the capital. One of these students, Fray Hernando Trejo, born in Asunción, Paraguay, became provincial of Lima and, in 1594, the first creole graduate of the University of San Marcos named a bishop. His two immediate successors as provincial were also creoles. The education the order provided and the presence of the University of San Marcos attracted enough students that in 1592 the viceroy of Peru reported that all friaries were populated. He recommended that the Crown send no further missionaries for any religious order.

As the number of friars from Spain declined rapidly starting in the late sixteenth century, religious orders realized that their expansion could come only through training creoles or, from their perspective, even less acceptable mestizos or indigenous men. Starting with the Franciscans in the early 1580s, the orders in Guatemala followed the Mexican example and established formal education and novitiates for creole youth.

Dominicans

In 1559, the Dominicans in Mexico prohibited the entry of any creole without the approval of the provincial superior: "[W]hether due to the climate of this land, or to other causes of which we are not aware, they do not appear to us to be as well suited to the religious state as they should be."[2] Despite these misgivings, by the late sixteenth century, nearly half of the Dominicans in New Spain were creoles, most of them undoubtedly native sons.

In Guatemala, the Dominicans initially accepted native son and other creole novices, but then pursued with increasing rigor a discriminatory policy against them. In 1562, the order mandated that creoles must submit to a "great examination of customs" before being authorized to take the habit. Six years later, the friars ruled that the provincial must give his explicit permission for a creole to be admitted. In 1570, the Order determined that "none of the so-called creoles shall receive the habit." Going beyond the American born, it further stipulated that peninsulars who had reached America before the age of 10 were also to be excluded. The discrimination rested on the belief that creoles' moral stature was low and that young peninsular boys adopted their unacceptable habits. According to the Order's seventeenth-century historian, "[T]he land was licentious in customs . . . and its sons took in vice along with their mothers' milk."[3] The discriminatory policy carried the seeds of the order's disappearance since after the 1570s the Crown reduced for over a half century the number of new friars it sent from Spain. Faced with a deteriorating reality and a potentially worse future, the Dominicans relented, making instruction in philosophy available to native son and other creole youth and accepting them as novices. More than 140 creoles, including the 20 most recent novices, had become Dominicans in Guatemala by about 1615.

Before the end of the sixteenth century, the Dominicans in Peru's Province of St. John the Baptist elected Salvador de Ribera, a graduate of the University of Salamanca, as the first native son provincial of any religious order in Peru. His two immediate successors were creoles as well, although not from Peru. Native sons and other creoles in the province asserted their power in Peru in 1592 when they passed an order prohibiting the admission of peninsulars into their province. Although the restriction proved short-lived, it demonstrated the depth of division based on birthplace.

Augustinians

Uniquely among the mendicants, the Augustinians had little hesitation about admitting creoles. Its friars reached Mexico in 1533 and in 1565 received autonomy from the province of Castile. Because of the distance from Spain, the environment of New Spain, and the erection of native parishes, the order became rooted in native-son society beginning in mid-century. By the early seventeenth century, its 79 friaries in New Spain were almost entirely composed of locally born creole younger sons, a consequence of an inheritance system that regularly favored their older brothers. Although these native sons frequently entered the order out of economic necessity rather than a true religious vocation, their ordination helped the order to expand. The division of New Spain into two Augustinian provinces in 1603 resulted in peninsular friars assuming control of the province of Michoacán, and native sons and other creoles enjoying dominance in the province of Mexico.

By the end of the sixteenth century, over 5000 regulars resided in the Indies. Less than a century later, the number had grown to 11 000. Probably almost 90% of them were born in the Indies and almost as many were serving in their province of birth. Declining immigration by peninsular friars, the growing number of native sons and other creoles in the religious orders, and the entry of American-born friars into leadership positions reduced conflict over regular clergy in native parishes. As this issue disappeared, however, a new one surfaced as the dwindling number of peninsular friars sought to retain control of their orders' highest elective offices in the Americas.

Rotation in the Orders' Provincial Offices

The religious orders were divided geographically into provinces whose highest ranking official, an elected provincial in every order but the Jesuits, resided in a regional capital. Initially, friars from Spain elected fellow peninsulars to their province's offices. This did not ensure unanimity, of course, and contested elections were common, at times dividing the friars into factions based on their regional origins; for example, Andalusians versus Castilians. The presence, especially in the sixteenth century, of peninsulars and creoles born outside of the province's boundaries but ordained in the province where they were serving, created another identifiable group (*domiciliarios* or *hijos de provincia*) in many ways comparable to *radicados*. As creole novices completed their training and became friars, their numbers and American birth added still another dimension to the elections. Initially, peninsular factions sought their support, but by 1600, native son friars in many provinces had joined together to form an identifiable, and in some places a majority, faction of their own.

Elections in the religious orders aroused a high level of interest encouraged by public processions and festivities that focused the populace's attention on the results. While friars from Spain frequently received political support from local high-ranking peninsular officials, native son friars and *hijos de provincia* enjoyed backing from families and friends in the city where the provincial was resident. The rivalry for office and, from the perspective of native sons, the deplorable restrictions imposed on their ambitions, can be seen clearly through an examination of the application of a rotational electoral policy to the Franciscans and Augustinians.

Franciscans

Heated competition for positions in the religious orders eventually led to a system of rotation (*alternativa* or *ternativa*) in the Franciscans' highest provincial offices. In 1602, Mexico's Province of the Holy Gospel elected to office 9 creoles, 24 *gachupines*, and 29 *hijos de provincia*. The creoles, most of whom were undoubtedly native sons, were dismayed since they totaled about one-third of the provinces' friars and obtained only 15% of the positions. As Viceroy Conde de Monterrey reported in 1604, the Franciscans were divided between creole and Castilian factions. But the dominance of the *hijos de provincia* terminated in 1611 with the imposition of a rotational system (*alternativa*) under which they would share offices equally with native sons. This solution was modified when it was realized that the new system omitted the *gachupines*! A revised procedure called for the three groups rotating in the highest offices but having proportional representation in the lower ones. While this *ternativa* specified that a creole (native son) would serve as provincial after every third election, the distribution of other offices meant that the peninsulars and *hijos de provincia* combined would always have more representation in the order's highest positions than their numbers justified. Already, in fact, *gachupines* were a minority in the province, and the number of *hijos de provincia* was declining.

During the seventeenth century, probably fewer than 300 ordained peninsular Franciscans reached Mexico. Although more than 500 *hijos de provincia* arrived between 1600 and 1650, fewer than 200 did so after the latter date. In contrast, nearly 1600 native sons entered the order, a figure roughly 50% greater than *gachupines* and *hijos de provincia* combined. Despite their overwhelming majority, native son friars' complaints about the inequitable *ternativa* formula used for rotational office holding proved fruitless, and the policy remained a disruptive and ongoing irritant.

In Peru, overwhelming creole majorities in the provinces of Lima and Cuzco elected mostly creole provincials between 1650 and 1678. The viceroy of Peru's support coupled with political intrigue and chicanery in Madrid and Rome enabled the provinces' peninsulars to emerge victorious over their native son rivals in 1683. For the losers, the imposition of the *alternativa* documented their relegation to second-class status. A decline in the number and social standing of subsequent Franciscans in Lima testified to the displeasure of the province's prominent families.

Augustinians

Augustinians became rooted in New Spain starting in the middle of the sixteenth century. Their number increased as native sons and other creoles entered the order and, by the early seventeenth century, it was almost entirely composed of American-born friars. In 1627, Pope Urban VIII ordered the Province of Mexico to employ the *alternativa*. The mandate infuriated the two creole factions whose numbers exceeded those of the peninsulars by almost 10 to 1 and whose control was so extensive that the successful leader became known as the "monarch." As was common throughout the orders, peninsular friars looked down upon the creoles as akin to indigenous and mestizos. While native son and other creole friars similarly disparaged these groups, they also denigrated the peninsulars who, they believed, were in the Indies because they lacked the ability to be successful in Spain.

Holding positions in their province was one way in which American Spaniards sought to demonstrate their equality with the peninsulars. The frustration at having to share offices with them led one friar to write about the "inscrutable mystery" that native sons govern and obtain the rewards of all nations except in the Indies. The *alternativa* functioned until 1658, when it was suspended for lack of the required 14 peninsular friars. The rotational system was not restored until 1675 when additional friars arrived from Spain.

The *alternativa* was the peninsulars' solution to their minority status. It enshrined continued European office holding within an order's province when native sons and other creoles composed the majority of the friars. More than an annoyance, its patent rejection of native sons enjoying the benefits of their majority permanently reminded them of their deprecation by European Spaniards.

Native sons and other creoles supplied the religious orders much needed manpower starting in the mid to late sixteenth century. They found, however, that their peninsular predecessors were never willing to grant them full equality. The resulting mandated rotation in provincial positions in the mendicant orders guaranteed a small number of peninsulars a disproportional share of authority and prestige. In a different setting, native daughters found that the Church provided them opportunities for personal and financial security, administrative responsibility, and spiritual growth. Disputes within the convents, however, could be nasty and had a way of leaking outside their walls.

Female Convents

Women lacked comparable opportunities with men in the patriarchal world of the Catholic Church as neither positions in the secular clergy nor as regular clergy active in missionary work were available to them. Nonetheless, convents or nunneries provided daughters of elite families both a socially acceptable alternative to married life and an opportunity for spiritual growth. In their final profession, all novices affirmed four vows: poverty, chastity, obedience, and enclosure. Every convent founded by Spaniards and Portuguese in the Indies was cloistered, and professed nuns spent the remainder of their lives within the physical space of their nunneries. In contrast, none of the male orders, for example, Franciscans, Dominicans, or Augustinians, were monastic, and their activities occurred outside as well as within their living community. Convent founders included both women and men who at times were bishops or archbishops.

Few nuns sailed to the Indies, a consequence of their vow to remain cloistered as well as the hardships and risks of transatlantic travel. Although four female religious accompanied Fernando Cortés on his return from Spain to Mexico in 1530, as *beatas* they belonged to no religious order, made only informal vows, and originally dedicated themselves to providing basic education to the daughters of Indian lords (*caciques*). In 1540, Bishop Juan de Zumárraga bestowed the habit of the Conceptionist Order on the *beatas* and founded La Concepción, the first convent in the Americas. In Santo Domingo, the initial nunnery was established at mid-century with 10 sisters of Saint Clare from Spain and 16 young women recruited locally.

In Lima, widowed peninsular Leonor de Portocarrero and her daughter established a community of lay sisters (*beaterio*) for women whose conquistador husbands had predeceased them; it became the convent of La Encarnación under Augustinian canonical rules in 1561. A dozen years later, the twice-widowed peninsular Inés Muñoz de Rivera devoted her fortune to creating the nunnery of La Concepción under the canonical rules of the Franciscans and entered it with her peninsular daughter-in-law. In 1640, Angela de Zárate y Recalde, a first-generation creole born in Santiago de Chile, left La Encarnación with four other nuns to open the stricter Convent of Our Lady of the Prado founded with peninsular Archbishop Pedro de Villagómez in the capital's port of Callao.

As the movement of Angela de Zárate illustrates, early nunneries often supplied the founders of later communities. Sisters from La Encarnación in Lima also initiated what became the city's largest and most prestigious convents – those of the Conceptionists, Santísima Trinidad, and Saint Clare. By 1580, the number of nunneries founded in the Indies reached 25; it exceeded 60 by 1610 when they were present throughout the empire from Mexico to Chile. In Brazil, the daughters of elite families had to travel to Portugal to enter a nunnery until the foundation of the Convent of Santa Clara do Destêrro in 1677. The early English colonies had no convents; the first opened in the state of Maryland in 1790.

Quintessentially urban institutions, convents attracted women and girls from throughout society, although their roles varied significantly.

Some 300 women lived in San Jerónimo in the city of Mexico in 1593. The largest convents in Lima, Quito, the city of Mexico, and Guatemala had from 800 to 1300 women residing in them in during the seventeenth century, although only a minority were nuns. As the Archbishop of Bogotá complained in 1618, the surfeit of servants with and without a habit was "common in almost all convents of the Indies."[4]

Women entered convents for reasons that included religious vocations as well as family pressure. Related attractions included spiritual benefits through nuns' prayers for their families and potential access to financial resources through loans from the convent. Impoverished conquistadors unable to provide adequate dowries or suitable spouses for their daughters' earthly marriages encouraged them to become "Brides of Christ," a path that sometimes required a lesser dowry while in a sense marrying the family to the convent.

Most native daughters of the elite entered nunneries known as "shod" or calced communities that allowed them to live a "private life" while cloistered. This type of community marked what became known as the "great convents"; those in Lima occupied many city blocks and each housed more than 1000 women of whom only 200–300 were nuns. Although the required dowry was small or even nonexistent, fewer women professed in the "barefoot," discalced, or Capuchin orders whose first nunnery in the Indies was founded in Puebla in 1604. Discalced communities enforced a "communal life" dedicated to an austere routine of prayer and poverty that included eating meals together. The severe lifestyle attracted comparatively few native daughters of the elite, and their size was much smaller than the great convents.

Young women who desired to enter a nunnery needed more than a deep religious vocation. They had to meet racial, social, and financial qualifications as well. In general, those who sought to be nuns of the black veil had to demonstrate their "purity of blood" (*limpieza de sangre*), legitimate birth, youth and virginity, and to provide a dowry unless patrons of the convent or the Crown had established endowment funds that would allow exceptions for a few poor candidates, for example, those of outstanding musical talent. In New Spain, dowries were in the range of 1000–1500 pesos in the sixteenth century, but climbed to 4000 pesos and in some cases substantially more by 1800. In Havana, elite families readily paid a required dowry of 4300 pesos for a daughter to enter the Convent of Santa Clara in the late eighteenth century.

Before profession, novices had to dispose of their worldly possessions and frequently relinquished their legal right to a subsequent share of their parents' inheritance, as did sons entering a religious order. Dowries were normally paid in cash, but a family might resort to mortgages to pay the expenses of the daughter's profession ceremony and wardrobe, make income available for her personal needs, buy a room for her in the convent, and in some cases purchase a slave to serve her. The total of these expenditures was understood to represent the nun's share of the family inheritance and those who received such assets often in turn provided resources for a poor relative, protégé, or other novice who lacked the funds to profess. In short, native daughter nuns typically kept resources flowing to other native daughters. Added to claustration, the financial dimension of profession served to limit peninsular women's interest in New World convents unless they had arrived as children and their family had committed to permanent residence in the Indies.

Within the nunneries, distinctive garb identified the diverse social and economic statuses of their residents. Nuns of the black veil occupied the highest rank and sang the canonical hours in the choir. Usually educated and cultured native daughters of elite families, these women enjoyed the honorific *doña*; held the convent's offices; were allowed to vote and participate in formal meetings; enjoyed private rooms, personal servants, meals to their taste, and many comforts; and sometimes taught young girls to read and write. Nuns of the white veil included mostly native daughters from modest families. While they also professed the four vows, they performed housekeeping tasks and were ineligible to vote, hold office, or sing the canonical hours. The *donadas* below them wore a nun's habit, but never took public vows. Generally of mixed ancestry, these poor, illiterate women performed menial tasks. Novices were candidates who spent a year being trained for profession of the required vows. Several hundred servants and slaves also lived in the "great convents."

Regardless of who founded them, convents within a few years routinely came under the domination of native daughters of local and regional elite families. This was true even for nunneries originally created to serve mestizas. In Cuzco, the Santa Clara convent established by *encomenderos* for their *mestiza* daughters in 1551 had a solid majority of Spanish nuns within a generation and developed into a haven for native daughters of the city's elite. Prominent families often supported convents for generations. An example of such long-term commitment occurred in Querétaro, Mexico. When a wealthy native daughter professed in the Convent of Santa Clara in 1751, she was the fifteenth member of her family to enter the nunnery since 1650; by 1800 another five family members had followed her.

Convent elections for abbess at times became heated factional contests that divided local elites for both family and financial reasons. Aside from the position's prestige, the abbess held considerable authority over the community's loan funds. As a result, relatives and prospective borrowers shared interest in the outcome with their widowed mothers, aunts, cousins, daughters, and granddaughters inside the nunnery. Civil and ecclesiastical authorities also took the elections seriously and for good reason. In an unprecedented and scandalous prelude to the election of an abbess of Lima's convent of La Encarnación in 1633, one nun killed another. When the same convent's nuns were preparing to elect an abbess in 1671, the viceroy of Peru posted a mounted guard to police the exterior of the premises. On election day, 100 infantrymen supplemented the mounted guard. Peace returned only after the completion of voting late in the evening.

While internal conflicts sometimes assumed a native daughter versus peninsular character, other issues could be much more important. A controversy in Mexico City's Carmelite Convent of San José in the mid-seventeenth century revealed that the peninsular nuns and all but two creole nuns refused to accept the authority of a creole vicaress named by the archbishop after he had forced out of office the abbess who supported the majority's desire to leave his jurisdiction for that of the Carmelites. The dispute also pitted the viceroy and his wife against the archbishop, although all three were peninsulars. Since the peninsular nuns had arrived in Mexico as young girls and thus were equivalent to *domiciliarios* as identified by the Franciscans, their support of the majority position is not surprising. Despite dissension and disorder associated with elections, the female orders escaped the mandated rotation in office (*alternativa*) imposed on their male counterparts, presumably because their divisions were not as clearly linked to their places of birth.

The Secular Clergy

Preference in Benefices for Creoles and Native Sons

The Royal Patronage gave Castile's monarch extensive power over the Church in nondoctrinal matters. This included the authority to name clerics from the lowliest parish priests to archbishops, although the latter required papal confirmation. The Concordat of Burgos issued by Ferdinand in 1512 contained the first provision for the appointment of creoles, although they were not yet known as such. After reiterating that the Crown would fill vacant "dignities, canonries, prebends, and benefices" as a right of the Royal Patronage, Ferdinand authorized a system of preference:

> All other benefices that become vacant . . . [after the first nomination and provision] shall be granted to legitimate children of the settlers and inhabitants who have come or will come to those kingdoms and take up residence in those parts, and of their descendants, and not to the sons of the natives who were there before the Christians settled. . . .[5]

This document reveals that, even before Cortés reached the American mainland, the Crown had granted future native sons and other creoles of legitimate birth a legal claim to ecclesiastical offices.

In 1525, Charles I informed the bishop and cathedral chapter of Darien, Panama, that the benefices of the bishopric should be given to "*hijos patrimoniales*" – priests native to the bishopric – who were properly educated and had the qualities required. A response to a request by the Spanish *vecinos* and early settlers in Panama, the order (*cédula*) added to the legal foundation for native son appointments in the diocesan clergy. Similarly, in 1542, the council of the city of Mexico sought explicit preference in ecclesiastical appointments for native sons. Thus, requests for native son clerics as well as the Crown's stated policy of using its patronage to favor them followed quickly on the heels of Spanish settlement. But did this policy take effect?

The Quality of Secular Clerics

The secular clergy in sixteenth-century Mexico had substantial room for improvement. A report by visitor Juan de Ovando on 95 priests in the archdiocese of Mexico in 1569 exposed that only 22 had university degrees and few were beyond the baccalaureate. By 1575, the dismal lack of education had improved modestly although still barely a third of the priests had an adequate education. Moreover, numerous peninsulars neglected their clerical responsibilities to pursue personal gain through ownership of mines, ranches, and other financial activities. As the Ordinance of Royal Patronage clearly recognized, the selection process for parish priests required revision.

The use of competitive examinations (*oposiciones*) began in Mexico in 1575. Prior to participating, competitors had to document their *limpieza de sangre*. During the exam they had to demonstrate knowledge of moral theology and administration of the sacraments plus their skill in either Nahuatl or Otomí. The language requirement gave native sons a definite edge over peninsulars while the Ordinance of Royal Patronage itself reiterated that descendants of the conquistadors and early settlers were to be favored for appointments.

By the early 1570s, regular clergy serving in indigenous parishes (*doctrinas*) was also an issue in the viceroyalty of Peru. The archdeacon of Quito's cathedral chapter complained in 1576 that most peninsular friars could not speak their parishioners' language. At the same time, sons of the conquistadors and early settlers who knew native tongues were unable to obtain benefices. Complementing the archdeacon's criticism, the city's representative (*procurador*) penned an argument that native sons who were secular clergy in the diocese should be preferred to clerics from Spain. In due course, a royal order in 1583 specified that diocesan priests were to fill empty indigenous parishes in Peru, but mendicants protested sufficiently that the Crown suspended it five years later.

The issue would not go away. Provincials of the orders charged in 1595 that the Bishop of Quito had ordained mestizos, mulattoes, and even shoemakers. The cathedral's canons, in turn, recounted in 1601 the peninsulars' deficiencies in indigenous languages and reiterated the familiar point that benefices, the only rewards available to the bishop, were patrimonial and therefore reserved for native sons. In the midst of these ongoing exchanges, the Archbishop of Lima estimated that more than a hundred secular clerics lacked positions; without opportunities to fill them, native sons would abandon their pursuit of a clerical career and become soldiers or take to the roads as brigands. The surfeit of locally born clerics was so great that the archbishop recommended – to no avail – that the Council of the Indies should order the superfluous clerics to Spain. Such complaints had already prompted the Crown in late 1593 to remind the *audiencias* of the Indies not to recognize appointments to native parishes given to clerics born outside of their jurisdictions.

No later than the 1570s, native son and other creole parish priests surpassed their peninsular counterparts in the archbishopric of Mexico.

The ranks of the native born continued to climb. By the early seventeenth century, over 95% of the priests in the diocese of Guatemala were born within its boundaries; this level of ascendancy continued for the remainder of the colonial era. In Charcas, creole priests began to outnumber peninsulars in the decade 1611–1620 and in the 1640s, native sons exceeded all other creole and peninsular priests combined. In Cuzco, native sons and other creoles accounted for 85% of the secular parish priests in 1657. Since few peninsulars in the diocesan clergy had interest in serving poor rural parishes, the royal policy of favoring native sons for parish benefices was ultimately successful almost by default. Ambitious, well-educated priests in rural benefices, however, frequently sought advancement to city parishes in their diocese's see. From there, the next step, available only to a few of them, was appointment to a cathedral chapter.

Cathedral Chapters

Each cathedral had an ecclesiastical chapter responsible for its governance and maintenance. Staffed by clerics known collectively as prebendaries, these men were named by the monarch following a recommendation by the Council or Cámara of the Indies or, for a small number of positions, after a formal local competition. The chapter advised the bishop or archbishop on matters pertaining to the diocese and was responsible for the distribution of revenues. Its highest ranks included the five "dignitaries" – dean, archdeacon, choirmaster, teacher or schoolmaster, and treasurer. Appointment as a dignitary usually required prior service as a priest in the three lower ranks of the chapter – canon, *racionero*, and *medio racionero* – that participated in the cathedral's religious services. Positions in the chapter, especially those of dignitaries, carried authority and prestige that included, for example, the privilege of incumbents to use the noble honorific *don*. Attractive in their own right, these positions also were valued because they placed dignitaries on a promotion ladder that led to advancement as bishop. This possibility made native sons particularly interested in them. Local elite families considered the cathedral chapter important for economic reasons as well, for it lent money at interest and was responsible for collecting the tithe, a task for which it contracted with tax farmers.

Native sons and other creoles secured substantial and often dominant representation on cathedral chapters, although their extent varied by

Figure 2.3 Interior of cathedral in Mexico City. Appointment to the cathedral chapter of Mexico was a high honor that numerous native sons attained.
Source: Pierre Frédéric Lehnert et al, *Album Pintoresco de la Republica de México* (Mexico, Estamperia de Julio Michaud y Thomas, 1850), 3. Reproduced by permission of the Mercantile Library at the University of Missouri-St. Louis.

location. Between 1650 and 1700, the chapter of Concepción, Chile, had a total of 23 prebendaries, all born in the kingdom of Chile. During the same years in Santiago, at least 27 of 32 prebendaries were Chileans and no more than 3 were peninsulars. In Valladolid de Michoacán, creoles constituted a majority of the cathedral chapter from at least 1630 to 1666. In the city of Mexico, after 1575, creoles obtained the greater part of appointments and by 1600 held over half of both the prebends and all other benefices (see Figure 2.3).

The Episcopacy

Archbishops and bishops were the highest-ranking clerics in the Indies. Their authority, prestige, and patronage ensured prominence throughout a tenure that normally lasted until either death or promotion. Both regular and diocesan clergy could become bishops and between 1500 and 1620, friars accounted for 70% of all bishops, and Dominicans were nearly half of them, a level of success that undoubtedly helped to attract aspiring native sons to the orders. Although previous parish service was not unusual for either mendicants or secular clerics, the latter routinely had experience as dignitaries of cathedral chapters, and many held advanced degrees in theology or canon law. Standard procedure was for the Council or Cámara of the Indies to recommend three candidates to fill a vacancy and the monarch to select one, usually the man listed in first place, and present his name to the pope for confirmation.

After naming only a handful of creoles earlier, the Crown named 6 in the 1590s and between 6 and 18 creole bishops in every decade except 1621–1630 for the remainder of Habsburg rule. As Table 2.1 reveals, between 1611 and 1687, the Crown appointed at least 12 native sons and 65 other creoles; combined, they accounted for more than one-third of all newly named bishops.

Among the earliest creole bishops were Franciscan Fernando Trejo de Sanabria and Alfonso de la Mota y Escobar. Born in Paraguay, Trejo entered the Franciscan Order in Lima in 1569 and received ordination in 1576. A "celebrated preacher in Potosí," he was the first creole elected provincial of his order and the initial creole bishop of Tucumán. He served in this position for many years and is remembered particularly for founding in 1613 the University of Córdoba. Mota y Escobar was the son of a conquistador. Born in the bishopric of Puebla in 1546, he learned Nahuatl as a boy, and graduated from the University of Mexico with a doctorate in theology. After ordination and service as a parish priest in rural New Spain and the mining district of Pachuca, he sailed to Spain and obtained a degree in canon law at the University of Salamanca. Returning to Mexico as dean of Michoacán's cathedral chapter, he

Table 2.1 First appointments as bishops in the Indies, 1611–1687.

	NS	%	OC	%	Pens.	%	Unk.	%	Total
Totals 1611–1687	12	5%	65	29%	142	63%	5	2%	224

Table developed from author's database.
NS, native sons; OC, other creoles; Pens., peninsulars; Unk., unknown place of birth.

advanced to the same post in Puebla and later in Mexico. In 1596, he turned down the bishopric of Panama, but the following year he accepted that of Guadalajara. Subsequently named a native son bishop of Puebla, he served until his death in 1625.

The first native son archbishop was Fernando Arias y Ugarte, born in Santa Fe de Bogotá in 1561 to a creole mother and peninsular father who was a notary (*escribano*) of the city council among other local positions. After his initial studies, Arias crossed the Atlantic, completed a baccalaureate at Salamanca, and obtained the licentiate and doctorate in law from the University of Lérida in Catalonia. After touring in Spain and Italy, he journeyed to Madrid where, after the Royal Council approved him to practice law, he worked briefly as an attorney. A judge advocate of the army sent to Aragon in 1591–1592, he refused three appointments as *corregidor* and was passed over in 1594 for positions as dean of the cathedral chapter of Bogotá and *oidor* of the *Audiencia* of Quito. Named *oidor* of Panama in 1595, he quickly moved to the *Audiencia* of Charcas, served as *corregidor* of Potosí, and then advanced to the court in Lima with an appointment in 1603. Granted permission to enter the clerical estate in 1605 and ordained in 1607, he continued serving commissions for several years before the Crown named him bishop of Quito in 1613 and three years later sent him to his home see of Santa Fe de Bogotá. Selected archbishop of Charcas in 1624, he advanced to Lima in the same position in 1629 and entered his new see in January 1630. The first creole to hold the viceroyalty of Peru's most eminent ecclesiastical office, he remained archbishop until his death in 1638. An author in Lima enthused in 1688 that that the viceroyalty had not produced a more illustrious subject.

Lima and Mexico provided 62 (over 80%) of the creoles and 6 of the 12 native sons appointed bishops from 1611 to 1687. This success reflected their viceroyalties' wealth, the high concentrations of Spanish settlement, and the presence of colleges, seminaries, and major universities in the capitals. More bishops in these years studied at the University of San Marcos in Lima than at Salamanca and more at the University of Mexico than at the University of Alcalá. The availability of higher education in the Indies facilitated the employment not only of native sons and other creoles in particular, but also that of peninsulars (*hijos provinciales*) who had reached America at an early age. From the former emerged writers who extolled their homelands and defended them from outsiders' criticism.

Clerics and Early Native Son Patriotism

Clerics were among the first Spanish authors to focus on the Indies. A significant subset of the literate population, they provided an audience for publications as well as contributed to a transatlantic debate over the New World's implications for both native-born and immigrant residents. Their perception of their homelands now goes by the name of "early creole patriotism."

Limeño Buenaventura de Salinas y Córdoba, a grandson of conquistadors, was born in 1592. He became a page to Viceroy Luis de Velasco at the age of nine and continued in the post under the two subsequent viceroys. In 1616, he joined the Friars Minor and later preached in provincial cities of Peru, observing the natives during his travels. In *Memorial de las historias del Nuevo Mundo* (1630), he condemned Spaniards' demands on the indigenous peoples, the harsh treatment they administered, and legislation that deprived descendants of conquistadors of their *encomiendas*.

Salinas advocated strongly on behalf of native sons, protesting their progenitors' loss of rewards and displacement by peninsulars from offices that were rightfully theirs. In addition, he denied the common European charge that America's climate induced physical degeneration and reduced mental acuity. Enthusiastically he outlined creoles' positive qualities and descent, in many cases, from Spain's "most illustrious and ancient houses." Wryly he commented about newly arrived peninsulars: "[T]he South Sea baptizes them, and places a '*don*' upon each: after arriving in this City of the Kings (Lima), all are dressed in silks, descended from don Pelayo and the Goths and Visigoths. They proceed to the palace of the viceroy to claim pensions and office."[6]

Salinas bestowed praise on creoles in general, but emphasized those who had secured high positions in the Church and state. He was among the first apologists to declare that creoles were superior to their peninsular ancestors. While a predecessor had averred in 1620 that "Creoles are children of the nobility, [but] improved by bravery . . . becoming more advantaged when transplanted here than [their parents] had been in their native land," Salinas claimed: "Creoles are extremely intelligent, lively, subtle, and well versed in all genres of science [for] the skies and climate of Peru elevate them and ennoble their spirit." His brother, *limeño* Franciscan Diego de Córdoba Salinas, added in a 1651 publication that "in general they are all of such elevated spirits that few are inclined to the arts and mechanic trades that their parents brought with them from Spain; for the sky, the climate, the abundance, and the richness [here] elevates them and ennobles their spirits and minds."[7]

To buttress his assertion of creoles' ability, Buenaventura Salinas proudly listed 13 creole alumni of the University of San Marcos who had become bishops and archbishops. Their ranks included the Archbishop of Lima, Fernando Arias de Ugarte, although he had incorporated rather than earned his degrees there. In addition, the author provided a roster of 16 alumni born in Peru who had secured appointments to *audiencias* and councils. Graduates, many boasting doctorates, had also obtained 26 dignities and canonries; a dozen came from Lima itself and the remainder from throughout its *audiencia* district, Quito, Charcas, and other American locations. Finally, Salinas noted that the Dominicans, Franciscans, and Augustinians had elected creole provincials. As did many other creole apologists, he received an appointment, Bishop of Arequipa, but died before assuming it.

Listing by name native sons and other creoles that received high-level positions of Church and state proved a popular way to document their ability. In the early 1640s, *limeño* Franciscan Balthasar de Bustamante cataloged creoles from the viceroyalty of Peru and the *Audiencia* of Santo Domingo in high ecclesiastical posts. Their ranks had increased noticeably since Salinas's 1630 publication. Bustamante's total of 28 bishops and archbishops was more than twice as large. Men born in the viceroyalty of Peru and the *Audiencia* of Santo Domingo holding dignities and canonries numbered 103, a total that omitted nine cathedrals. Creole provincials included 20 Dominicans, 12 Franciscans, seven Augustinians, two Mercederians, and one Jesuit. The Salinas brothers and Bustamante were only three of the seventeenth-century friars who lauded creoles. It remained for a secular cleric from New Granada to focus specifically on native sons' rights to high-ranking clerical appointments.

A Creole Cleric's Protest, 1634

In 1634, Luis Betancur y Figueroa, a native of Antioquia, New Granada, was resident in Madrid as representative of the cathedrals in the Indies. The son of a Spaniard born in the Canary Islands and a native daughter of New Granada, he studied in the Jesuit College of San Bartolomé in

Bogotá, received ordination, served as a curate in the Cathedral of Lima, and garnered an appointment as advisor to the Tribunal of the Inquisition. While in Madrid, he published a treatise of some 50 pages that presented a legal foundation for advancing to bishop a cathedral's dignitaries and especially the native sons of its diocese. Although the author modestly termed his publication "an informative memorial" in 1634, interest in the issue was sufficiently high that it was republished in 1635 and 1637 and once more in a Madrid periodical in 1789.

The context for Betancur's tract was the few appointments as bishop going to native sons and other creoles as well as discouragingly rare naming of prebendaries with experience in the Indies. Although the 20 creoles first selected bishops or archbishops between 1594 and 1633 were approximately one-fifth of those appointed, creole prebendaries in the Indies' cathedral chapters found this number unacceptable. It meant their chances of elevation to a see were modest, especially since the record showed that peninsulars filled the vast majority of vacancies.

Betancur's publication rested on a surfeit of legal texts and scripture. The arguments can be summarized as follows. Divine, natural, canon, and civil law, and the statutes of Castile and the Indies bestowed preference to native sons for positions in their place of birth, province, and kingdom precisely because of their local nativity and citizenship. Specifically, legislation supported this advantage for every rank of prebend, bishop, and archbishop. Since the importance of birthplace outweighed other qualifications, for example, adequate age and experience, intelligence, education, knowledge, virtue, and personal merit, the many capable native son prebendaries should be favored for elevation as bishop in the cathedrals they served. As Spaniards filled the sees in Spain, creoles should receive those in the Indies. Only in the absence of worthy native sons should the Crown name "foreigners," that is, peninsulars.

Betancur recognized the direct relationship between the growth of universities in Spain and the pursuit of Church and royal positions. Similarly, he noted, the presence of universities in Mexico and Lima had stimulated many native sons to study in the expectation of rewards. Their advancement required only the implementation of existing legislation. Indeed, when he was writing, seven university professors at San Marcos were also prebendaries on Lima's cathedral chapter; in a like manner, six professors at the University of Mexico held prebends. Eleven of these 13 clerics were creoles. In addition, an existing pool of beneficed clerics was available to fill university chairs vacated by promotions.

Moreover, the advancement of native sons and long-serving prebendaries yielded identifiable benefits; in contrast, naming foreigners, that is, peninsulars, brought inconveniences. For example, native son appointments provided deserved recognition to the descendants of the conquistadors and settlers who had given the Crown enormous territories and wealth. The provision of foreigners, in contrast, brought despair among native sons. Pointedly, Betancur referred to the *encomenderos*' revolt in Peru (1544–1548) and the earlier Comunero Rebellion in Castile (1520–1521) at the beginning of Charles I's reign as consequences of the Crown's disregard of this broad principle.

Promotion within cathedral chapters and from them to prelacies, Betancur observed, honored the Church while failure to advance the prebendaries showed it contempt. To support his argument, he pointed out that the Indies in 1634 had six archbishoprics, 32 bishoprics, and 360 prebends. Although the Crown had named 8 archbishops and 28 bishops in the preceding 5 years, it had promoted only 1 dignitary in the Indies. Since the Church's founding in the Indies, moreover, the monarchs had elevated only 23 prebendaries of the same see and 22 from other cathedral chapters when filling 369 appointments of bishop and archbishop. In addition, it had appointed far more friars than secular clerics in the cathedral chapters.

Thus, Betancur insisted that the best appointments of bishop were those that advanced native son prebendaries. As one of his sources noted, it seemed a punishment from on high that a recent arrival (*advenedizo*) should govern a native son. Furthermore, peninsulars frequently refused appointments to the Indies in order to seek better ones and as a result, dioceses went long periods without a bishop. For example, the see of La Plata had remained vacant for nine years after the promotion of Fernando Arias de Ugarte to Lima in 1626.

Naming native sons and prebendaries as bishops had another advantage; they left their earnings in the diocese rather than remitting them to Spain. Arias de Ugarte served as a model. While archbishop of Bogotá, he founded a nunnery for the daughters of conquistadors and *beneméritos* and purchased facilities for the diocese from his prior earnings and remuneration as archbishop.

In sum, Betancur demonstrated the undeniable, ongoing preference that peninsular clerics enjoyed in gaining appointments as bishop and archbishop. His memorial pointedly reminded Philip IV that the Council of the Indies ignored explicit legislation to favor native sons. Although he accepted that originally the so-called Republic of Spaniards in the Indies represented a "new colony dependent on Spain," native sons had subsequently taken advantage of the universities in Mexico and Lima and then served as parish priests, university professors, and prebendaries. The resulting availability of clergy qualified for elevation as bishops proved that the Crown had no need to send peninsular prelates to the Indies.

Betancur, his protest, and its arguments did not simply fade into oblivion. In 1636, he received an appointment as choirmaster (*chantre*) of the cathedral in Quito. Obtaining a license to return to the Indies in 1637, he was named the first creole inquisitor of Lima in 1642. Although elected bishop of Popayán in the 1650s, he turned down the appointment to remain in Lima, where he died in 1659. It is impossible to say whether or not his memorial directly influenced subsequent appointments as bishop and archbishop. Of 126 identified new prelates appointed between 1635 and 1699, however, at least a third went to creoles. This represented progress but certainly not perfection.

In the regular and secular clergy as well as in nunneries, the Church offered opportunities for native sons and daughters and other creoles to obtain potentially positions with power and prestige. The male clerics also found in the Church multiple opportunities for earning a living. At the same time, the first Spanish clerics in the Indies were peninsular mendicants who by virtue of seniority authorized and implemented regulations on admission to novitiates and ordination. The discrimination against creoles that originally marked their admission to the orders continued under the anti-creole policy of rotation in office. Moreover, the Crown never systematically excluded peninsulars from consideration for positions of bishop and archbishop. While Betancur's arguments received attention and he ultimately was named a bishop, it was not to his home diocese. Native sons continued to claim that they should receive preference both for the services of their ancestors in conquest and settlement and because they were native sons of the dioceses in which they wanted to serve. But the Crown persisted in naming peninsular bishops – the foreigners in Betancur's tract.

3

Native Sons in Office

Spaniards and Portuguese in America recreated patriarchal societies modeled on those in Iberia. Thus, by natural right men held extensive authority over women, children, and slaves. This prerogative started with the king, proceeded to nobles with jurisdiction over vassals, and included the power of fathers over wives and children, and masters over slaves. The gender system ensured that, aside from royalty, women held no positions in administration, the ecclesiastical hierarchy, or religious orders other than those women who were in convents. Even there, a male bishop or provincial of an order held authority over the abbesses. Although women sometimes affected male appointments through dowries and royal grants received by widows as a reward for the services of a deceased husband, father, or other relative, the following discussion of native sons in office necessarily focuses principally on men.

Office provided salary in some cases and opportunities for financial gain in others that, in many cases, was based on control over indigenous labor and economic production. Consequently, securing local and royal positions was vital to native sons and their families. Despite legislation that favored them, the lack of its systematic implementation underscored their complaints about appointments bestowed on peninsulars from the sixteenth to the nineteenth century. The core argument initially rested on the services of ancestors who had paid their own expenses during the conquest, suffered hardships, wounds, and even death, and settled in the Indies to retain it for the Crown. These sacrifices, as petitioners viewed them, obligated the king to provide offices to descendants whose presence protected his New World realms. As their ancestors became the

Spaniards in the Colonial Empire: Creoles vs. Peninsulars?, First Edition. Mark A. Burkholder.

stuff of legends, the supplicants turned to a second contention, the legal benefits inherent in status as a native son. Just as Fernando Arias de Ugarte had started his career as a royal official and then embraced an ecclesiastical vocation, a change facilitated by his university education, the arguments moved easily from clerical to civil employment.

Americans never questioned the Crown's prerogative to name officials, and monarchs employed this power to exert authority over the conquistadors through administrative and judicial institutions erected in both Spain and the Indies. In the sixteenth and seventeenth centuries, however, the financial pressures of Spain's war against rebels in the Netherlands and involvement in other European conflicts progressively led the Crown to sell municipal offices and subsequently appointments to royal positions. Native sons never received what they considered their due, and creole writers articulated their frustration in published tracts that emphasized their legal claims to appointments. While marriages between native daughters and peninsular officials served to integrate the latter into the elite in a given municipality, they failed to provide the direct participation in office that native sons believed was their right.

The Crown's Conquest

When conquest and settlement replaced Columbus's dreams and hyperbole, the Castilian Crown became seriously interested in the New World. Accordingly, it started to withdraw privileges and duties willingly granted to entrepreneurial leaders when success was uncertain. Originally vested with administrative oversight, tax collection, and judicial authority over whatever non-Christian peoples and lands he found, Columbus's inability to execute these charges effectively made him the earliest casualty of the Crown's emerging policy. After stripping the admiral of his power, in 1502, Ferdinand and Isabel sent a new governor, Nicolás de Ovando, to Española accompanied by some 2500 settlers. His charge was to stabilize Spanish settlement on the island and to make it profitable. The next year the monarchs created a House of Trade in Seville, Spain, to oversee a monopolistic commercial system and to license ships and passengers. Erection of the Council of the Indies followed in 1524. This body would legislate for the rapidly expanding settlements in the New World, serve as an appellate court for certain civil cases originating there, and, crucially for native sons, recommend candidates for many civil and ecclesiastical positions.

To establish its authority in the Indies, the Crown turned primarily to Castilian precedent, imposed the use of Castilian law, exported a variety of administrative and judicial institutions, and named their officials. Starting in Española in 1511, it created *audiencias*. To counter Fernando Cortés's power in New Spain, the Crown established a second *audiencia* in the city of Mexico to serve, along with treasury officials, as its representatives in the distant kingdom. In general, each *audiencia* enjoyed first instance jurisdiction in its seat, served as a regional high court with appellate responsibilities, advised the chief executive, for example, viceroy or captain-general, and legislated in conjunction with him. Its judges received commissions to undertake special assignments. During the sixteenth and early seventeenth century, the Crown created tribunals in Panama, Guatemala, Lima, Guadalajara (New Galicia), Santa Fe de Bogotá, La Plata (Charcas), Quito, Chile, and Manila. When the first tribunal in Mexico proved an ineffective executive body, Charles I turned to the office of viceroy used in the Crown of Aragon and parts of Italy. Antonio de Mendoza, the first appointee, was a younger son of one of Castile's most prominently titled noble families. He reached the capital of Mexico in 1535 to initiate the position. Lima became the capital of the viceroyalty of Peru authorized in 1542.

Treasury officials routinely accompanied major expeditions of conquest to collect tax revenue. When appropriate, they founded treasury offices at important mining centers, ports, and administrative capitals. Named to oversee the Crown's fiscal interests, they commonly devoted considerable effort to their own. An early example was *hidalgo* treasurer Alonso de Estrada who arrived in New Spain in 1523 with his wife, a son, and five daughters. Besides official duties and pursuit of *encomiendas* for himself, Estrada and his spouse were soon busily arranging marriages for their children that would place them in the emerging *encomendero* aristocracy.

Starting in the 1530s in New Spain and the 1560s in Peru, the Crown began to subdivide *audiencia* jurisdictions into smaller units known as *corregimientos*, *alcaldías mayores*, and *gobernaciones* depending on the provincial official's title: *corregidor*, *alcalde mayor*, or governor. The viceroys initially appointed for a one- or two-year term salaried *corregidores de indios* to oversee native officials who collected tribute not assigned to an *encomendero* and to administer justice by handling appeals from indigenous villages within their district. In less than 20 years, their jurisdiction was extended to encompass *encomiendas*. In New Spain in the 1550s, they were authorized to handle civil and criminal cases in their district involving both Indians and Spaniards. Thus, the expanded use and authority of *corregidores* who served in effect as short-term *encomenderos* placed natives under direct royal authority. This change accompanied a gradual reduction in the number of *encomenderos*. By the end of the sixteenth century, some former *encomenderos* and their heirs were receiving appointments as *corregidores*, the term used in Peru, and *alcaldes mayores*, as most provincial administrators became known in New Spain in the seventeenth century.

Municipalities were the territorial building blocks of empire, and aldermen (*regidores*) of cities and towns established after conquest were among the earliest officeholders. As prominent founding citizens, they received lots near the central plaza as well as property for agriculture and grazing outside the municipality's core. Other officials ranged from a sheriff and judge to an inspector of foodstuffs sold in the market. By 1630, Spaniards had created well over 300 municipalities as the initial step of settlement and transfer of Spanish culture.

The Crown's right to create this array of institutions and to name their officials went unquestioned. The issue was whom the Crown would name. This, in turn, rested on the nature of the relationship between the Crown of Castile and the Indies, individuals' claims for recompense based on merit and service, and patronage networks.

What Kind of Kingdoms?

Two models existed for incorporating the "kingdoms" of the Indies, for example, New Spain, New Granada, and Quito, into the Crown of Castile. Since the relationship rested on conquest, the Crown could rule them as it pleased in an "accessory" union. The alternative was to incorporate the lands as a juridically equal realm of the composite monarchy that formed the ruler's patrimony. In this relationship, each kingdom, for example, Aragon and Castile, retained its own laws and customs and formed part of what became known during Habsburg rule as "Greater Spain" or "The Spanish Monarchy." The person of the monarch, rather than common institutions, laws, and privileges, linked the separate realms. Charles I explicitly declared in 1519 that "we are Lord [*Señor*] of the West Indies, Islands and Mainland of the Ocean Sea, both discovered and to be discovered, and they are incorporated into our Royal Crown of Castile."[1] His declaration meant that Castilians in America could expect a contractual relationship between service and reward and confirmed that American Spaniards were Castilians and governed by that kingdom's laws except when specific legislation for the Indies superseded them.

As settlement replaced conquest, the growing number of native sons in America increasingly saw themselves as belonging to kingdoms that were distinct patrimonial realms enjoying the rights of Castilians. The names "Kingdom of New Spain" and "New Kingdom of Granada," for example, conveyed this claim. During this evolution, the Crown never clarified explicitly whether the kingdoms of the Indies were joined to Castile through "accessory" union or as a distinct patrimonial entity directly tied to the monarch. Of significance to native sons, the Habsburg Crown rarely if ever referred to the Indies as colonies rather than kingdoms. Consequently creoles considered their relationship to the monarch to be patrimonial, an identification that conveyed specific rights including "distributive justice."

Reciprocity between Crown and subject and the concept of "distributive justice" were central to the Spaniards' exploration and settlement in America. The monarch had the responsibility to recognize services that individuals performed for the Crown and to reward them according to their worth. Each individual in a political or ecclesiastical jurisdiction, in turn, possessed the right to receive – according to his status, service, and merit – a just reward. As the ultimate fount of favor, the monarch's actions created personal ties with vassals that obligated them to continued service. Importantly, the rewards went not only to the vassals who performed the service, but also to their descendants. In this way royal patronage bound together an effective monarchy. Distributive justice and the obligation of royal reward thus formed the context that conquistadors, early settlers, and their descendants employed when seeking *encomiendas*, offices, and other forms of recognition. The great distance between Spain and the Indies, however, meant that monarchs delegated much of the responsibility for implementation to the viceroys of New Spain and Peru. This proved to be an important and ongoing problem, for native sons fully recognized the benefit of holding office.

Offices

The Value of Holding Office

Conquistadors in Mexico quickly sought to solidify their descendants' position in the emerging society of New Spain. The Crown responded in 1531 by ordering the *Audiencia* of Mexico to favor them, their relatives, and their retainers in making land grants. Continued awards to newly arrived peninsulars led earlier residents to press their case, and in 1543, they obtained another royal injunction that directed officials not to privilege newcomers. The conquistadors' anxiety over grants of every kind arose from the decline and, in some cases, collapse of *encomiendas*, first in New Spain and then in Peru, as a result of native depopulation caused by smallpox, typhus, and other diseases whose impact had been worsened by *encomenderos*' excessive labor demands and abuse. In addition, the reversion of *encomiendas* to the Crown began quickly with the largest ones tending to pass into royal control first. Although they could be reassigned, the Crown preferred to retain them and designate pensions from their income. Several examples illustrate the changes.

Martín Monje, a conquistador of Mexico, received an *encomienda* that diminished from 3000 tributaries in 1524 to 800 in 1550. One assigned to another conquistador in New Spain in the 1530s still had 8000 tributaries in 1570, but fell to fewer than 1100 by the early 1640s when its tribute reverted to the Crown. *Encomendero* Francisco Hernández Retamoso found that his grant in the Colca Valley of Peru no longer produced enough revenue to maintain payments on his debts. The deteriorating value of *encomiendas* as well as uncertainty about the Crown's willingness to allow another "life" for one's heir made offices an attractive alternative.

Offices provided prestige and usually income through fees, salaries, and opportunities for personal gain. The modern conception of office as a public trust had not yet replaced the belief that office should provide benefits to the incumbent, his relatives and *paisanos*, and others in his network. A variety of restrictions prohibited royal officeholders from having family and economic ties within their district of service and thus sought to encourage the upright administration of justice and to limit illicit gain. Nonetheless, officeholders routinely engaged in practices that today are considered corrupt. Moreover, the Crown undercut its policy in the seventeenth and first half of the mid-eighteenth century by granting or selling exceptions to restrictive legislation, for example, the prohibition of marriage to a local woman, with such frequency that exceptions became the norm.

Types of Offices

The Crown named officials for either a term or life. Term offices included viceroy, captain-general, governor, president, *corregidor*, and *alcalde mayor*. Lifetime appointments went to treasury officials, *audiencia* ministers, and officials in various administrative agencies. The men named received legal income through either fees for service or salaries. Fee offices included notaries (*escribanos*); sheriffs (*alguaciles*); municipal inspectors of weights and measures; and officials in the royal mint among others. Viceroys, *audiencia* ministers, treasury officials, and their staffs received salaries and, in some cases, additional perquisites. Provincial officials, for example, *corregidores*, were paid modest salaries, often a percentage of the revenues they collected. They made up for this inadequacy by extralegal means, notably the forced sale of merchandise, distribution of raw materials, and loans to indigenous in their district. Aldermen comprised the largest group of offices without salary or fees. As with the post of municipal standard-bearer, men sought these positions for the prestige, precedence, and local influence they offered. Some conquistadors and early settlers became aldermen when they established new municipalities, although as early as 1525, a royal appointee to the post appeared in the city of Mexico and others followed there and elsewhere.

Municipal Offices

Native sons started to serve as aldermen (*regidores*) almost as quickly as the first reached the required age of 18. In Lima's municipal council, every alderman named through 1560 was a peninsular. Three young *limeños* shattered this monopoly when they became aldermen in 1561. After losing their majority in 1575, peninsulars subsequently outnumbered native sons only from 1595 to 1605. For more than two centuries, native sons enjoyed overwhelming domination of Lima's city council.

Many municipalities throughout the empire mirrored the local preeminence on Lima's city council. The council in Mexico City had a creole majority by 1590, as did Quito soon afterward. In contrast, half of the identified aldermen on the municipal council of Guatemala City in the late seventeenth century were peninsulars, and just under half were native sons. The remaining two were creoles from outside Guatemala. By the 1630s, Popayán's most prominent families dominated the *cabildo*, but the body experienced considerable turnover as incumbents sold rather than bequeathed their positions. Local notables also comprised the municipal councils in Brazil, although aldermen were elected by their peers rather than purchasing their posts. Landed interests dominated the council in Salvador, Bahia, but some merchants were also present. Of all offices in the Indies, native sons' representation was strongest in municipal councils.

Native Sons, Other Creoles, and Offices

As they came of age, native sons and other creoles beseeched the Crown to reward appropriately the merit and services of their ancestors and themselves. Sons of conquistadors and first settlers initially sought *encomiendas* through inheritance and new grants. Overlapping these increasingly unsuccessful requests, they sought appointment to royal offices. Their pursuit rested on economic necessity, especially from the final decades of the sixteenth century onward. Younger sons in particular studied in a novitiate or acquired a university education to prepare for a career in the Church or royal employment.

Native sons applauded legislation issued in 1538 that ordered the appointment of American-born descendants of conquistadors and early settlers to office in recognition of their ancestors' services. Especially pleasing was the provision that, with the important exception of judicial posts, they were to be named to positions where the services had been performed, that is, typically in their region of birth. Although the exception ruled out native sons for *audiencia* appointments, enterprising creole jurists expounded why the king could and should ignore this limitation. The Portuguese Crown also followed a general policy of not naming such officials to their home district, although it selected a few Brazilian magistrates to the high court of Bahia in the years after the expulsion of the Dutch from northern Brazil in 1654.

Viceregal Patronage and Illicit Sale of Appointments

Viceroys during Habsburg rule embodied the monarch in New Spain and Peru through authority, symbols, ritual, public display, and patronage. One sign of their status was the power to grant, at least on an interim basis, an assortment of offices. The many posts of *corregidor* and *alcalde mayor* in particular made them a valuable part of viceregal patronage as well as a source of illicit income.

Viceroys during Habsburg rule (1516–1700) invariably reached their posts with a substantial entourage that emulated the royal household on a smaller scale. One incoming viceroy of Peru, for example, brought a confessor, chamberlain, majordomo, master of the horse, secretary, captain of the guard, physician, a dozen ladies-in-waiting to attend to his wife and mother-in-law, a number of gentlemen of the chamber, pages, valets, a pastry chef, an accountant, and a variety of lower servants to take care of cooking, the wardrobe, and other more menial chores. Often a viceroy also brought a physician and captain of the guard. The consequence was numerous new arrivals (*advenedizos*) that the viceroy, as patron of this clientele, had to reward in order to confirm his elevated position and to demonstrate the favor his retainers and clients enjoyed.

The predominance of peninsular newcomers in a viceroy's entourage was central to native sons' complaints. They knew correctly that most had the single goal of self-enrichment. One creole of New Spain complained: "It is a great affront that requests for honors by descendants of Conquistadores are hopeless unless they are aided and preferred by a member of the viceroy's entourage."[2] The author fully recognized that many positions were a means to gain and extend control over indigenous labor, a major source of prosperity. *Visitador* of New Spain Juan de Palafox stated explicitly in 1641 that viceregal appointments angered creoles "when they see that a viceroy's chamber servant, who rose to this post from less than page, has precedence over the grandchildren and heirs of those who participated in the conquest."[3] Native sons and other creoles, in contrast, received such appointments only by paying substantial sums to the viceroy. Viceregal appointments of recent arrivals thus conflicted with what *beneméritos* considered theirs by law. Consequently, viceroys had to balance the kings' repeated orders to reward the *beneméritos* against their own obligation to provide for their retainers. In general, they did better by the latter and stimulated repeated protests by individual creoles and the municipal councils that represented them. Besides attacking viceregal appointments of relatives and peninsular retainers, critics objected to some viceroys' practice of favoring relatives of *audiencia* ministers as a way to garner support. The evidence is clear that viceroys regularly and intentionally failed to implement legislation granting preference to native sons.

Appointments by early seventeenth-century viceroys in Peru illustrate the issue's magnitude. Viceroy Luis de Velasco (1596–1604) awarded *encomiendas*, administrative offices, and positions in the viceregal guard to his retainers. Marquis of Montesclaros (1607–1615) granted *corregimientos* to his secretary, master of the horse, a gentleman of his chamber, a page, and a servant of his wife. His successor, the Prince of Esquilache (1615–1621), however, put Velasco and Montesclaros to shame. The Prince's entourage of 174 persons included his wife, two daughters, retainers, servants, musicians, and Italian comedians. Even before officially entering his post, he started to name followers to office. His favorite Martín de Acedo not only proposed to him candidates for posts and received their monetary payments for this consideration, but also secured at least five offices for himself and married the sister of a prominent creole cleric. A critic charged that of 100 positions available, the viceroy gave 70 to his retainers. These included a *corregimiento* to a Portuguese musician of his entourage. The Prince also favored dependents of ministers on Lima's *audiencia*, intentionally ignoring *beneméritos*. In response to local complaints about Esquilache's patronage, Philip III issued a stricture in 1619 that again forbade viceroys from naming relatives and retainers and ordered them to give preference to *beneméritos* and men from the district (*hijos patrimoniales*).

Viceregal appointments of provincial officials were commonplace and lucrative for nearly a century and a half. In the 1670s, allegedly the viceroy of New Spain pocketed 375 000 pesos annually through the private sale of appointments and the viceroy of Peru some 150 000 pesos. This source of revenue suffered a major blow in the late 1670s when the Crown briefly withdrew their prerogative of naming provincial officials. Two years later it granted each viceroy the right to name a dozen retainers to specified provincial positions ranked from first to third class. Charles II's objective of removing most of these positions from viceregal patronage was not to chastise viceroys, reward native sons, or benefit the indigenous. Rather it was to turn the posts into a source of regular revenue by selling appointments on behalf of the royal treasury.

The Sale of Offices and Appointments

Sale of Municipal Offices

Citizens of municipalities initially elected officeholders in the Indies, but soon the Crown intervened, appointing aldermen as a favor or reward for service. Charles I began the sporadic sale of municipal offices in Castile for the treasury's benefit in 1523 and more systematically in the years 1540–1545. Philip II continued the practice and, despite occasional attempts to suppress offices established solely to be sold, the list of saleable positions expanded. The year after the Crown's "bankruptcy," in 1558 Philip II authorized the sale of local and fee-producing offices in America, thus extending the transformed concept of office as a royal grant to one of royal income. Beginning with fee-collecting positions, most notably that of notary (*escribano*), saleable offices expanded to include all municipal posts except those of the elective local magistrates (*alcaldes ordinarios*). Many sales permitted the purchaser to arrange for a deputy to perform the actual work. Gradually the Crown added the right to sell or bequeath purchased positions in order to increase their value. Forcing the owner to pay a tax based on the sale ensured that the Crown would receive ongoing income from alienated offices. Once begun, the number of posts sold for a lifetime expanded; grants followed that allowed a second life or even perpetuity.

Philip III brought uniformity to the process in 1606 when he formally created for the Indies, but not for Castile, an official class of "saleable and renounceable offices" as a form of property that allowed all purchasers to sell or bequeath their positions upon payment of a tax. This decision guaranteed that native sons throughout the empire would continue to hold substantial local authority. By succeeding either peninsular or creole fathers, they could legally dominate the municipal councils and their elective positions of local magistrate. While prices varied by location and date, at times some offices could be very costly. In the city of Mexico, peninsular merchant and financier Baltasar Rodríguez purchased the post of sheriff (*alguacil mayor*) for the princely sum of 125 000 pesos. The Crown also sold positions in the colonial mints. In Mexico City, prominent wholesaler and founder of the merchant guild (*consulado*) Diego Matías de Vera, a native of Seville, and his wife, Ana de Ureña, paid for the mint's directorship and the right to bequeath it for the enormous and unprecedented amount of 250 000 pesos in cash. They then used the post as the basis for an entail for their creole eldest son. The assayer position sold for 140 000 pesos in 1609 and 160 000 pesos in 1633 while the post of weigher at the mint sold for only 7000 pesos, but provided an annual income of 1600–1700 pesos in the late sixteenth century.

By designating certain offices saleable and transferable property, the Crown enabled owners to include them in their daughters' dowries and thereby provided a way for peninsular sons-in-law to be incorporated formally into municipal oligarchies. Additionally, by sanctioning inheritance of these positions, the Crown ensured that native sons would frequently own the most desirable municipal posts and hence effectively eliminated them as a potential major source of conflict between native sons and peninsulars. A close study of the city council of Lima, moreover, revealed no examples of conflict between native son and peninsular aldermen.

The Sale of Appointments to Royal Offices

The Crown's continued search for revenue soon spread to salaried royal positions. Sales began in the 1630s with treasury appointments, expanded to provincial posts in the late 1670s, added *audiencia* positions in the late 1680s, and even included appointments as viceroy before 1700. Sale of treasury and provincial appointments continued until the mid-eighteenth century, as did *audiencia* appointments during years of war. The sale of appointments as viceroy proved ephemeral. The Portuguese sold virtually all offices in Brazil except for those of governors and magistrates on the colony's equivalent of the *audiencias* in the Spanish realms.

Unlike the sale of offices, the Spanish Crown's sale of appointments did not convey property rights. Rather it was buyer beware. Without a special provision in the title of appointment, a purchaser who died soon after assuming his post lost his money for there was no office to bequeath or for his heirs to sell. Buying these appointments was consequently most attractive to young men and especially young native sons willing to pay a premium for exemptions to legislation designed to limit ministers' personal and economic ties within their jurisdiction.

The evolving process documented the Crown's willingness to abandon its commitment to naming native sons and other creoles on the basis of descent from conquistadors and early settlers in exchange for cash. This transformation affected differently the major jurisdictions of the empire. In some regions, native sons queued up to purchase appointments, especially those on *audiencias* and in treasury and accounting offices. In others regions, the market for appointments as *corregidor* and *alcalde mayor* resulted in peninsulars becoming especially active purchasers. Overall, the sale of appointments resulted in more native sons and other creoles holding office at the end of the seventeenth century than a century earlier.

Term Appointments: Provincial Officials

Several hundred provincial officials (governors, *corregidores*, and *alcaldes mayores*) held their posts for a term rather than for life. Although regular, as distinct from interim, appointments as a provincial official were initially for one or two years, tenure for three years for viceregal provisions, and five years for appointments made in Spain became common. The Crown paid governors 2000–3000 pesos; *corregidores* in Peru, 1000–3000 pesos; and *alcaldes mayores* in New Spain, about 500 to over 1300 pesos. Some offices also provided perquisites termed "the same benefits as your predecessors"; these could include, for example, administering textile manufactories (*obrajes*) of the district in Quito for the recipient's personal benefit.

For provincial officials, the opportunity to engage in the *repartimiento de mercancías*, or forced sale of goods and distribution of raw materials on credit to the indigenous of the district, was more valuable than the salary. Depending on location, the goods could include mules, tools, cotton to weave into cloth, and a plethora of other items. This *repartimiento* of merchandise made the offices of *corregidor* and *alcalde mayor* especially attractive in populous jurisdictions. In Oaxaca, Mexico, an *alcalde mayor* operated a credit system also known as *repartimiento*. He served as a moneylender, advancing sums at a fixed rate of interest to local producers of cochineal and cotton cloth who needed credit and had no alternative source. He later received the red dye and cotton cloth as payment. In addition, he forced the indigenous peoples to purchase livestock, notably oxen and mules. As was common elsewhere, *alcaldes mayores* used assistants (*tenientes*) to help distribute goods and cash as well as for the more difficult task of collecting.

Whether born in Spain or the Indies, provincial officials routinely turned to wealthy, usually peninsular merchants or, less frequently, the Church to provide the bond required before assuming office. The surety served to assure the Crown that the official would collect tribute and other required revenues. The merchants, in turn, expected to sell goods to the indigenous population of a district through the officials they had bonded and the assistants they had named. Profits were divided between the bonding merchant and the provincial official. Although men could hold provincial offices more than once, a single term was the norm, for these posts did not constitute a career or even a step in an identifiable career path. Consequently the officials sought to maximize profits during a single term of office through the use of *repartimiento*. Cooperation between the officials and their bondsmen was essential for success, regardless of the participants' place of birth.

Life Appointments: Fiscal Offices

Treasury officials reached Española in 1502 and subsequently accompanied or arrived shortly after expeditions of conquest on the American mainland. Treasury offices located in the capital of each *audiencia* and in some ports and mining camps both documented the Crown's desire for revenue and provided posts to be filled. The most important treasury offices were in the viceregal capitals of Lima and Mexico. Their officials oversaw the collection and disbursement of revenues and the receipt of surpluses from other treasuries. Tax farmers did most of the actual revenue collection into the eighteenth century. The creation of tribunals of accounts in 1605 in Lima for Peru, the city of Mexico for New Spain, and Cartagena de Indias for New Granada complemented the treasury offices. The tribunals' major responsibility was to audit public accounts for which a dedicated accounting office did not exist. Peninsulars were the first appointees.

The Crown named only two native sons to the accounting tribunal in Lima before the sale of its appointments began in 1633 and but 2 creoles out of 10 new appointees to the treasury office between 1613 and 1633. Purchased appointments conveyed life tenure, but not property rights unless specifically stated in the official title of appointment. Consequently, buying an appointment was most advantageous for young and inexperienced native sons, often with little background in accounting, who planned to serve for many years. By mid-century, purchasers were a majority in both the treasury and tribunal of accounts. Because these positions were few, to increase income, the Crown also sold *futuras*, the right to fill the first available vacancy in order of seniority. Between 1633 and 1660, sometimes six or seven futures were outstanding in Lima. Probably 10 of the 12 men that bought them for this tribunal of accounts during these years were creoles, and most of them almost certainly were native sons. Overall, purchasers accounted for more than 80% of appointees to the treasury and the accounting tribunal of Lima between 1633 and 1700.

The small number of purchasers who were not native sons or other creoles included peninsulars long resident in Lima. Among the first buyers were two *radicado* merchants. Juan de Quesada y Sotomayor was a prosperous merchant from Galicia married first to a *limeña* daughter of a couple born in Seville and then to a woman from Seville. His wealth enabled him to provide a dowry of 25 000 pesos in 1636 when his daughter María married. He assumed his post as treasurer in the same year, gained the additional office of admiral of the Pacific fleet in 1637, and secured command of the fleet that carried treasure to Panama in 1648. Quesada was also an agent for the Inquisition of Lima. He took advantage of his positions to engage in contraband trade, smuggle unregistered silver from Callao, and extract bribes from other merchants.

Not all sales worked out. In 1641, peninsular Juan de Medina Avila bought an appointment as auditor of the Tribunal of Accounts in Lima for 9000 pesos. His purchase included the right for his son to enter the office when he had reached the age of majority. In the meantime, Juan would serve. His service was brief for it quickly became clear that he could neither write nor do arithmetic. While his son had those skills, he was not bright enough to do the job. Juan alleged that his memory had failed and he had forgotten how to do accounts, but would be fine within two months. The time passed without his memory improving and finally he was removed from office.

The sale of treasury appointments in the city of Mexico was common as well. Between 1635 and 1679, three-quarters of the 32 appointments to treasury posts in Mexico were sold. In the subsequent years to 1750, peninsulars bought nearly two-thirds of the appointments sold. One purchaser was Francisco de Rodezno of Madrid, a government auditor who had left the Old World for the New in 1677. After buying his appointment, he subsequently devoted himself to wringing a profit from his investment. One source of private income was a warehouse in the city of Mexico stocked with sugar, olive oil, and cinnamon. He married a *criolla* from Puebla in the fall of 1680, and by the end of the decade had at least one son. Considered prosperous by 1689, Rodezno left a complex estate in Mexico upon his death in the mid-1730s. By then his son José, born and educated in the capital, had been established for years. Undoubtedly aided by his father's cash, while still a minor he bought an appointment in 1710 as a supernumerary judge on the *Audiencia* of Guatemala, where he served for 30 years. The immigrant auditor not only had prospered, but also was able to place his creole son in a more prestigious position.

The sale of appointments to treasury offices and the tribunals of accounts increased the power of local elites comprised primarily of native sons and peninsulars at the expense of royal authority. While native son purchasers obviously had local family and economic interests, other purchasers either were already *radicados* or soon became them. A native daughter's marriage to a treasury official was one way for the bride's family to gain access to persons of influence and wealth and, if he were a peninsular or creole from elsewhere, to integrate him into prominent society of the city.

Life Appointments: Audiencia Ministers

Audiencias were arguably the most important royal institution in the colonies. Unlike the six-year term appointments used in Brazil's high court, *audiencia* ministers in the Spanish possessions were named for life. Many spent decades in a single location, often investing in the local economy, marrying a native daughter of an important local family, and subsequently arranging for children to marry into other elite families as well. The powerful and prestigious *audiencia* positions were extremely attractive to native sons with university training in law (*letrados*). Securing a position in their home districts was often difficult, particularly in the viceregal capitals prior to the late seventeenth century, but especially enticing.

Creoles began to obtain *audiencia* appointments in the late sixteenth century, but through 1610, the Crown had named only a handful. Among

Table 3.1 First appointments of *audiencia* ministers in the Indies, 1611–1687.

	NS	%	OC	%	Pens.	%	Unk.	%	Total	%
1611–1687	8	2%	92	22%	243	59%	71[a]	17%	414	100%

Table developed from author's database.

[a] Although not definitively identified, all or nearly all of these ministers were peninsulars.

NS, native sons; OC, other creoles; Pens., peninsulars; Unk., unknown place of birth.

them was Simón de Meneses, the son of Dr Gaspar de Meneses. The Council of the Indies noted years later that Gaspar had provided "very good" services in the discovery of Peru and during the rebellion led by Gonzalo Pizarro. A first-generation native son of Lima, Simón studied at its College of San Martín before spending a decade at the University of Salamanca where he graduated with a licentiate degree. Returning to the City of Kings, he practiced law and taught at the University of San Marcos before sailing again to Spain, this time to pursue an *audiencia* appointment. The Council of the Indies considered him for a post in Mexico, where, the councilors pointed out, the issue of birth in the district was not a problem. In 1591, Meneses was named an *oidor* of the *Audiencia* of Santo Domingo.

Creole appointments to *audiencias* increased substantially between 1611 and 1687, although native sons received few of them (see Table 3.1). From 1611 to 1630, 16 Americans obtained the coveted posts; 19 more were named in the following decade and another 18 from 1641 to 1650. By late 1687, creole appointees totaled 100, but only eight were native sons, one as a result of a royal dowry. *Limeño* Alonso de Zárate y Verdugo's appointment as a criminal judge of the *Audiencia* of Lima in 1660 resulted from his marriage to *limeña* Luisa Sotomayor y Córdoba, niece of a favorite of Philip IV. His naming included an explicit exemption for being a native son of the City of Kings, one of the few such men who had yet been named to an American *audiencia*.

Disappointed by their very limited success, native sons took advantage of opportunities to bargain with the Crown. When Philip IV sought financial support in 1636 for a naval squadron in the Caribbean, the council of the city of Mexico sought concessions in return. One was that creoles born in New Spain receive half of the *audiencia* positions in the empire, a remarkable aspiration considering that no more than five men native to the viceroyalty had received *audiencia* appointments. The request proved unsuccessful.

Native Sons

Legislative Preference

In 1538, Charles I decreed that, "merit" being equal, descendants of the first discoverers, conquerors, settlers of the Indies, and persons born there were to receive preference in appointments so that they and especially married men "would be occupied and rewarded where their ancestors served."[4] Soon afterward, the New Laws of 1542 acknowledged the Crown's obligation to the explorers, conquistadors, and settlers:

> And because it is right that those who have served in the discoveries of the said Indies, and also those who assist in the settlement thereof and have their wives there, be preferred in the advantages, We ordain that in conferring *corregimientos* and other emoluments whatsoever, our Viceroys, Presidents, and Auditors of our said *Audiencias* prefer the original Conquistadores, and after them the married settlers, being suitable persons, for such offices, and that until these are provided for, as aforesaid, no other person be provided for.[5]

In a clarification the following year, Charles I observed that he had been informed that some sons of conquistadors (i.e., native sons) of New Spain were impoverished. As a result he instructed the viceroy to provide "*corregimientos* and other remunerative offices" to sons of the original conquerors of New Spain "who have no *repartimiento* of Indians, and remain poor" but are of legitimate birth and have ability and the requisite age.[6] A law of June 4, 1548 noted that rewards for services were to be where the claimant or his ancestors had performed them. An exception made in 1569 was to prohibit *encomenderos* from serving as *corregidores, alcaldes mayores,* and other officials engaged in the administration of justice in the jurisdiction of the *encomienda*, but this restriction was subsequently lifted for descendants of explorers, settlers, and "pacifiers" in the Indies who had provided services that merited compensation.

Viceroys were not to fill offices with persons who had engaged in "oficios mecánicos" nor with relatives, retainers, servants or others who had gone to the Indies with them or with presidents, *audiencia* ministers, treasury officials, and other ministers. As these examples illustrate, the Crown repeatedly recognized as its side of reciprocity that it owed rewards to the descendants of explorers, conquistadors, and early settlers.

However much they might have encouraged native sons, policy statements were not actions. What these men wanted was for the Crown to take seriously the decline of the *encomenderos* as well as their heirs' longing to hold honorable occupations in their homeland that would enable them to continue in their local elite as it had developed since the conquest. Ironically, the initial native son appointed to an American *audiencia* lacked these characteristics.

The First Native Son Named to an American Audiencia

Almost a century and nearly 300 new appointees after the first designation of an *audiencia* minister in America, in 1602, Philip III selected Alonso Bravo de Sarabia as *alcalde del crimen* of the *Audiencia* of Lima. As the first native son, second *limeño*, and among the initial handful of creoles to receive any *audiencia* appointment, Alonso's success was an early precedent that subsequent aspirants could use to support their pretensions. At the time, of course, no hopeful American *letrados* could know that the election of a second native son for an initial *audiencia* position would not take place until 1637 after another 180 appointments. In short, Alonso's selection was a fluke, a circumstance that makes the case worth examining.

Alonso's profile differed from the descendant of a conquistador whose *encomienda*'s decline in value caused him to seek appointment to office. His parents were peninsulars. If born a little later, he would have been a Chilean rather than a Peruvian, for his father, after serving 16 years on the *Audiencia* of Lima, was the first president of the short-lived *Audiencia* of Chile established in Concepción in 1565. He studied briefly at Lima's University of San Marcos before sailing to Spain with his parents. After spending some time in Soria, where his father died in 1577, Alonso entered the University of Salamanca and in due course graduated with a baccalaureate degree in canon law. Moving to Seville, he entered the university's postbaccalaureate residential college of Santa María de Jesús, also known as Maese Rodrigo, becoming its rector in 1602 and at the same time pursuing *audiencia* positions in the Indies. In 1611, he entered the Order of Santiago because of his brother Juan's participation in the Cortes of Castile.

Alonso's great advantage was to belong to an extended family of successful peninsular *letrados.* They obtained high-ranking royal positions, secured knighthoods in military orders, and belonged to a network that included men from the Crown of Castile's six most prestigious and influential postbaccalaureate residential colleges (*colegios mayores*) and provided access to the corridors of patronage in Madrid. His father, the first *colegial* of the Colegio of San Clemente at the University of Bologna to serve on an American *audiencia*, devoted more than a quarter-century to serving his monarch on New World tribunals. Alonso's sister Mariana wed a peninsular whose years in the *Colegio Mayor* of Santa Cruz at the University of Valladolid facilitated his appointment to the Chancellory of Granada, advancement to the Council of the Indies, and promotion to the Council of Castile. His presence on the recently created *Cámara* of the Indies, an advisory committee that recommended to the king candidates for *audiencia* appointments, unquestionably influenced Alonso's assignment on Lima's tribunal.

Alonso's familial ties to successful *letrados* extended from the realms of Spain to the Indies and included multiple generations. His wife's sister married a peninsular *colegial mayor* who served on the *Audiencia* of Lima and then as President of the *Audiencia* of Quito. His niece, Mayor de Sarabia, born in Santiago, Chile, married a peninsular *colegial* of Santa Cruz named *oidor* of Lima in 1598. Their *limeño* son Juan Jiménez de Montalvo y Sarabia was a *colegial mayor* at Salamanca and ultimately reached the Council of the Indies; his daughter married a Knight of Montesa and member of the *Cámara* of Castile whose father had been a member of the Council of Aragon. Juan's sister María Jiménez de Montalvo y Sarabia benefited from her widowed mother, receiving a grant of an *audiencia* position as a daughter's dowry and married peninsular Sancho de Torres y Muñatones, the son of a minister of the Chancellory of Valladolid. An *oidor* of the *Audiencia* of Santa Fe de Bogotá, Sancho ultimately returned to Spain to serve on the Chancellory of Valladolid. Another of Juan's sisters, Marina, married a peninsular *colegial mayor* at Salamanca who was named *oidor* of Bogotá in 1629 and entered the Order of Alcántara in 1640.

The examination of native son Alonso Bravo de Sarabia's familial relationships in a well-connected *letrado* network in Spain reveals that he had an inside track when seeking an *audiencia* appointment. It also suggests implicitly the difficult competition faced by candidates lacking similar ties; few if any other creoles in the seventeenth century could boast comparable bonds. Noteworthy is that all of these *letrados*, as well as Alonso and the several creoles that preceded him to an *audiencia* in the Indies, were resident in Spain when named.

The unusually favorable circumstances that influenced Alonso Bravo de Sarabia's appointment did not reduce local pride in his success, for his appointment was a precedent, an example that demonstrated the ability of native sons to hold high office. Accordingly, a compilation of 1643 entitled "First Fruits of Peru in Sanctity, Letters, Arms, Government, and Nobility" placed his name at the top of 38 men named to *audiencias* in the Indies. He was also remembered in a more extensive list published in 1688: "El Doctor Don Alonso Bravo de Sarabia, of the Order of Santiago, Peruvian, son of this Royal University [of San Marcos] Alcalde de Corte of Lima, and *Oidor* of Mexico."

Alonso's success occurred at about the same time that native son *encomenderos* petitioned the Crown to extend their grants for a "fourth life." Echoing their forebears' plaints, these *beneméritos*' anguished refrain focused on the loss of their patrimony to a Crown that had forgotten the services of their conquistador and early settler ancestors. Inadequate initial rewards had left the heirs impoverished. Worse, the rapacity of recently arrived peninsulars with royal offices had deprived them of both income and positions. As descendants of conquistadors, the *beneméritos* believed it their birthright to serve as the Crown's political representatives and to be the primary beneficiaries of their homeland's human and natural resources. Creole apologists took up the challenge and began to pen legal treatises demonstrating that native sons had a legitimate claim to all positions in their American *patrias*.

Native Sons Lament

A litany lamenting insufficient royal gratitude and the resulting poverty formed the monotonal chant of native son resentment that linked *beneméritos* to conquistadors. The authors frequently resided in the viceregal capitals of Mexico City and Lima, home to original *encomenderos* and their descendants alike and thus centers for disgruntled conversations. Writing in New Spain in 1599, native son Gonzalo Gómez de Cervantes specifically requested "a general and perpetual distribution of Indians to the sons, grandsons and other descendants of the conquerors and first settlers." Nostalgically recalling the conquistadors' aspirations, he called for *encomenderos* to receive titles of nobility with recognition as "perpetual lords with civil and criminal jurisdiction."[7] Complete with entailed properties, the self-interest of this rich and powerful aristocracy would safeguard New Spain. Gómez de Cervantes ignored the obvious reasons that his proposed nobility did not exist. The Crown not only opposed the creation of a legally protected aristocracy located an ocean away but also recognized that high-ranking officials of Church and Crown reached the Indies with the obligation to provide for their retainers. In addition, competition from hardworking, peso-pinching peninsular merchants and their young, often related, assistants worked to the disadvantage of *beneméritos* who believed themselves above commerce and manual labor and had no hesitation to share their conviction. Mining was always risky and agriculture required oversight by careful administrators. Much better were *encomiendas* that provided income without the *encomendero*'s labor.

Another native son author in New Spain was Baltazar Dorantes de Carranza, heir of a conquistador who had accompanied Núñez Cabeza de Vaca on his astonishing trek from Florida to Mexico. Dorantes recognized that *encomiendas* were on the way out and turned to public office, especially the position of *corregidor*, as central to the *beneméritos*' survival. For viceroys' benefit, he distinguished conquistadors' creole descendants born in wedlock from mestizo descendants of illegitimate birth. His manuscript *Sumaría relación de las cosas de la Nueva España* (1604) revealed that fewer than 200 families with only 934 resident males spread over four generations remained in New Spain, out of more than 1300 Spanish conquistadors of Mexico. The author also complained that recently arrived peninsulars assumed the guise of noblemen despite the lowly retail positions they filled. Faced with royal favor given to European Spaniards and competition from the despised *advenedizos*, the *beneméritos*' bitterness was understandable.

In the early seventeenth century, creole apologists with degrees in civil and canon law began to publish treatises to remind the Crown of the legal foundation underpinning native son claims for appointment.

Born in Lima, the city of Mexico, and Bogotá among other places, they usually obtained their formal education in the Indies and subsequently traveled to Spain to represent both a corporate body, for example, a municipal council, and themselves as they solicited an appointment to office. Among the first Peruvians to assemble a case for preferential appointment of native sons and other creoles to offices of state (and Church) was Juan Ortiz de Cervantes. Born in Peru, he graduated from the University of San Marcos, was a licensed attorney, and taught both civil and canon law at the university. A *vecino* of Cuzco, the city's *encomenderos* named him to represent them in Madrid in arguing for the transformation of their grants from a single life to perpetuity. Despite a published memorial addressed to Philip III on the topic, Ortiz de Cervantes proved unsuccessful; the Crown had no interest in changing a royal policy in effect for nearly a century. Simultaneously pursuing personal interests, he published, probably in 1620, another tract entitled *Information in favor of the right that those born in the Indies have to be preferred for their prelacies, dignities, canonries, and other ecclesiastical benefices and secular offices.* His point was unmistakable: "The first consideration, which is of divine law, is that offices shall all be held by members of one nation, land, or lineage."[8] In short, native sons should have a monopoly on posts in their *patria*, not just preference for them. The following year he authored an additional brief publication in which he congratulated Philip IV his accession to the throne and again emphasized the birthright of native sons to hold all positions in their patria. Although his efforts failed to change royal policy, Ortiz de Cervantes received subsequent *audiencia* appointments in Bogotá. In the early 1650s, another *limeño* lawyer, Alonso de Solórzano y Velasco, specifically rejected a 1609 order to the *Cámara* of the Indies not to recommend native sons for *audiencia* appointments. In his publications, he emphasized both the capability of fellow graduates and professors (*catedráticos*) from the University of San Marcos and their right to high-level offices in their *patria* of Peru.[9] Like Ortiz de Cervantes, Solórzano did not secure the desired alteration in royal policy, but later was named an *audiencia* minister in Chile, Buenos Aires, and Charcas.

In 1667, creole Pedro Bolívar y de la Redonda published while in Madrid a memorial to Charles II and the *Cámara* of the Indies. His thesis was explicit: "the Spaniards who were born, studied, and served in the Indies should be preferred in *all* civil and ecclesiastical appointments."[10] His father José Bolívar de la Torre was sheriff for the Inquisition in

Cartagena and later *corregidor* of Arequipa, Peru. He entered the Order of Santiago in 1641 and a decade later paid 12 000 pesos for an appointment as a supernumerary auditor on the Tribunal of Accounts of Lima. Pedro was born in Cartagena de Indias, as were his parents. An attorney educated in Lima, he sailed to Spain in 1663 and the Council of Castile approved him to practice law. Subsequently, he became a knight of Santiago. Reflecting a personal agenda, his memorial emphasized the qualifications for *audiencia* appointments.

Pedro Bolívar reviewed the numerous types of law that gave Spaniards born, educated, and serving the king in the Indies preference in appointments to all royal and ecclesiastical positions there. Creoles (although he rarely referred to them as such) able to speak indigenous languages were precisely the type of clerics needed among the native peoples. Their qualifications also made them the most worthy candidates for designation as bishops. As Betancur had argued earlier, the realms conquered, settled, and maintained at no cost for the Crown of Castile gave creoles the right to secular offices as well. While the King knew and legislation confirmed creole rights and preference, the problem was that the *Cámara* of the Indies ignored it. Moreover, Bolívar contended that creoles possessed the requisite qualities to be *audiencia* ministers: intelligence and education; ancestors from prominent noble families in Spain who had participated in the conquest, settled in the Indies, and had held offices there; and adequate wealth to serve without succumbing like peninsular appointees to the lust for riches. He emphasized that the appointment of newly arrived foreigners, that is, Castilians, grieved the *beneméritos* because it suggested that the Crown considered them unworthy and incapable. In order to prove their honor and good reputation by securing appointments, creoles left their families and *patrias* and embarked on long, risky, and expensive voyages to Spain. As had Betancur three decades earlier, Bolívar identified royal advisors and administrators as responsible for failing to execute pro-creole legislation.

Bolívar recognized the existence of legislation that prohibited native sons from holding judicial posts in their *patrias*. He averred, however, that the king had the right to name native sons at his pleasure and good reasons to do so for they were superior to Castilians in a variety of ways. They knew and loved their *patrias*, were qualified, and deserved remuneration for their birth, studies, and service in the Indies. Like its predecessors, Bolívar's memorial failed to produce a policy change regarding native sons, but he benefited personally from his residence in

Madrid, receiving an appointment to the *Audiencia* of Panama in 1676. Bolívar and other creole apologists before him emphasized their desire for native son appointments but understood that the Crown's policy of naming outsiders prevented creoles from serving at home except in rare cases.

The Crown's reluctance to name native sons to high office arose from the same foundation as its policy against officials' marriages to native daughters. Both cases produced conflict of interest. From the royal perspective, officials holding executive, judicial, and treasury posts should be free of local ties that impaired their ability to implement royal directives effectively or administer justice impartially. Native son appointments and outsiders' marriages to native daughters threatened these goals. Consequently the Crown issued and reissued legislation designed to prevent its officials from establishing local ties. The restrictions prohibited marriage between royal officials and their children to native daughter or native son spouses. They also banned specified godparentage relationships and outlawed a variety of economic and financial activities. As with its earlier decisions to sell positions and appointments, however, the Crown yielded to financial demands and sold individual exemptions to the restrictions. Its need for revenue and the willingness of officeholders to pay cash in exchange for legal ties to local elite families through marriage and other relationships were simply too great to make effective enforcement of the restrictions possible.

While the arrival of peninsular newcomers prompted annoyed and at times insulting commentary by local elites, an unwed peninsular who carried an appointment as an *audiencia* minister or treasury official typically stimulated marital interest in established families with eligible native daughters. When the newcomer was married and brought children with him, the odds were favorable as well that one or more children would marry locally. Creole apologists could write learned treatises insisting that native sons should have all positions, but the Crown's appointments demonstrated its disagreement. As a result, native daughters' marriages to peninsular officials and merchants were the best available means for long prominent but often relatively poor families of the local elite to retain their status. Continued financial need, however, led the Crown in late 1687 to start selling *audiencia* appointments accompanied with exemptions from any and all restrictions on local ties.

4

The Heyday of Native Sons and Daughters, circa 1630–1750

About 1630, local elites that included native sons and daughters as well as successful peninsulars integrated through marriage were beginning to add the honorific trappings of nobility. Underpinned by wealth derived from Indian labor, land, mining, trade and office, they pursued knighthoods, gained titles of nobility, and followed a suitably lavish lifestyle. These publicly displayed attributes enhanced long-voiced claims of noble status based on conquistador and early settler ancestors, Old Christian relatives in Spain, exemption from direct taxation associated with commoners in Castile and indigenous and free blacks in the Indies, and a variety of privileges historically encapsulated by *hidalguía*.

Associated with elite status were inheritable offices important for their honorific, financial, and social value, and for their use in dowries. An increase in purchased royal appointments between the early 1630s and the late 1680s included those of provincial administrator, treasury official, and *audiencia* minister. The greatest local dominance occurred in the *Audiencia* of Lima, a tribunal with an extraordinary number of native sons as well as other creoles and *radicado* ministers. In contrast, although the *Audiencia* of Mexico briefly had numerous local-born ministers, the Crown assigned a visitor to investigate their activities and in 1720 he ousted seven. This set the stage for Juan Antonio de Ahumada, a New Spain attorney, to assemble and publish a detailed argument for native son appointments in the 1720s. Also during the creole heyday, Spaniards born in the Americas obtained or continued majority representation in cathedral chapters and numerous appointments as bishops. A compari-

Spaniards in the Colonial Empire: Creoles vs. Peninsulars?, First Edition. Mark A. Burkholder.

son of the incumbent bishops and *audiencia* ministers in 1750 documents the extent of native sons, other creoles, and peninsulars in these positions at that time. For men and women with worldly success in hand, the sainthood of Santa Rosa of Lima and the recognition of Our Lady of Guadalupe as patroness of Mexico, the remainder of New Spain and Guatemala, and finally all Spanish realms confirmed God's favor toward them.

Social, Financial, and Political Capital

Sources of Native Son and Daughter Prominence

Native sons and daughters held considerable social, economic, and at times political power. While males monopolized formal authority associated with royal offices, they shared informal influence with women from prominent families who possessed tangible property, wealth, and patronage. Ongoing sources of consequence included ancestry, if linked to conquistadors, early settlers, or undisputed nobles, and accumulated family merit; physical assets of agricultural and pastoral land; mines and their equipment; urban property; wholesale and retail inventory; slaves; ships; offices; loans receivable; and family and business networks inherited from or related to one's parents, relatives, and in-laws. Although entail (*mayorazgo*) was used less commonly than in Spain, it remained an important device to limit the division of property as otherwise mandated by Castilian statute. The result was land concentration made possible by marriage between elite native daughters and grooms of either peninsular or local birth.

By the mid-seventeenth century, native sons dominated most municipal councils and saleable and inheritable offices, although not infrequently these posts were transmitted via native daughters' dowries. Local presence in treasury offices was overwhelming in Peru, although not in New Spain, as a result of purchased appointments dating from 1633. Just over 50 years later, a new avenue opened when the Crown began to sell *audiencia* appointments. Unprecedented numbers of native sons bought these provisions, but other creole buyers were even more abundant.

Predominant patronage for regular appointments to the provincial offices of *corregidor* and *alcalde mayor* shifted in the 1670s from viceroys in Mexico City and Lima to the royal treasury in Madrid where peninsulars proved to be the primary purchasers. The administrative change reduced native sons' clamor about viceroys favoring their retainers, although enterprising executives turned to interim appointments for a remunerative source of illegal income. As the eighteenth century progressed, the bulging entourages that accompanied Habsburg viceroys lessened as Bourbon monarchs favored men with professional military credentials instead of grandees, and frequently advanced captains-general already employed in the Indies.

Formal education continued to determine eligibility for posts in the Church and some in royal administration. In the College of San Martín in Lima, the number of *limeños* reached parity with other creoles between 1695 and 1699, by which time peninsular students had fallen to only 2 among the 100 young men that enrolled. The major universities of Mexico and San Marcos in Lima remained preeminent, but higher education in the seventeenth and eighteenth centuries had become available in other locations, for example, in Guatemala, Quito, and Bogotá.

Immigrants who arrived with networks of relationships in Spain found opportunities in the Indies to expand them. A thick web of interpersonal relationships among privileged families was most evident in cities, but interrelated elites dominated lesser municipalities as well. While guarding claims of "Old Christian" nobility against the expanding multiracial population beneath them, well-placed families remained open to peninsular talent and capital. The marriage of native daughters to peninsulars of stature and promise was the primary way to turn these outsiders into *radicados*.

A provincial example of elite native sons and daughters incorporating peninsulars can be found in Mérida, Yucatan. By the mid-seventeenth century, population decline had diminished considerably the value of *encomiendas*. As a result, *encomenderos*, traditionally a largely endogamous group of native sons that controlled local offices, began to marry their daughters with greater frequency to peninsular royal officials and the more numerous successful merchants from Spain. The latter marriages provided the advantages of economic diversification, while husbands from the royal administration brought political benefits. At the same time, native son *encomenderos* maintained an air of superiority over peninsulars who lacked their lineage. This aristocratic attitude encouraged Castilian immigrants to seek *encomenderos*' daughters as brides, thereby to raise themselves and their children into the established elite.

Immigrants' goals in Mérida were straightforward: marriage into the *encomendero* elite, membership on the city council, and an *encomienda*. They saw native daughters as the means for securing one or more of these. For example, *benemérita* Catalina Pacheco, a daughter and granddaughter of conquistadors of Yucatan, married treasury official Gil Carrillo de Albornoz. Their native son Gerónimo in turn married a *benemérita* whose grandfather, father, and brother were members of the municipal council. While treasury officials had the prestige of their office and the opportunities and protection their post provided, merchants, mostly of peninsular origin, offered little but capital to recommend them. *Encomenderos* were willing to have their daughters, especially younger daughters, marry these men, however, because of their wealth and connections at a time of increased business opportunities. The prestige and position of his wife's family transformed the relative newcomer into a *radicado*. At the same time, his in-laws benefited from an improved patrimony. In Yucatan, successful merchants typically married daughters of local elites; in the city of Mexico, it was more common for merchants' daughters with large dowries to marry sons of local aristocrats.

Late seventeenth-century Santiago de Guatemala offers another example of native daughters marrying successful peninsulars. Between 1660 and 1697, 14 native sons and two other creoles made up half of the 32 identified aldermen. Most of the native sons' mothers but only about half of their fathers were born in Guatemala. Marriage often linked native daughters of peninsulars with later Spanish immigrants, primarily prosperous merchants who thus joined the elite with little difficulty. Despite the ease of bequeathing purchased aldermanic positions after 1606, few aldermen passed them directly to an heir and in no case did more than three consecutive members of a single family hold the post. The result was ongoing circulation within the municipal elite of Guatemala City in which *radicados* marginalized native sons of reduced wealth.

A review of marriages by aldermen on Lima's city council indicates that the incorporation of peninsulars into Lima's elite via marriage to native daughters increased in the seventeenth century. Of those who entered the council from 1620 to 1661, at least half married native daughters, several wed other creoles, and only two definitely entered matrimony with women from Spain. Peninsular aldermen from 1561 to 1619, in contrast, wed peninsular women in over half of the cases. Not surprisingly, native son aldermen married a higher proportion of native daughters but only 1 of the 38 entering the council from 1561 to 1661 contracted marriage with a peninsular woman. The centrality of native daughters in elite integration in the seventeenth century is clear.

The Nobility

Beneméritos, as descendants of conquistadors and first settlers were often known in the seventeenth century, considered themselves ennobled by their ancestors' services. They assumed the highest level of a social hierarchy that grew out of the initial divisions between conquerors and conquered, owners and slaves. Peninsular women and their creole daughters quickly assumed the honorific *doña* and creole sons used *don* within a generation or two. Although successive monarchs prevented the emergence of a nobility with inheritable seigneurial jurisdiction as existed in Castile, the Crown clouded the issue by exempting Spaniards in the Indies from tribute, a direct tax analogous to the *pecho* paid only by commoners in Castile. It also allowed explorers, conquistadors, and first settlers to bear both offensive and defensive arms, a traditional privilege of the nobility. To emphasize the point, it denied this privilege to Indians, mestizos, blacks, and mulattoes. In addition, Philip II explicitly declared that first settlers and their descendants were *hidalgos* with "all the honors and preeminences" of nobles in Castile. Later immigrants demanded and usually received the same benefits. As two eighteenth-century observers noted: "[T]he precedent established at the time of conquest gave all Spanish settlers the right to enjoy the privileges of the nobility . . . [Those who immigrate] acquire in the Indies the two things they esteem most but which they cannot enjoy in Spain – wealth and nobility."[1]

Regardless of birthplace, Spaniards sought honors and recognition that would confirm or elevate their family's place in white society. The outstanding example was Fernando Cortés, whose rewards included a title of nobility (Marquis of the Valley of Oaxaca) and, in a rare exception to general practice, an *encomienda* awarded in perpetuity. Moreover, the king granted a knighthood in the Order of Santiago to Martín Cortés, the conquistador's son by his indigenous mistress and translator, variously known as Marina, Malinche, and Malintzin. The queen's decision in 1527 to award noble status to the 13 men who remained with Francisco Pizarro on Gallo Island, off the coast of Ecuador, supported as well the principle of reciprocity that made service in conquest a justification for royal recognition, in this case explicit social advancement.

Figure 4.1 A well-to-do Chilean woman with servant. White women of any means usually had one or more servants.
Source: John Constanse Davie, *Letters from Buenos Ayres and Chile* (London: R. Ackermann, 1819), 314. Reproduced by permission of the Mercantile Library at the University of Missouri-St. Louis.

Spanish society in the Indies was homogenous only to the extent that it considered everyone else inferior. Aside from birthplace, whites differed greatly in wealth, status, and occupation, although even the poorest claimed to be above all persons of color (see Figure 4.1). For those with the means and requisite genealogy, knighthoods confirmed a family's nobility, *limpieza de sangre*, and *limpieza de oficios*, that is to say absence of a father or grandfathers who had engaged in "vile" occupations, such as hangmen, mule drivers, tanners, butchers, cobblers, dancers, and town criers. To become a knight thus demonstrated one's membership in the elite.

Knighthoods

A knighthood in a military order, notably Santiago, Calatrava, and Alcántara, publicly confirmed the nobility and unsullied ancestry of the recipient and his family. Originally, knights were mounted warriors in the Reconquest and the military orders received rich rewards of land and jurisdiction over its inhabitants. Later, military service disappeared as a requisite. Philip II awarded an average of 169 knighthoods per decade. His successor Philip III granted many more, although the total was less than 1000. Even greater inflation of honors occurred during the reign of Philip IV (1621–1665). As the king informed the President of the Council of State in 1625, "Without reward and punishment no monarchy can be preserved. Now rewards may be either financial or honorific. Money we have not, so we have thought it right and necessary to remedy the fault by increasing the number of honors."[2] Accordingly, the Crown began to sell knighthoods, a step that increased their numbers to unprecedented levels. By 1643, about 20% of the awards since 1621 had been sold. Subsequently, sales were not made openly, but certainly could have occurred. Philip IV conferred some 7000 knighthoods, although not all recipients could demonstrate the necessary *limpieza de sangre* to gain entry to an order.

Spaniards in the Indies observed the wholesale distribution of knighthoods with considerable interest and soon participated. From the knighthoods awarded to Martín Cortés in 1529 and Diego Colón, grandson of Christopher Columbus, in 1535 until 1800, nearly 850 creoles entered the military orders. The highest average per year occurred between 1621 and 1709 when, excluding knighted siblings, 360 entered the military orders. Native sons from Peru comprised almost half of the total, far ahead of men from New Spain, New Granada, and other American regions. New Peruvian knights continued to outnumber those from New Spain by more than two to one for the remainder of Spanish rule.

Knights' maternal lines were more established in the Indies than were paternal lines. Almost three-quarters of their mothers were creoles while nearly two-thirds of their fathers were peninsulars. In fewer than one-third of the cases did knights have both parents born in the Indies; just over one-fifth had two peninsular parents. To have both two parents and four grandparents born in the Indies was extraordinary, with only 13 cases. Much more frequently knights' parents and four grandparents were born in Spain. With a substantial majority of knighthoods going to first-generation creoles on the paternal side, the benefit of peninsulars entering local elites was apparent. Familial duplicates aside, between 1529 and 1819, over 430 American knights entered the Order of Santiago. Four of seven knights named in the sixteenth century entered the order in the 1590s, the decade in which Americans started to receive *audiencia* appointments. The three Basque Provinces and Navarre shared the benefit of "universal nobility" and provided almost half of the parents and grandparents of Americans who entered the Order of Santiago.

Many native sons helped their cases for knighthood by residing in Spain while the process of examining their genealogy was underway. A few went as children; others made the voyage to study at a university in Spain, claim an inheritance, or follow a military career. Combining the quest for a knighthood with that for an appointment to office was not unusual. Alonso Pérez Castellanos of Quito, for example, secured a provision as *contador mayor* of the Tribunal of Accounts of Lima in 1677 and entered the Order of Santiago in 1679. While knighthoods added luster to the individual recipient, noble titles provided even more splendid recognition.

Titles of Nobility

A noble title documented royal confirmation that one's family and ancestors were among "the elite of the elite" as it highlighted *limpieza de sangre*, religiosity, honor in relationships, and responsible citizenship. In contrast to knighthoods, awarded only for the recipient's life, titles were inheritable and women could hold them. Since peninsular males typically married much younger native daughters and often predeceased them, their widows often held titles of nobility for years. *Limeña* Ignacia Carrillo de Córdoba, for example, retained the title Countess of Vistaflorida for more than three decades after her peninsular husband's death. In Mexico, females accounted for about one-quarter of the titled nobility, although few were the original recipients and only five never married. Only males could be both a titled noble and a knight, but more frequently, other members of a family would divide these honors with the eldest son or, in the absence of a brother, a daughter receiving the title.

Castilian monarchs awarded only 17 titles of nobility to the Indies before 1665. During the reign of Charles II (1665–1700), the number of recipients increased with 22 creoles and 31 peninsulars receiving new titles. Another 28 creoles and 37 peninsulars joined their ranks during the reign of Philip V (1700–1746). While more peninsulars than creoles received titles in the Indies, inheritance practice dictated that the latter would ultimately hold most of them.

As with knighthoods, the Crown resorted to selling titles of nobility, at times earmarking the money paid for a specific worthy cause. For example, Ferdinand VI (1746–1759) authorized the sale of three titles free from any taxes to reimburse the former bishop of Concepción, Chile, for expenses in rebuilding that city's cathedral following an earthquake in 1737. A purchased title, however, did not mean the family would continue to be wealthy. In 1721, the viceroy of Peru provided a compilation of 27 titled nobles in the City of Kings. Some he noted had "great wealth," or were "rich" or "very rich"; others were "poor" and even "very poor." The only two peninsulars on the list were "poor," a reminder of the wealth that some creole families enjoyed. In Mexico, titled noblewomen married both native sons and peninsulars and at times first one and then, after his death, the other. Unlike in Spanish America, no Brazilians received noble titles and only a few received knighthoods. Noble status (*fidalguia*) itself was best brought to Brazil, for Portuguese monarchs were notably stingy in awarding it to immigrants or their *mazombo* descendants.

Living Like a Noble

Titles of nobility and knighthoods ratified their holders' station in a local elite but also imposed the responsibility of living appropriately. Opulent surroundings that included servants and slaves, porcelain from China, imported coaches with matched pairs of horses or mules, generosity, hospitality, religious beneficence, and public display of loyalty to the monarch marked a noble lifestyle and indicated a family's honor. Failure to exhibit a home environment and personal behavior deemed appropriate for titled nobles of Castile cast a long shadow on counterparts in the Indies.

Even if the recipient had not purchased a title, as many did in the seventeenth and eighteenth centuries, the expenses of a titled family were high. Their peers expected them to support the Church through means such as establishing chantries, constructing chapels, supporting missionary activities, and even building churches. Lavish religious ceremonies, for example, baptisms and funerals, could cost tens of thousands of pesos. Erecting a church was even more expensive, while suitably furnishing it was costly as well. Since anyone leaving a will had to contribute to pious works, some nobles left thousands of pesos to demonstrate their piety. Creating a chantry to pay for masses to speed a noble's soul through Purgatory was common, although it often also provided a mundane income for a younger son or other male relative. As a matter of course, titled nobles were expected to contribute when the king requested "donations." For males, this took the form of outfitting a militia unit, an activity that frequently also brought the noble or his son an appointment as an officer.

Sumptuous conspicuous consumption included exquisite clothing and diamonds, gold, and jewels worn by elite noblewomen. A French traveler who visited Lima in 1747 commented on the dress of wealthy creoles and others' efforts to emulate it:

> The women here are so richly dressed, that one of no high station would make a very brilliant appearance at a French theatre. Their hair is twisted and tufted with diamonds, pearls, and artificial flowers: they wear a black hat, embroidered with large earrings of diamonds and pearls. Some of the better sort of the mulatto and negro women, also aim at this extravagance.[3]

Legislation sought to prevent nonwhites from emulating Spaniards in dress and perquisites of status. In New Spain in the sixteenth century, laws prohibited black women from wearing gold, pearls, silk, or other signs of luxury unless married to a Spaniard, a rare occurrence. In the following century, the Lima city council banned black and mulatto women from wearing silk cloth and gold lace. Such proscriptions were never very effective. Toward the end of the seventeenth century, the

Crown banned any use of silk, lace, or precious stones and limited gold and silver for use in buttons only. Spain and its colonies, of course, were not unique in sumptuary legislation. Portugal issued similar laws that affected Brazil, and in seventeenth-century Massachusetts, sumptuary statutes sought to prevent "the people of mean condition" from dressing in the "garb of gentlemen." Similarly, Virginia strictly limited those allowed to "wear gold in their clothes, or to wear silk."[4]

For the elite, "honor" was tangible, a quality they could pass to their heirs. It rationalized the social hierarchy, giving the few families at the top privileges and access to positions while justifying discrimination against everyone else in general, and non-Spaniards in particular. The Crown abetted this attitude by legislating restrictions to prevent non-Spaniards, especially those of illegitimate birth, from inheriting *encomiendas* when they were important and from holding specified positions subsequently. Yet honor was also variable as members of local elites determined who among them possessed it.

The purchase of knighthoods and titles of nobility separated the highest level of the empire's elites from other Spaniards, regardless of birthplace, as well as persons of mixed race (*castas*), indigenous, and both freedmen and enslaved Africans. During reigns in which the Crown put a price on honors, it is not surprising to find the sale of appointments to virtually every royal position, including, at the end of the seventeenth century, that of viceroy. More than perhaps any other single cause, sales and accompanying dispensations were responsible for an age of native son and other creole success that signaled in essence a reversal that made Spain more dependent on the Indies than vice versa.

The Sale of Appointments

Provincial Administrators

Appointments of *corregidor, alcalde mayor*, and governor went on sale in the 1670s and remained available until the mid-eighteenth century for native son, other creole, and especially peninsular purchasers. In the *Audiencia* of Quito, almost two-thirds of identified buyers between 1701 and 1750 were peninsulars; of their American counterparts, a majority were native sons and the next largest contingent was from the neighboring *audiencia* district of Lima. Notably, native son and other creole purchasers in the district of Quito were a significantly higher percentage than American buyers throughout the empire had been from 1674 to 1700. Purchasers of appointments to the post of *corregidor* in Zacatecas between 1696 and 1748 divided equally between creoles and peninsulars.

As the eighteenth century opened, viceroys still arrived from Spain with substantial retinues. Although restricted from the late 1670s to only a dozen retainers holding posts of provincial administrator simultaneously, they found ways to benefit themselves, their dependents, and their local clients. Short-term interim appointments, which they frequently sold privately, served as an excellent source of both income and patronage. The viceroy of New Spain, Duke of Alburquerque, sailed with nearly 100 dependents to run his court and to ensure that the daily tasks of his service were carried out. During his tenure from late 1702 to late 1710, he made 280 usually short-term appointments of *corregidor*, *alcalde mayor*, and governor. Few were to the most profitable districts, however, for the Crown sold them on its own account. Rumors claimed that the duke charged men who had bought their appointments from the Crown another sum that might equal the purchase price in order to enter their posts. He named at least 26 retainers to positions in New Spain, usually to provincial administrative posts, with many of them receiving two appointments. Since provincial administrators frequently arranged for a lieutenant to do the actual work associated with the position, work that included handling the profitable *repartimiento*, such assignments offered income with little labor. When Alburquerque returned to Spain, a majority of his retainers accompanied him, confirming what native son apologists had long claimed; such peninsulars saw the Indies only as a place to gain riches they could take back to Spain. Those who remained had become *radicados* through marriage, a permanent appointment to office, or economic ties.

The Audiencia of Lima: The Native Son Stronghold

By the end of the seventeenth century, Lima and its *audiencia* district had become a stronghold for successful native sons. More Peruvians became knights and titled nobles than in any other *audiencia* jurisdiction in the colonies. Frequent marriages between local women of good family and successful merchants and royal officials created and extended social networks that often stretched to Spain. *Limeños* dominated their city council for more than two centuries. With the sale of treasury and Tribunal of Accounts appointments, they quickly outnumbered peninsulars in these posts as well. Their greatest success, however, was as native sons in the *Audiencia* of Lima and secondarily as other creoles with family ties to Lima who served in the *audiencias* of Santiago de Chile, Quito, Charcas, and Panama.

Men born of good family in Peru had the great advantage of a university in Lima that provided courses of study in civil and canon law from the 1570s. Many also benefited from their parents' ability to support their travel to Spain. By the early seventeenth century, a growing tradition of success in securing high positions in the Church and posts on New World *audiencias* served to inspire young *limeños*. The first native son to start an *audiencia* career in his home tribunal, Alonso Bravo de Sarabia, was from the City of Kings. By late 1687, 50 other Peruvians had been named to American tribunals, although only three were native sons at initial appointment. In contrast, creoles from the *Audiencia* of Mexico obtained only 16 *audiencia* positions while those from the *audiencia* district of New Granada, with the third largest number, contributed only 9. In Brazil, the High Court of Bahia between 1609 and 1751 had only 10 identified native sons, partly because the colony lacked a university.

When the Spanish Crown began to sell *audiencia* appointments systematically in November 1687, Peruvians immediately responded. Purchases enabled an unprecedented number of native sons to join the tribunal in Lima, and other Peruvians to obtain appointments elsewhere. By 1712, when sales were temporarily halted, 41 men from Peru had obtained *audiencia* appointments, at least 3 dozen by purchase. In the following year, 10 native sons, 1 other creole, and only 6 peninsulars held appointments to Lima's court. New Spain was the second most frequent place of birth for Americans who reached a high court. Purchases enabled native sons on the tribunal to increase from 1 in 1700 to 12 in 1712. In 1715, the court's composition included 11 native sons, 2 other creoles, and 8 peninsulars. Sales had enabled native sons to become a majority on the *Audiencia* of Mexico for the first time. In contrast, the Portuguese Crown apparently never sold appointments to its high court in Bahia.

The War of the Spanish Succession (1702–1713) resulted in the confirmation as monarch of Philip V, the grandson of the French monarch Louis XIV, over his Habsburg rival, and the installation of the Bourbon Dynasty in Spain. The war's conclusion enabled the new monarch to respond to the problems caused, at least in part, by the sale of appointments during the conflict. Between 1717 and 1720, the Crown suspended 26 ministers, most of them creole purchasers. As part of this attack, in 1720, Philip named peninsular Francisco de Garzarón as visitor-general to investigate the *Audiencia* of Mexico. Already resident in the capital as an inquisitor, within months the visitor suspended 11 of 18 *audiencia* ministers and exiled them from the capital. Most were purchasers; seven were native sons. Although the charges were nothing unusual – influence peddling and routine peculation – the Council of the Indies upheld their deposition. By the end of the year, only three native sons and two other creoles remained on the tribunal.

The reduction of native sons, which also occurred to a lesser degree in several other *audiencias*, fit into a broader imperial environment. After the War of Spanish Succession, Philip V explicitly targeted native sons in the kingdoms of the Crown of Aragon when he abolished the kingdoms' historic regional privileges in 1716. Accustomed to locally born judges filling their *audiencias*, Aragon's kingdoms could no longer claim even a guaranteed minimum of their positions for native sons. The elimination of native son and other creole ministers in the Americas did not go unnoticed. A Mexican attorney, in Spain because of a legal case, took the opportunity to publish a major treatise on native sons' statutory claims to appointments.

Juan Antonio de Ahumada's "Representation"[5]

Juan Antonio de Ahumada became involved in a judicial case involving native sons and peninsulars in the city of Mexico. Two peninsulars who claimed to be from the mountains of Burgos were arrested as accomplices in a robbery, and sentenced by three creoles of the few remaining ministers on the *Audiencia* of Mexico to serve in textile manufactories (*obrajes*). A large group of peninsulars and creoles calling itself "the Spanish nation" signed a legal petition stating that the sentence dishonored all Spaniards and accusing one native son judge in particular of hating peninsulars. The group also hired four representatives in Madrid to press the case for reversing the sentence and to secure the transfer of several *audiencia* ministers. Because the case involved native sons, it posed a particular threat to lawyers like Ahumada who almost certainly aspired to an *audiencia* appointment. Fearing that the Crown would further tighten its renewed policy against native sons visible in the Garzarón investigation, Ahumada went to Madrid to represent his client and while there published in 1725 a "*Representation*" to Philip V that voiced native son frustration. The *Representation*'s full title spelled out what the author wanted – an explicit declaration by Philip V that Spaniards born in the Indies (*Españoles indianos*) had no legal impediment prohibiting their appointment to offices in America; moreover, they should be preferred for *all* ecclesiastical, political, and military positions. This statement would quash what the author claimed was a rumor that the king had ordered the *Cámara* of the Indies not to propose them for these posts.

Ahumada drew upon early creole apologists to outline why the Crown should favor native sons with appointments as well as the adverse consequences of not doing so. Since natural law called for the appointment of those who had labored on the king's behalf, the monarch owed the *beneméritos* for their own service, their ancestors' conquest and settlement in America, and the Crown's enrichment. A Spaniard became a citizen of a municipality at birth and thereby had a claim to its honors. Never should the Crown name foreigners, recent arrivals, or transients, that is to say, peninsulars. Since European Spaniards enjoyed by law all offices in their respective kingdoms, the author inaccurately asserted, why should Americans not enjoy the same benefit?

Following his predecessors, the lawyer referred to existing legislation that gave preference in appointments to the descendants of conquistadors and early settlers as well as to other Spaniards born in America. Since the appointments were to be to posts in the province where the services had been performed, legislative intent was to name native sons for *all positions* – political, military, and ecclesiastical – in the Indies. Failure to do so shamed them by implying they were unsuitable for royal appointments. The performance of those selected earlier, moreover, demonstrated that creoles served the king well.

As had Pedro Bolívar y de la Redonda more than a half century earlier, Ahumada argued that *americanos* possessed appropriate qualifications for any employment in the Indies: education and good judgment; knowledge of the jurisdiction's physical environment and its peoples' customs; noble birth as required for higher magistrates and demonstrated by either ancestors in the conquest or descent from younger sons of eminent noble families in Spain; and the wealth needed to assume a position. Given the legal right to seek royal employment in accord with natural, civil, and royal law, native sons should receive all appointments in the Indies. As for positions in Spain, Americans had no interest in them. Unlike native sons who loved their *patria* in the Indies, European Spaniards, whom Ahumada variously referred to as "foreigners" (*extraños*) "pilgrims" (*peregrinos*) and "recent arrivals" (*advenedizos*), typically sought only to make their fortunes in order to return to Spain wealthy. These foreigners lacked detailed knowledge of American regions, their inhabitants, and the law employed in the Indies.

Noting that native sons were like legitimate offspring in a family in which Europeans were adopted or legitimated, Ahumada asserted that a king with many kingdoms had to treat each as if it were his only one. A ruler who had remarried could not give sons of his first wife the dowry of the second and vice versa. Thus, the sons of the second wife – America – should enjoy in the Indies the same rights as belonged to the sons of the first wife – Spain – in her realm. Because Americans were qualified for office, there was no reason to send European Spaniards to posts in the Indies. Admittedly native sons had local bonds, but officials from Spain frequently married there, establishing ties that eliminated this theoretical advantage.

The need to spend time and money at court resulted in European candidates for office accumulating debt prior to appointment. Additionally, travel to an American post left the appointee owing 6000 pesos or more if he were single. Journeying with a family increased the cost and resulted in high-interest loans. These expenses and the resulting debt forced a European officeholder to seek illicit income. In contrast, American appointees were spared much of this expense. This was a disingenuous analysis, of course, since Ahumada was himself at court and surely knew that the ministers ousted from the *Audiencia* of Mexico in 1720 had purchased their appointments and, in some cases, traveled to Spain to buy them.

Ahumada recognized the existence of old legislation that prohibited native sons from seeking judicial appointments, but contended that custom had largely corrected this. Even this proscription, however, did not affect adjoining provinces; for example, a Mexican could serve in another *audiencia*. In any case, the anti-native son legislation dated to before Columbus reached the Indies. The lawyer also examined "other objections made by enemies of the *Indianos*." These grew out of the immutable fact that Americans were born in the Indies. The charge that the Americans would conspire against the king was simply absurd. As for the claim that "the Americans hate the European Spaniards" and would harass them if they held the highest offices, Ahumada reversed the charge and asserted that Europeans hated Americans without cause. Furthermore, the popular European canard that Americans' use of reason started to diminish after the age of 30 was baseless.

Ahumada's *Representation* thus reviewed the multiple arguments that favored native son appointments. Although he mentioned the well-established point about *beneméritos*' right to reward, he devoted most of the treatise to examining native son claims to preference based specifically on birthplace. Indeed he went so far as to say that custom and subsequent appointments superseded existing legislation forbidding native sons' appointment. The disadvantages in naming outsiders received ample attention, but the bold assertion that Europeans hated Americans staked new ground for an apologist's tract to a monarch.

Philip V did not declare native son preference as Ahumada sought, for his already articulated position was the reverse. On March 31, 1720, he had ordered the Council of the Indies neither to grant native sons judicial positions nor to approve licenses for officials to marry women of the district. In addition, as a result of the case in which Ahumada represented a native son judge, the monarch in 1727 again ordered the *Cámara* not to propose or select creoles for posts in the Indies, a mandate the *Cámara* interpreted as meaning for *audiencia* positions. In fact, general adherence to this policy had started in 1713. Between then and 1739, only three new men named, all to Lima, were native sons on their initial appointment; a fourth native son returned to Lima after an appointment in Chile. Two of the four native sons were the only documented purchasers of these years, but the floodgates for sales were about to open.

A Renewal of Sales

The Crown's renewed sale of *audiencia* appointments accompanied the War of Jenkins' Ear and associated extraordinary expenses. Between 1740 and 1750, sales accounted for over half of the tribunals' new ministers and men from the *Audiencia* of Lima again comprised the largest group of purchasers. Sixteen native sons bought appointments to the courts of Lima, Guadalajara, Panama, Chile, Quito, and Charcas. This final period of sales left the *Audiencia* of Mexico with far different results than the first. Although two purchasers joined it, neither was from New Spain. The reason was security. With war underway, the Crown explicitly recognized that *Audiencia* of Mexico, both as a court and as a region, was too important to risk compromising by the sale of appointments to native sons.

In 1750, two ministers in Guadalajara were the only native sons whose initial appointments had been to one of five *audiencias* in the viceroyalty of New Spain. Among the six tribunals in South America, native sons held initial appointments in all but Santa Fe. Together the 11 *audiencias* had 19 native sons, the largest number ever; 19 other creoles including numerous *limeños*; and only 16 peninsulars. Especially in South America, native sons and other creoles had unprecedented representation on the tribunals. Even though the Crown had removed some purchasers after the War of Spanish Succession, no South American of the time echoed Juan Antonio de Ahumada. Native sons were doing well enough in royal offices and the Church to avoid rocking the boat.

Native Sons and Other Creoles in the Clergy and Royal Offices

By the second half of the seventeenth century, numerous native son friars and priests were spread throughout the empire. Their presence in the mendicant orders was extensive; they virtually monopolized the parishes of the secular clergy, and they also formed a large number of chaplains and other nonparish clerics. Furthermore, they were well represented in the higher ranks of the diocesan clergy.

Cathedral Chapters

Prebendaries of cathedral chapters often spent many years, sometimes an entire career, slowly gaining advancement based heavily on seniority. Often including native sons, the prebendaries either arrived with local connections or soon developed them. Hence, they brought the world of the local elite into the cathedral and did not hesitate to use its influence for their own purposes. The Church was a source of material benefit and political influence as well as spiritual comfort.

By the mid-seventeenth century, overall native son and other creole representation was strong in cathedral chapters, at least partly because many peninsular clerics lacked interest in settling in modest cities with limited possibilities of advancement. In La Plata, creole appointees surpassed peninsulars from 1611 to 1620 and during the next 40 years almost all were native sons, a majority by the 1640s, and other creoles. In Santiago, Chileans steadily took over the cathedral chapter starting in 1634 and for more than 150 years, no new peninsular prebendary arrived. In the diocese of Concepción, all prebendaries named between 1650 and 1700 were native sons and over half were from the diocese itself. This pronounced local presence continued into the eighteenth century. In Valladolid de Michoacán, creoles accounted for just over two-thirds of the prebendaries between 1630 and 1666, increased to more than three-quarters in the years to 1691, and reached their highest level, nearly nine-tenths, between 1691 and 1730, a time when native sons of the bishopric comprised almost half. In the New World's most prestigious cathedral chapters, creoles in 1700 constituted about three-quarters of the prebendaries in the city of Mexico and about nine-tenths in Lima. During the first half of the eighteenth century, America-born clerics outnumbered all others in the chapter in Mexico; in Lima, native sons of the city itself comprised a majority.

Bishops

Overall, secular clergy and members of the religious orders in the Indies far outnumbered *letrados* in royal positions. At any given time, however, substantially more *audiencia* ministers held appointments than bishops. Between 1504 and 1750, about 500 bishops in the Indies received appointments; the Crown named more than twice that many new *audiencia* ministers. Divisions based on birthplace identified bishops as they did *audiencia* ministers, but it took some years before a pool of creoles with university education and appropriate experience was available. Only 27 had been named by 1629, but by the end of 1650, 10 creoles including 1 native son were among the 28 bishops. Fifty years later, 8 creole bishops including 2 born in New Spain were prelates in its dioceses.

Creole bishops increased noticeably during the remainder of the seventeenth century with 63 selected. Table 4.1 shows the bishops chosen between 1687 and 1750. Although over 40 percent were Americans, the

Table 4.1 Initial appointments as bishops in the Indies, 1687–1750.

	Native sons	%	Other creoles	%	Peninsulars	%	Unknown	%	Total
Bishops	17	13	38	29	74	57	0	0	129

Table developed from author's database.

native son monopolization that Ahumada, Betancourt, and others had sought remained a fantasy.

Empire-wide figures obscure the frequency of native son bishops in specific locations. The first Chilean bishop of Santiago was Alonso del Pozo y Silva. Educated in Chile and ordained in 1690, he became prelate in 1723 after serving in the cathedral chapter of Concepción and then as bishop of Tucumán. A Peruvian followed Pozo's promotion as archbishop of Charcas in 1730, but was replaced after his own advancement to Cuzco in 1734 by another Chilean, Pedro Felipe de Azúa y Iturgoyen, son of a successful Basque immigrant and his Chilean wife. Azúa studied in Lima and graduated from the University of San Marcos with a doctorate in civil and canon law. The *Audiencia* of Lima approved him to practice law, and he returned to Santiago where he held various *letrado* positions. After winning the post of canon in the capital's cathedral chapter, he obtained ordination so he could serve it. He advanced within the chapter and several years later was selected bishop of Concepción. Named archbishop of Santa Fe in 1744, he was replaced by native son José Toro y Zambrano of Santiago. Toro studied initially in Santiago, but then traveled to Lima where he obtained a doctorate in civil and canon law and practiced law until returning home in 1705. After service as *relator* of the *audiencia*, he competed as the only candidate for a position of canon in the cathedral. The governor of Chile noted that the city of Santiago would receive very well the appointment of "its son" to the post.

Bishops born in the Indies also served in other parts of the empire. Between 1608 and 1750, all eight creole bishops in Antequera, Mexico, were born in New Spain. The initial American bishop in Guatemala was chosen in 1617; by 1750, six more, including one from San Salvador, were selected. Panama's first creole bishop was named in 1662 and seven others followed by 1750; none were native sons. Only rarely were native sons and other creoles selected as archbishops of Mexico, Lima, or Santa Fe de

Bogotá. Between the founding of the diocese and 1750, only one of three creoles named, the single native son, actually assumed the see in Mexico; he died shortly afterward. In Lima, only one creole, Fernando de Arias y Ugarte, was among the 15 prelates named. He was also the sole native son among four creoles appointed bishop of the diocese of Santa Fe.

Peninsulars' strong presence in appointments in Mexico City and Lima was a consequence of the size of the capitals' populations, the wealth of the dioceses, and the prestige and power of the position of archbishop. On more than one occasion, archbishops served as viceroys. Unlike a bishop in a modest see such as Concepción or Tucumán, the prelates of Lima and Mexico could be confident that appropriate officials in Madrid would read and answer their correspondence. The position's importance also ensured that the selection process in Spain would favor candidates known to members of the Council and *Cámara* of the Indies, candidates who for the most part were peninsulars.

Networks

Spanish societies in the Indies rested on social and patronage networks based on families, marital ties, local and regional origins, and common objectives that included wealth and appointment to office. The backbone of the elites' relationships over generations was native daughters whose adherence to the values of chastity before marriage and faithfulness afterward provided the legitimacy that underpinned their families' continued high status. The example of José Bernardo de Tagle Bracho and his family in Peru illustrates multigenerational success built on networks of native daughters and peninsular entrepreneurs.

A noble born in Ruiloba, Santander, José Bernardo settled in Lima in the early eighteenth century. There he could benefit from family and regional connections with the established wholesale merchant Francisco Sánchez de Tagle y Castro Velarde of Santillana del Mar, a town less than 8 miles from Ruiloba. After several years of working together, the two peninsulars' bonds tightened in 1707 when José Bernardo married his employer's daughter. Rosa Juliana Sánchez de Tagle e Hidalgo was born in her mother's birthplace, the town of San Jerónimo de Sayán, some 65 mi from Lima. As her dowry, Rosa brought José Bernardo capital totaling 11 000 pesos; at the time, he had nothing but prospects and his father-in-law's confidence.

After marriage, José Bernardo's fortunes advanced rapidly. He benefited from both legal and contraband trade; financing, often with partners, a variety of business operations; seizing a foreign ship and sharing the prize; and offices, including the purchased post of paymaster of the garrison at Callao with rights of inheritance and the elective position of prior of the Consulado of Lima. His collaborators included his brother Francisco who had settled in Chile; his father-in-law until his death in 1712; a cousin in Cuzco; and nephew Juan Antonio Tagle Bracho y Calderón, a future prior of the Lima merchant guild and knight of Calatrava, whom he recruited from Cigüenza, a town near Ruiloba. Both José Bernardo and Juan Antonio obtained titles of nobility: Marquis of Torre Tagle for the former, and Count of Casa Tagle de Trasierra for his nephew. José Bernardo constructed a palatial residence in Lima, purchased a rural estate worked by slaves, and owned urban property that included a grocery store. At his death in 1740, he left his wife instructions to found two entailed estates. As was typical in marriages of native daughters and peninsular merchants, Rosa outlived her husband. Designated by José Bernardo as tutor and executor for their many children, for more than 20 years, she was the pillar of the extended family, overseeing financial affairs and maintaining tranquility.

The lives of their children reveal the Tagle Bracho family's expanding social and economic network. Although daughter Rosa Isabel entered Lima's Convent of Santa Catalina, three other daughters married. Daughter Serafina followed her mother in wedding a successful peninsular merchant. Born less than 20 mi from his father-in-law's birthplace, Gaspar Quijano Velarde y Ceballos became the first Count of Torre Velarde, a knight of Calatrava, a magistrate of Lima, and, like his father-in-law, prior of Lima's merchant guild. Their son José became a judge on the *Audiencia* of Bogotá. Daughter Águeda Josefa entered matrimony with a merchant born in a town near to Ruiloba, Manuel Hilario de la Torre Quirós. Named *corregidor* of Canta in 1749 and a knight of Calatrava from 1753, Manuel worked closely with his father-in-law and his cousin Juan Antonio de Tagle Bracho. Native son Matías married María Josefa de Villalta y Santiago Concha, the daughter and granddaughter of *limeño* ministers on the *Audiencia* of Lima; she provided a dowry of 25 000 pesos. Daughter María Josefa brought an enormous dowry of 80 000 pesos to her marriage with peninsular Alfonso Carrión y Morcillo, a criminal judge of the *Audiencia* of Lima and nephew of Archbishop and interim viceroy of Peru Diego Morcillo Rubio de Auñón. By marriage to peninsulars, native daughters Serafina, Águeda, and María Josefa enabled a continuation of the Tagle-Sánchez de Tagle prominence in wholesale trade, brought a tie to the *Audiencia* of Lima, and increased the number of knights and titled nobles in the family. Marriages and careers of native son brothers expanded the Tagle-Sánchez network as well.

Eldest son Tadeo inherited the title of nobility and office of paymaster general. He married María Josefa Isasaga y Vázquez de Acuña of Pisco, a native daughter of creole parents and heiress to several entails in Spain and a large hacienda in Peru. Her patrimony joined her husband's entail and their progeny would extend the family's network. *Limeño* grandson José Bernardo Tagle, Marquis of Torre Tagle, was briefly president of Peru in 1822 and 1823. Three sons of José Bernardo and Rosa Juliana entered the clergy. One became a Franciscan, another a Dominican, and the third served for years in the cathedral chapter of Lima, thus creating a direct link to this important institution. Two sons purchased appointments on *audiencias*. José Severino, who never married, reached the *Audiencia* of Lima as a native son at the age of 25 and held commissions as judge of the Merchant Guild (*Consulado*) of Lima and the Mining Tribunal. Pedro Antonio served on the *Audiencia* of Charcas and later advanced as a native son to the tribunal in Lima. A knight of Calatrava, probably by purchase, he married *limeña* Mariana de Zamudio de las Infantas, widow of the third Count of Villanueva del Soto, native son protector of the Indias for the *Audiencia* of Lima and granddaughter of the Count of Monclova, viceroy of Peru, through his illegitimate daughter.

The example of peninsular José Bernardo de Tagle Bracho and his descendants demonstrates the importance of native daughters for the ongoing incorporation of peninsular males into the family through marriage and the successful placement of sons in both royal offices and the regular and secular clergy. Given the land inherited by wives and purchased by offspring as well as the opulent residence constructed in Lima, the Tagle Bracho family was diversely and effectively invested in real estate, commerce, offices, and the Church.

Native Sons and Other Creoles in Office in 1750

In the mid-eighteenth century, native sons and daughters were entrenched throughout the Spanish empire. They included *hacendados*, plantation owners, miner owners, and merchants. Native daughters were prevalent in the 130 convents and often served as abbesses. Native sons held a variety of royal posts and constituted an overwhelming majority of churchmen below the rank of bishop. They dominated the faculty and student bodies of the universities as well as the legal profession.

As *audiencia* ministers, native sons were most evident in Lima in 1750, although also present on the tribunals of Charcas, Chile, Quito, Panama and Guadalajara. Strikingly, 18 sat in the six tribunals of Peru, but only one in the tribunals of the viceroyalty of New Spain. Since *radicado* ministers were more common in the tribunals of New Spain than in those of Peru, local interests were well represented on every court as Table 4.2 shows.

Among the 30 bishops with appointments to American dioceses at the end of 1750 were 9 native sons and 12 other creoles. As in the *audiencias*, both groups were better represented in Spanish South America than in New Spain. The archbishops of Mexico and Lima, however, were peninsulars.

At mid-eighteenth century, the Crown's appointment policies had placed unprecedented numbers of native sons and other creoles in high civil and ecclesiastical offices of America. They were not spread equally

Table 4.2 Native sons and *radicados* on *audiencias* in 1750.

Audiencia	Native sons	Radicados	Total
Mexico	0	14	14
Guadalajara	1	4	5
Guatemala	0	2	2
Manila	0	3	3
Santo Domingo	0	3	3
Total: Viceroyalty of New Spain	1	26	27
Lima	13	2	15
Charcas	1	3	4
Chile	2	3	5
Panama	1	1	2
Quito	1	3	4
Santa Fe	0	4	4
Total: Viceroyalty of Peru	18	16	34
Grand total	19	42	61

Table developed from author's database.

among the *audiencia* capitals to be certain, but every capital had seen one or more arrive as either an *audiencia* member or a bishop. Because purchased appointments brought both extra (supernumerary) ministers and other men holding promise of future appointments (*futuras*), they clogged the lines of promotion leading to the courts in Mexico and Lima. The result was that ministers throughout the empire remained in one location for many years and established extensive local ties. While wealthy native sons and daughters were the base of elites throughout the empire, *radicado* peninsulars joined them generation after generation.

Santa Rosa and Our Lady of Guadalupe

Accompanying the satisfaction that native sons had in their compatriots who had reached *audiencias* and become prebendaries, bishops, and provincials was elation at the glories of the Church in the Indies. Among other signs of God's grace between the mid-seventeenth and mid-eighteenth centuries, they could boast that Saint Rose of Lima became the first American saint and the Virgin of Guadalupe became patroness of Mexico, the remainder of New Spain and Guatemala, and finally all Spanish realms. Born in Lima in 1586, Isabel Flores de Oliva entered the Third Order of Saint Dominic and took the name Rosa de Santa María. The name recognized both her beauty and that she wore a crown of roses on top of her veil and another of thorns beneath it. Her life was one of piety, chastity, prayer, seclusion, and mortification of the flesh. Contemporaries associated her with numerous and exceptional miracles. Eight days after her death in 1617, the Dominicans started to compile the dossier necessary to document her sanctity. Her beatification in 1668 and canonization in 1671 provided the Indies with its first native-born saint and a source of great pride.

In 1648, native son priest Miguel Sánchez of the city of Mexico published an account of the miraculous apparition in 1531 of the Virgin Mary to a humble Native American named Juan Diego at Tepeyac, about 40 mi from the capital, and the equally remarkable imprinting of her cape in the presence of Archbishop Juan de Zumárraga. Although the Virgin had appeared to an indigenous male rather than a creole, Sánchez considered her proof of divine favor toward native sons of Mexico. In 1660, a Jesuit published a shortened edition of Sánchez's work that attracted a broader readership. The cathedral chapter of Mexico took an interest in

1666 and shrines, altars, and churches were dedicated to Guadalupe at locations outside of the capital, where the original devotion was centered. A visitor-general in New Spain returned to Castile with enthusiasm for the devotion and subsidized the publication of the abridged account in 1662. Mexican native sons in the seventeenth and eighteenth centuries emphasized that the Virgin had selected them uniquely as the new chosen people. After the Virgin was credited with ending an epidemic in 1736–1737, her cult spread beyond New Spain to other Spanish realms. It proved attractive to the indigenous peoples, and the Church employed it in an evangelization campaign. The devotion emphasized the primacy of the city of Mexico and its archbishop within New Spain even as it provided a single patron for the viceroyalty and overshadowed both regional and racial differences. The city of Mexico proclaimed Our Lady of Guadalupe as its principal patron in 1737, and this honor was broadened to the whole of New Spain and Guatemala in 1746 and to all Spanish realms in 1757.

Saint Rose and Our Lady of Guadalupe represented miraculous interventions unique to the Indies. Their recognition just before and during the heyday of native son power provided religious content to a growing sense of American identity. Thus, they strengthened a belief in entitlement due to favored people formed in a special American environment. By the mid-eighteenth century, entrenched local elites that included substantial native son and other creole officeholders as well as native daughters and *radicado* peninsulars were benefiting from over a century of diminished royal authority. “Creole” had become an appellation worn with pride by those who increasingly termed themselves “Americans.” The royal assault that began around 1750, however, inaugurated decades of royal efforts to regain lost control and revenues and provided ample justification for renewed American complaints of discrimination.

5

Reforms, Commentaries, and Officials, 1750–1808

Between 1750 and 1808, the Spanish Crown sought to regain control of its American realms that it had sacrificed by the sale of offices and appointments to native sons, other creoles, and *radicado* peninsulars. In addition to seeking to curtail abuses by more careful attention to appointments, it expanded administration and took steps to reduce the privileges and influence of the clergy, increase legal trade, and strengthen its military forces in the Indies. At the same time, European writers associated with the Enlightenment launched a new round of denigrating commentaries on the Americas in general as well as its climate, peoples, and fauna in particular. Insulted by foreigners' commentaries and travelogues on the one hand and facing heightened discrimination in their pursuit of office on the other, native sons became ever more aware of their distinctiveness from Europeans.

The Indies at Mid-eighteenth Century

Spain enjoyed almost a generation of peace after the War of Jenkins' Ear (1739–1748). With military expenditures reduced and registered silver production rising in both Mexico and Peru, Ferdinand VI's powerful chief minister the Marquis of La Ensenada (1743–1754) was able to initiate or extend policy changes that affected trade, the *repartimiento* of merchandise, the clergy, and royal administration. A commercial treaty with Britain in 1750 terminated that country's gains by the Treaty of

Spaniards in the Colonial Empire: Creoles vs. Peninsulars?, First Edition. Mark A. Burkholder.

Utrecht: a monopoly on the African slave trade to the Spanish Indies and the "annual ship" that carried legal exports but also served as a cover to introduce contraband goods. An agreement with Portugal in the same year sought to conclude the boundary dispute between the Río de la Plata and Brazil. The years at mid-eighteenth century, in short, opened a new era in the Americas.

Register Ships and Silver Production

The British destruction of Portobello in 1739 ended the fleet sailings that sustained legal trade with the viceroyalty of Peru. In response, the Crown authorized an expansion of single register ships sailing around Cape Horn, a change that forced merchants along the Pacific coast of South America to adjust to new conditions. From 1741 to 1750, registered silver production in Mexico and Peru reached its highest level to date as the northern viceroyalty's output exceeded 100 million pesos and surpassed Peru's by almost 60 million pesos. The total of 148 million pesos was nearly 20 million pesos greater than the largest amount during the Habsburg years, 129 million from 1631–1640.[1] While the quantity of contraband silver produced is unknown, unquestionably it added millions, if not tens of millions of pesos to the taxed amount.

Repartimiento of Merchandise

An institution long needing reform was the *repartimiento* of merchandise. Its value had risen with native population growth in Mexico and Peru. This benefited *corregidores* and *alcaldes mayores* as well as wholesale merchants who provided the required bonds for provincial administrators and then supplied them with products they imposed on the natives of their jurisdictions or, in some locations, raw materials that the officials later bought as finished goods. The use of credit throughout the chain contributed to its profitability. In the early 1750s, the Crown legalized *repartimiento*, but sought to control exploitation by establishing quotas, quality levels, and prices for items distributed in each jurisdiction. The reform effort threatened all merchants and officials involved in the practice, but the Crown lacked the capability to enforce the new regulations consistently.

Secularization of Indigenous Parishes

In 1749, the Crown revived an initiative that had failed in the 1570s. The Marquis of La Ensenada persuaded Ferdinand VI to order the replacement of mendicants by secular clerics in all indigenous parishes of the archdioceses of Mexico and Lima. Four years later, the monarch extended the mandate to his other American realms. Within the bishoprics of Mexico, Puebla, and Michoacán, approximately 150 regulars needed replacement. Although most regulars were located in cities by the mid-eighteenth century, the secularization program represented a long-delayed victory for advocates of Christianizing indigenous peoples on the frontiers of empire rather than ministering to the descendants of Native Americans converted in the sixteenth century. Viceroy of New Spain Count of Revillagigedo (1746–1755) and the bishops moved quickly. Viceregal agents seized rural churches and turned them over to secular clergy. At times soldiers forced clerics to depart with little but breviaries and the clothes they were wearing. In addition, the Crown ordered religious houses with few residents closed. The viceroy's successor acted with greater prudence and the process dragged on until the early 1790s when the last regulars in native parishes died.

Despite assurances from the archbishop of Mexico that replacing the mendicants would not pose a problem, for his jurisdiction had sufficient clerics able to preach in indigenous languages, reality forced the creation of new schools to teach Castilian to Native Americans. Clerics often drew students from their villages' most distinguished families in the hope of turning them into priests. The Crown encouraged this in 1769 by requiring a significant minority of indigenous and mestizo students in seminaries. This reduced the secularization program's anticipated opportunities for native sons.

Religious orders' recruitment of novices declined with the shift of their responsibilities from central Mexico to the less attractive northern frontier. In addition, the Crown restricted the number of novices that the orders could recruit. As intended, implementation of these policies reduced the friars available. From the Crown's perspective, the program of secularization had worked; from the regulars' perspective, the program was needless, mistaken, and detrimental to their mission.

Rebellion in Venezuela

In 1749, Canary Islanders among cacao planters in Venezuela led a rebellion against the Basque-dominated Guipúzcoana Company established in 1728. Besides displeasure over the company's monopoly of the legal cacao trade, large-scale elite planters, composed primarily of native sons residing in Caracas, objected to the governor's increased authority in the growing regions. Added to record-low prices for cacao beans, the stage was set for conflict. The arrival of a Basque employee with a dozen men to stop smuggling in one of the production centers triggered a march on Caracas led by Juan Francisco de León with the encouragement of prominent, although anonymous, planters.

Many Canary Islanders and an assortment of other whites, free blacks, runaway slaves, and indigenous peoples participated. Their primary objective was to drive the company's agents from Venezuela. After initial exchanges demonstrated the rebels were serious, the governor disguised himself as a priest, fled to the fortress at La Guaira, and declared the protestors in rebellion. When León and his followers advanced, the governor defused them by banning the Guipúzcoana Company's executives from Venezuela and suspending the monopoly, pending review in Madrid. The royal response was harsh. The Crown ordered troops from Spain to join those already dispatched from Santo Domingo, to terminate the remnants of the uprising, and to punish those involved. As a result, the Crown augmented its authority in Caracas, favoring peninsulars, but not Basques, over native sons for offices. It stationed a garrison, revamped the militia, reformed taxes, and created additional posts on the city council to be filled with men who supported the new policies. Although Canary Islanders had initiated and led the rebellion, native sons found they were also paying the price of failure.

Royal Support of Modern Ideas

In a less well-known action that spoke directly to Americans' abilities, Ferdinand VI forbade written attacks on Benedictine Friar Benito Feijóo, the influential publicist of modern ideas on whom he had already conferred honors of the Council of Castile. Americans regarded the

Benedictine highly for he had condemned the widely held European view that their intelligence developed rapidly, but then deteriorated precipitously, leaving them, but not Europeans, with premature senility. Asserting that creoles were as capable intellectually as Europeans, Feijóo argued that if they turned to idleness, the cause was discrimination that limited their opportunities to serve in offices of Church and state. Native sons, of course, had repeatedly made the point earlier and Feijóo's authority was welcome reinforcement.

A Snapshot of Society in Mexico City, 1753

While native sons, native daughters, and *radicado* peninsulars dominated local elites throughout the empire, the capital of New Spain offered the most royal and ecclesiastical positions, the largest concentration of wholesale merchants, a full spectrum of artisans, numerous blacks employed as household servants, and a multitude of *castas* and Native Americans. Internal migration to the city resulted from food shortages and disease in the countryside as well as greater perceived opportunities. Pressure on existing housing and a crime wave blamed on "beggars, vagabonds, loiterers, shiftless and illegally employed" led the viceregal government to order a census to inform its decision about how to deal with crime in particular.[2] Although incomplete, the enumeration of 1753 distinguished peninsulars from creoles (mostly native sons) and complemented more anecdotal materials.

The surviving materials document the presence of almost 3000 native sons and other creoles but fewer than 300 peninsulars in the capital. American and European Spaniards virtually monopolized elite occupations, but the former outnumbered the latter by almost 10 to 1. As elsewhere in the Indies, European Spaniards were particularly prominent in wholesale trade. Native sons occupied many important royal, local, and ecclesiastical offices and were active merchants, especially in retailing. With other creoles, they accounted for almost 4 out of 5 shop owners, including over 1000 artisan proprietors. This snapshot confirms the overwhelming presence of whites at the apex of society in the city of Mexico. Importantly, it reveals that over 80% of peninsulars were shop owners rather than in an elite occupation. More native sons and other creoles worked as artisans than had their own shops, and a small number were domestic servants and laborers. Strikingly, about one out of seven white women was in the workforce, with the largest number employed as servants and nearly as many engaged in spinning or working as seamstresses. While the Spanish population thus extended through the entire range of occupations, an overwhelming majority of whites, regardless of birthplace, were *not* among the city's elite in the mid-eighteenth century.

Commentaries

American Degeneracy?

Sixteenth-century arguments that America's inhabitants suffered adverse effects because of their environment enjoyed new life in the eighteenth century. In a multivolume *Natural History* that started to appear in the late 1740s, the French writer Count Buffon established himself among the most dogmatic critics. Expounding without benefit of firsthand experience, he declared that the New World had fewer indigenous species of animals than the Old. Excepting some types of deer, they were also smaller and weaker; no elephants, rhinoceroses, camels, or giraffes were to be found. The horses, donkeys, sheep, goats, dogs, and other animals introduced by Europeans had lost stature and weight. Even the original human inhabitants were neither numerous nor strong. "The savage is feeble and small in his organs of generation; he has neither body hair nor beard, and no ardor for the female of his kind."[3] In contrast to indigenous humans and quadrupeds, American insects were uncommonly large. Buffon blamed these remarkable differences on the humidity and cool environment of a new, young world more recently emerged from the seas than the Old and not yet adequately dried out.

While other European writers emphasized one or another of the failings claimed by Buffon, it was the Dutch Abbé Cornelius de Pauw who pushed the diatribe to its limit. In *Recherches philosophiques sur les Américains* published in 1768–1769, de Pauw portrayed a humid, unhealthy world that made American natives degenerate, savage, weak, and stupid. "The whole human [pre-conquest] race was indubitably weakened and rendered degenerate in the new continent." Indeed, "it is without a doubt a great and terrible spectacle to see half the globe so thoroughly maltreated by Nature that everything in it was either degenerate or monstrous."[4] Immigrants from Europe and their offspring declined as well, losing fertility and often dying at a young age. The survivors suffered mentally. At the age of about 20, "stupidity suddenly develops. . . . They regress instead of advancing, and forget so much of what they have learned that one has to give up their education and abandon them to their fate."[5] Creoles were unable to learn as well as true Europeans and consequently, no American university had produced a scholar of significant reputation. Persons of mixed ancestry were even less capable, and the poor indigenous "hardly merit the name of rational men."[6]

The claim of America's degeneracy stimulated substantial, ongoing interest. Abbé Guillaume-Thomas Raynal drew upon both Buffon and de Pauw. His *Histoire philosophique et politique des établissements et du commerce des Européens dans les deux Indies* was published initially in 1770, revised, translated into numerous languages, and issued in more than 70 editions by the end of the century. For Scottish author William Guthrie, creoles were degenerated versions of their peninsular progenitors. They "have all the bad qualities of the Spaniards from whom they are descended, without that courage, firmness and patience which makes the praiseworthy part of the Spanish character. Naturally weak and effeminate, they dedicate the greatest part of their lives to loitering and inactive pleasures." "Pride and laziness are the two predominant passions . . . the manners of old Spain have degenerated in the colonies."[7]

Scottish historian William Robertson helped to disseminate the ideas of Buffon and de Pauw widely. In 1771, he published *History of America*, a work of immense popularity that was quickly translated and reprinted into the mid-nineteenth century. For Robertson, America's original inhabitants were "rude and indolent," its animals were "inactive and timid" and those introduced from Europe had degenerated and become smaller. Even the birds sang less sweetly. He noted the "competition for power and wealth" between *chapetones* and creoles (he used both words) and asserted that their "hatred is violent and implacable." The latter suffered from "the enervating influence of a sultry climate" among other things and "the vigour of their minds is so entirely broken, that a great part of them waste life in luxurious indulgencies." "Sunk in sloth" and "languid and unenterprising," most considered trade beneath them and left it to the *chapetones*.[8]

Spaniards understandably took umbrage at these charges. Peninsular Minister of the Indies José de Gálvez was so furious with the anti-Spanish content of Raynal's work that he dealt with "those who have endeavored to introduce some surreptitious copies [of the *Histoire philosophique*] into the Spanish colonies in the light of criminals guilty of high treason against God and man."[9] In 1778, the Crown prohibited Robertson's *History* in Spain and the empire and suspended a project to publish a translation.

Exiled Jesuit Francisco Clavijero, a native son from New Spain, and other Americans wrote to counter the defamation of de Pauw, Raynal, and Robertson. Some paranoid creoles even believed that de Pauw was in league with the Crown and his denigration of them was at the suggestion of peninsulars. Mexican native son Fray Servando Teresa de Mier asserted in 1813:

> Ever since the Prussian [de] Pauw worked for nine or ten years, like a beetle concocting his pellet of dirt, collecting together everything bad their rulers had said about America and its inhabitants, the Spaniards have persisted in making merry with this putrefaction, and throwing it in our faces as if we were the *indios* of old.[10]

Travelers' Commentaries

Stereotypes of native sons and European Spaniards in Peru, solidly in place before the mid-eighteenth century, provided ammunition for those who sought to profit from publications about the Indies and their inhabitants. Travelers' accounts routinely popularized hostility between locally born creoles on the one hand, and *gachupines* and *chapetones* on the other. In 1717, French military engineer Amedée Frezier published a book of his travels that described Lima as he had found it several years earlier. Referring to the antipathy between its creoles and the "brutes," as he stated they termed the peninsulars, Frezier noted: "I believe one of the principal reasons of that aversion is because they always see those strangers in possession of the prime places in the state and driving the best of their trade, which is the only employment of the whites, who scorn to apply themselves to arts for which they have no relish."[11] While peninsulars were indeed preeminent in the wholesale trade, the sale of appointments to royal posts to native sons and other creoles meant that Frezier greatly exaggerated the presence of peninsulars in "the prime places in the state" in Lima.

The popular *A Voyage to South America* (1748) was the product of young peninsular officers Jorge Juan and Antonio de Ulloa whom Philip

V had sent to South America in 1735 as part of a French scientific expedition. Subsequently, they collaborated on a confidential description and analysis of conditions in Peru requested by the Marquis of La Ensenada in the late 1740s. In *Discourse and Political Reflections on the Kingdoms of Peru*, which circulated only in manuscript until its publication in England in 1826, the authors spelled out in damning detail what they termed the "factions or cliques of Europeans and Creoles."[12]

According to Juan and Ulloa, by virtue of birth in Spain, *chapetones* were anti-creole from the time they reached the Indies. Conversely, simply being born in the Indies made creoles hate peninsulars. Ties of kinship and marriage, they avowed, could not staunch the antipathy evident wherever both factions were present. Mutual hatred was most prevalent in municipalities in the Andes where few peninsulars arrived to trade; there it entertained whites that lacked other diversions. The greater commercial interaction with peninsulars common to cities and towns in the valleys (where most of them resided) spared them much of the factional strife.

The authors identified two principal causes for the conflict. First was "the excessive vanity, presumption, and pride which pervade the creoles"; second, "the miserably wretched condition of the Europeans who arrive in the Indies from Spain." Most immigrants came from the lower ranks of the commoners while the others, in the view of the two noble authors, had "undistinguished lineages." Through hard work and the support of relatives and friends, a European who obtained financial success was often able to wed a very prominent native daughter. In the first quarrel with his creole in-laws, however, they reminded him of his modest origins, and factionalism based on birthplace ignited. Elite native sons emphasized their own lineage obsessively and missed no opportunity to point out defects in their neighbors' lineage; these, in due course, reciprocated. Since rarely did a family "not have impure blood or some other equally significant defect," a peninsular unavoidably knew the misrepresentations in his in-laws' genealogical claims, and, in heated arguments, hastened to point them out.

Dedication to trade made peninsular males attractive husbands. Their thriftiness and commercial success enabled them to become aldermen, local magistrates, and prominent political leaders. While Juan and Ulloa claimed that native sons disdained trade because of their vanity, they admitted that in the seaports and Lima, one could see American Spaniards "do as much business as Europeans" and observed that without peninsular merchants, "creoles would do it all." At the same time, they remarked that many Europeans believed they could become wealthy in the Indies without hard work and considered their birth in Spain required them to avoid "inferior occupations." These peninsulars "always live a totally wretched, miserable, destitute existence and are of no use to anyone."

The travelers contended that native son children of peninsular fathers quickly developed anti-European sentiment because of their creole relatives' influence. Some even claimed that "they wish[ed] to rid their father's Spanish blood from their veins so it would not be mixed with the blood they acquired from their mother." Juan and Ulloa commented from a stereotypical peninsular perspective: "This is foolish, but even more foolish is that if they had the chance to purge themselves of their Spanish blood, nothing would run in their veins except the blood of Indians and Negroes." The comment is ironic because Ulloa subsequently married a young native daughter from a titled family of Lima.

Juan and Ulloa comprehended native sons' desire for offices in Church and state and refused to support fully the notion that they were "not apt for governing." Still, they maintained that Americans who served in high-ranking royal and ecclesiastical positions were a primary cause of factionalism and thereby justified discrimination against their pretensions for positions. A traveler in the early nineteenth century, the distinguished German naturalist and author Alexander von Humboldt, made a similar point about discrimination against native sons of New Spain. Although overstating the case, he asserted that the government's suspicion of them led it to grant the highest offices, indeed "all employments," to peninsulars. "The result has been a jealousy and perpetual hatred between chapetones and the creoles. The most miserable European, without education and without intellectual cultivation, thinks himself superior to the whites born in the new continent." From the 1780s, Humboldt added, one heard creoles declare "I am not a *Spaniard*, I am an *American!*"[13]

Repeated contemporary comments highlighting discord between native sons and peninsulars over royal positions document real antipathy. The extent of their validity, however, varies by date and region. In general, the number of creoles surpassed the number of native sons in a jurisdiction's royal offices. At the same time, marriages between native daughters and peninsulars almost certainly muted anti-native son sentiment while giving members of the local elite access to the corridors of power.

The Peninsular Offensive: Royal Offices

Soon after 1750, native sons understood that the inconsistent actions of the first half of the century had merely prefaced a more organized, coherent, and sustained effort to enhance royal revenues and reduce the local power of wealthy, extended families. Central to these initiatives was the appointment of peninsulars to both newly created and long-established offices. In 1750, Ferdinand VI effectively ended the sale of appointments to *audiencia* positions and the provincial posts of governor, *corregidor*, and *alcalde mayor*. Coupled with a renewed effort to enforce prohibitions that forbade officials from marrying in their district of service and creating other compromising ties, these decisions heralded an unmistakable attack on native sons' direct political influence through service in royal offices as well as on the indirect influence personified by *radicado* officeholders and their prominent native daughter wives. While the Crown failed to achieve all of its objectives, creoles throughout the Indies correctly appreciated that the royal offensive begun during the reign of Ferdinand VI (1746–1759), expanded through the rule of Charles III (1759–1788), and to some extent continued under Charles IV (1788–1808) signified an age of increased royal authority and heightened discrimination.

Against a backdrop of royal initiatives since mid-century, the British seizure of supposedly impregnable Havana in 1762 provided the imperative for further change. The action shocked Charles III and his advisors. With good reason they believed that another war with Britain was inevitable, and improved military defenses in the Indies were essential. Military expenditures, however, required additional revenue that the Crown expected the Indies to provide. Improved collection of revenue, tax increases, and new sources of income such as tobacco monopolies demanded an improved administrative structure, a structure the Crown chose to staff primarily with peninsular officials dedicated to carrying out its agenda. Imposing new or increased taxes, however, was always risky. As a peninsular *audiencia* minister noted in 1765, "[T]here is no American who does not reject any novelty whatsoever in the management of taxation."[14]

Increased taxation provoked rebellion in Quito in 1765 and in Peru and New Granada in the early 1780s. Heightened discrimination against native sons accompanied the expansion of regular military forces, although the reorganized militia offered them opportunities, for a price, to become officers. New royal offices and reinvigorated discrimination against native son appointments to prominent posts in the state and Church provoked increased local elites' resentment and formal responses. Royal efforts to strengthen its authority over the Church included the expulsion of the Jesuits and an often poorly received attempt to impose a rigorous, communal lifestyle in convents. Empire-wide demographic expansion led to greater emphasis on broadly defined individual and family "quality" rather than on ancestry, a modification that promoted upward social movement by *castas* into the "white" population. In short, royal initiatives on many fronts marked the Spanish Empire from the mid-eighteenth century to the early nineteenth century.

Military Reorganization

Military reorganization was the Crown's first order of business. While conquistadors, indigenous allies, and blacks used force of arms to establish Spanish rule, few professional soldiers had been stationed in the Indies. As codified in 1719, the Crown limited creoles to only 20% of the enlistees and required them to be at least four years older than the minimum for peninsulars. Despite explicit anti-creole regulations issued in 1748, no quota was specified and gradually, the number of creole officers increased. The introduction of "fixed" (*fijo*) units begun in the reign of Philip V expanded after the British took Havana and the Crown sought to create a credible military presence through a combination of regular army officers and soldiers and reorganized "disciplined" militia units. The "disciplined" militia was more attractive to most native sons for it provided prestige to officers, who purchased their appointments, without requiring them to leave their home province. Yet even when native sons dominated some units and *castas* or *pardos* others, peninsular officers trained them.

The regular army provided an important arena for discrimination against native sons. In general, senior peninsular officers were predominant immediately after reform but declined in number over time. Ten of 17 senior officers in the Regiment of the Crown in Mexico were peninsulars in 1788. Throughout America in 1800, peninsulars still comprised more than 70% of all lieutenant colonels, sergeant majors, colonels, and brigadier generals in the regular army. Creoles formed a majority of the officers from the rank of lieutenant downward. Opportunities for them started at the rank of cadet and years of service and a willingness to serve wherever one's unit was assigned were necessary for advancement to the ranks of captain and above.

A Tax Revolt in Quito, 1765

Despite successful negotiation with the Cuban elite to increase taxation in return for freer trade and opportunities in an expanded military, Charles III and his ministers had no interest in the back and forth discussion between officials and local elites that had characterized Habsburg rule. A tax revolt in Quito demonstrated widespread opposition to the new approach and laid bare how quickly popular anger focused on peninsulars.

In 1764, the viceroy of New Granada sent a European administrator to Quito to place under royal officials the collection of the sales tax and the Crown's monopoly for production and sale of cane liquor (*aguardiente*). The former threatened owners of estates (*hacendados*) that produced the beverage; the latter excited householders and traders of the city. With the *audiencia*'s approval, the city council, dominated by native sons, held an open session to discuss the measures and decided to oppose them. The viceroy had no intention of negotiating and, in early February 1765, arranged for 200 troops to enforce the changes.

A crowd that included artisans, retailers, and people from the lowest levels of Quito's population, rioted and destroyed the tax office in May. Few members of the local elite supported the authorities' efforts to quell the demonstrators and some may have promoted the riot, although this was not proven. Anonymous placards posted in Quito in June demanded the expulsion of peninsulars and aroused heightened sentiment against them. A melee ensued when the *corregidor* of Quito led a group of *chapetones* to confront the protestors and two rioters were killed. A Cadiz merchant alleged to have fired shots into the crowd soon found his house besieged and ransacked. The mob proceeded to the central plaza, attacked the royal government's headquarters (the *audiencia* palace), and made itself master of the city.

The June riot was a political action against peninsulars and especially the *corregidor*, who despised the plebeians, rather than a renewal of the May agenda. The *audiencia* capitulated and granted a general pardon, but was able to limit the expulsion of Europeans to unmarried males. Only by turning to the native son elite and religious orders was the tribunal able to regain its authority. The tax system, however, was in shambles. In September, the viceroy confirmed the general pardon issued by the *audiencia* and thereby ended the confrontation. The violent popular response was the first reaction to the Crown's attempt to increase revenue under peninsular officials and resulted in the city's *chapetones* becoming scapegoats. In the following year, 1766, the city's peninsulars formed a volunteer cavalry company for protection. The uprising in Quito would not be the last.

A Flood of Peninsular Officials

Charles III and his ministers fully comprehended the prominence and influence of native son and other creole officeholders. Indeed, Julián de Arriaga, Minister of the Indies from 1754 to 1776, had American experience as the official sent to restore order in Venezuela after rebellion began in 1749. The Crown also recognized that marital, family, and economic ties in a particular jurisdiction turned peninsulars into *radicados*. Consequently, it began to pay unprecedented attention to both the birthplace and marital status of men assigned to posts in the Indies.

José de Gálvez led the peninsular offensive. Born in the province of Málaga, Spain, he was a lawyer in Madrid whose career blossomed under Charles III. In a policy paper written for the monarch in the early 1760s, Gálvez emphasized the low overall quality of government officials in the Indies and carefully distinguished among them. Recognizing that native sons held *audiencia* positions, he recommended that, despite some being capable, they should be transferred to other tribunals. As Juan and Ulloa had noted, when serving at home, local creoles belonged to factions detrimental to the upright administration of justice. Gálvez also considered creoles named to *audiencia* presidencies, governorships, and captaincies-general typically inadequate. These men had purchased appointments or secured them through influential patrons. Both routes enabled merchants to become high-ranking officials for the sole purpose of increasing their fortunes. He recommended that the Crown appoint military officers in order to improve the quality of administration.

Regarding the provincial positions of *corregidor* and *alcalde mayor*, Gálvez noted that creoles who served them were frequently of low social status, little education, and often associated with retail trade. Peninsular appointees usually had no future in Spain and many purchased appointments only to enrich themselves through exploiting the indigenous. The lawyer encouraged the king to reward lower-level bureaucrats in Spain with these positions, either forgetting or not yet knowing that in New Spain *alcaldes mayores* received no salary after 1717.

In early 1765, Charles III named Gálvez visitor-general of New Spain with extensive responsibilities and wide-reaching authority. The visitor disembarked in Vera Cruz later in the year and initiated his assignment by suspending a number of customs officials for corruption and replacing them with his own clients. He soon found confirmation of his expectation that many officials were of low quality and did not hesitate to recommend transfers or "promotions" to Spain for well-entrenched officials who hindered the *visita* or were hostile to the Jesuits' expulsion in 1767. Thus, he arranged unsolicited appointments on the *Audiencia* of Barcelona for the *radicado* creole Francisco Xavier de Gamboa, a criminal judge on the *Audiencia* of Mexico, and to the Chancellory of Granada for *radicado* peninsular *oidor* Juan Antonio de Velarde y Cienfuegos.

Responsible for much more than personnel matters, Gálvez took actions in New Spain that increased silver production, established the tobacco monopoly as a vital source of royal revenue, and improved tax collection. He also provoked the ire of many who crossed his path, most notably by resorting to military force to punish rioters expressing opposition to both the expulsion of the Jesuits and the imposition of new taxes and other regulations.

Royal Officials

Gálvez served on the Council of the Indies after returning to Spain in 1772. Named its governor and also Minister of the Indies in 1776, he held the posts until his death in 1787. Harking back to his own successful *visita* in New Spain, among his first actions was to send peninsular visitors-general to Peru and New Granada. He also expanded the size of most *audiencias*, a structural change followed by an avalanche of peninsular appointments in 1776 and 1777.

Strengthening the number of peninsulars on the *audiencias* was intentional. As a result of purchases, native sons and other creoles were an overall majority on the courts in 1750. Their numbers declined slowly

Table 5.1 New ministers named to *audiencias*, 1751–1808.

Years	Native sons	%	Other creoles	%	Peninsulars	%	Total	%
1751–1775	1	1	9	13	58	85	68	99
1776–1777	1	3	3	9	28	88	32	100
1778–1808	5	3	45	28	111	69	161	100
Total	7	3	57	22	197	75	261	100

Table developed from author's database.

during the following quarter century as 85% of new ministers were peninsulars. In 1773, the *Cámara* of the Council of the Indies ordered its officials to note place of birth (*de donde es natural*) by each name on the list of office seekers (*pretendientes*) for a given position. There would be no cases of mistaken identity among the appointees. By 1775, only nine native sons remained on the tribunals. Gálvez's pro-peninsular policy resulted in European Spaniards totaling 28 of 32 new ministers named in 1776 and 1777. Continued discrimination against native son and other creole ministers caused their numbers at mid-century to plummet (see Table 5.1).

The results were dramatic. In 1808, 6 native sons, 22 other creoles, and 65 peninsulars held *audiencia* appointments; in 1750, there had been 27 native sons, 21 other creoles, and 40 peninsulars. Native sons were big losers; peninsulars were winners.

In 1776, the Crown created a fourth viceroyalty, carving it out of the truncated viceroyalty of Peru previously dismembered in 1739 by the erection of the viceroyalty of New Granada. Its capital in Buenos Aires, the new viceroyalty of Río de la Plata included the future countries of Argentina, Bolivia, Uruguay, and Paraguay. The Crown created an administrative structure and staff almost from scratch, from the viceroy and his secretariat down to expanded tax, accounting, and royal monopoly positions. From 1776 to 1810, peninsulars accounted for nearly two-thirds of the appointees and often filled the highest posts in each agency. Native sons, totaling less than 30%, usually occupied the lower level positions; other creoles made up a mere 7%. These appointments demonstrated that the Crown excluded neither native sons nor other creoles from the bureaucracy in Buenos Aires. Nonetheless, the 10-fold expansion of the bureaucracy generally placed them at the lower end. The establishment of a new *audiencia* in Buenos Aires in 1783 also required staffing, as did two other courts created in the 1780s in Caracas and Cuzco; all of the initial ministers in Buenos Aires and Cuzco, and all but one, a Cuban, in Caracas, were born in Spain.

The Crown's decisions to replace tax farmers with royal officials, create or transfer tobacco and other monopolies to direct royal control, expand the number of accounting and treasury offices, and enlarge customs offices produced a significant increase in royal bureaucrats. Employees associated with royal revenues nearly tripled in Chile and the number of well-paid officials rose as well. With two native sons on the *audiencia* in Santiago, native Chileans enjoyed respectable representation in the higher levels of financial administration and, complemented by *radicados*, dominated lower level posts. No revolution in government occurred in the distant colony. In New Spain, a shift to peninsular provincial officials in the mining center of Zacatecas began in 1752. Five of the six previous *corregidores* had been creoles; three of them, including Juan Antonio de Ahumada, had paid for their appointments. After 1752, only one creole has been identified of the nine named before the office was replaced under the intendant system. In Lima, the number of civil officials more than doubled between 1700 and 1790; most of the growth took place after 1776.

The capstone of the Crown's efforts to improve administration in America was the intendant system first introduced in Cuba in 1764. The instructions to visitor-general Gálvez specifically charged him to recommend whether or not it should be extended in New Spain. In due course, he strongly advised the appointment of intendants to replace *alcaldes mayores*, whom he described in terms reminiscent of native sons' description of peninsular officials:

> [T]hey generally do not overlook any means, however unjust or extraordinary, that may be conducive to the accomplishment of their ends [of accumulating wealth]. Since they cannot attain their desire without evident harm to the interests of the king and of his vassals, they are equally prejudicial to the king's treasury and to his people.[15]

As Minister of the Indies, Gálvez supervised the introduction of intendancies throughout the mainland empire, with the exception of New Granada. The post of intendant was prestigious and powerful, carried a substantial salary, and provided each incumbent with a secretary and a legal advisor (*teniente asesor*) to handle judicial matters. Responsibilities fell into four categories: justice, general administration, finance, and war.

The Crown paid careful attention to selecting well-qualified intendants and limited appointees to Spaniards born in either Spain or America. Although the creole viceroy of Río de la Plata specifically recommended in 1783 that native sons be named in the viceroyalty, his proposal brought no such appointment through 1808. Creoles were eligible as legal advisors only outside of their homelands. The nearly 100 intendants with royal appointments between 1764 and 1808 included no native sons and only seven other creoles. New intendants most frequently boasted experience as army officers, but a few naval officers, treasury officials, lawyers, and professional administrators secured appointments as well. Since Spain's military officers were primarily peninsulars, this track disadvantaged creoles.

Reporting to the intendants were subdelegates, the district officials who assumed administrative responsibilities held by the previous *corregidores* and *alcaldes mayores*. They were to be Spaniards regardless of place of birth, but recruiting peninsulars proved difficult because of low pay based on the collection of native tribute and the abolition of the *repartimiento* of merchandise. When they sought appointment, however, they received preference even if native sons had superior qualifications. In Peru at least, local creoles secured a majority of the subdelegate appointments. Indeed, peninsular Jorge de Escobedo, a former visitor-general of Peru who advanced to the Council and *Cámara* of the Indies, recommended that normally they should be named. Old habits lingered, however. In 1802, the viceroy of Peru complained that candidates paid intendants to propose them as subdelegates. Several years later, the president of Cuzco reported that he had heard appointments were sold "like pears in the marketplace."[16]

Under the intendant system, administration of justice devolved from the former provincial officials to locally elected municipal judges (*alcaldes ordinarios*). As one peninsular intendant griped, these magistrates "are natives of the country and in many cases related by marriage to each other." The result was "they become despots, oppressing the poor and unfortunate." For these political appointments, "natives of the country [native sons] are not suitable, because they are extremely difficult to dissuade from the customary ways ingrained in them even in contravention of the laws; they lack that mode of thinking, at once pure, sincere and impartial, prevalent in Spain, and even Spaniards [peninsulars] who live for some time in these parts come to acquire the same or worse customs."[17] No wonder native sons believed the Crown discriminated against them. It did.

By the late 1770s, it was obvious to any interested observer that the Crown was favoring peninsulars for office with great regularity. The greatest losers by this discriminatory treatment were native sons. Creoles willing to pursue appointments outside their homelands sometimes obtained them, but the pool of these candidates was small whether the prize was a commission in the regular army, a judicial position, or a post as intendant. Civil and military positions, however, were less numerous than desirable places in the Church. Did native sons fare better in the kingdom of God?

6

The Church, Complaints, and Social Change, 1750–1808

Spain's eighteenth-century Bourbon monarchs embraced "regalism," the idea that the state should increase its authority vis-à-vis the Church. Negotiations with the papacy resulted in several formal agreements or concordats that expanded royal patronage over the Church in Spain. In addition, the Crown sought to reduce the clergy's legal privileges (*fuero*) by giving civil courts broader jurisdiction. Royal confidence in its policy was demonstrated in the expulsion of the Jesuits from Spain and the Indies in 1767. At the same time, regalist bishops supported simpler religious behavior rather than the lavish, Baroque exuberance visible, for example, in church decoration, funerals, and festivals. This pursuit of austerity made its way to the convents and provoked substantial controversy between advocates of "communal life" and devotees of "individual life." The royal financial crisis that accompanied involvement in the wars of the French Revolution and the rise of Napoleon extended from Spain to the Indies at both individual and family levels when the Crown demanded that the Church exchange various forms of assets for royal bonds, forcing an unprecedented effort to call in mortgages from a wide range of borrowers that included native sons, peninsulars, and others.

Significantly, a screed written by the Archbishop of Mexico provoked the Mexico City Council formally to protest a decreed quota system that would permanently limit native son appointments to the offices of Church and state. In New Granada, increased taxation produced a rebellion, while in Lima, the readily perceptible drop in native sons serving on its *audiencia* underpinned one of its complaints in the early 1790s.

Spaniards in the Colonial Empire: Creoles vs. Peninsulars?, First Edition. Mark A. Burkholder.

Buoyed by rising silver production and growing population, the elite of Mexico City enjoyed a high level of prosperity in the late eighteenth century. Rich magnates there and in Lima, however, should not obscure the plight of "poor whites." Overextended financially and self-described as "poor," they simultaneously witnessed a rising number of families accepted as creoles by virtue of "quality," a collection of attributes that reduced the importance of putatively pure Spanish ancestry.

Clergy and Convents

Clerics

Native sons remained predominant in both the secular clergy and the mendicants throughout the Indies the eighteenth century. In the archdiocese of Guatemala they were all but 4 of nearly 300 priests and auxiliary priests in the late 1760s. Although peninsular friars sometimes arrived, four-fifths of the Franciscans in 1780 were creoles as were three-fifths of Dominicans in 1800. Undoubtedly nearly all of these mendicants had been born in the captaincy-general of Guatemala.

In New Spain, parish priests born in the capital comprised about a third of the total in the archdiocese of Mexico. The other clerics in the archbishopric were primarily native sons, perhaps 5% were other creoles, and peninsulars accounted for the remaining several percent. In Guadalajara, about one-third of the parish priests were born in Mexico City, probably another third were native sons from the city of Guadalajara, and nearly all of the remainder came from elsewhere in the diocese. As a sign of peninsulars' disdain, in 1757, none applied for a vacant curacy there.

In Lima between 1750 and 1820, an estimated 90% or more of the priests and pastors were born in America; the remainder were peninsulars. Of the Americans, a majority were from the capital, a minority from elsewhere in Peru, and less than 5% from other locations in the Indies. Although officially only students considered of Spanish origin were admitted to the Seminary of Santo Toribio and Colegio of San Carlos in Lima, several of the clerics were mestizo or indigenous.

Cathedral Chapters

Americans were also well represented in cathedral chapters at mid-eighteenth century. In Valladolid de Michoacán, nearly three quarters of the prebendaries between 1730 and 1760 were creoles and over half were native sons. Between 1760 and 1786, however, the percentage of creoles declined to 53% and peninsulars surpassed native sons for the first time since the mid-seventeenth century.

In Santiago de Chile, the Crown named 40 native sons and 10 outsiders (*foráneos*), including one from Spain, as prebendaries to the cathedral chapter between 1700 and 1810. During the same period, all 23 prebendaries presented for Concepción were from Chile. In Lima, over 85% of the prebendaries named in the 1750s and 1760s were creoles. This percentage dropped to under 60 in the 1770s, but rebounded nearly to previous levels for the remainder of the century. Creoles in Mexico City's cathedral were a smaller percentage than in Lima but held more than 75% of the prebends in the 1750s and 1760s. This percentage also diminished, to 45%, in the 1770s, but surpassed 50% in the 1780s and reached almost two-thirds in the 1790s. Almost certainly a majority if not most of the creoles were native sons.

Bishops

In 1750, creoles held nearly two-thirds of the bishoprics on the American mainland, Cuba, and Puerto Rico; 9 of the 21 American Spaniards were native sons. Although the number of bishoprics had increased, by 1808, the number of creoles had fallen from 21 to 10, only three of whom were native sons. Table 6.1 demonstrates the commanding majority of peninsulars named to bishoprics from 1751 to 1808. Among bishops, 73% were peninsulars and 15% were native sons. The change in appointment policy did not go unnoticed.

Table 6.1 Men named to first bishopric in Indies, 1751–1808.

Years	Native sons	%	Other creoles	%	Peninsulars	%	Total	%
1751–1775	9	16	10	17	39	67	58	100
1776–1777	0	–	2	33	4	67	6	100
1778–1808	13	15	7	8	66	77	86	100
Totals	22	15	19	13	109	73	150	101

Table developed from author's database.

Expulsion of the Jesuits

Parishioners' fairly modest protest to the secularization program begun at mid-century, coupled with the earlier expulsions by Portugal and France, perhaps encouraged the Crown in its unprecedented attack on the Society of Jesus. Using the pretext that Jesuits had helped to foment a riot in Madrid that caused him to flee the capital, Charles III in 1767 expelled the Society from his realms. As part of the expulsion, the Crown took possession of the Society's substantial wealth that included churches, educational institutions, and numerous profitable rural properties, some with slaves. Although the expulsion spared no priest in the Indies because of his place of birth, it affected more native sons and other creoles than peninsulars and foreigners combined. One detailed account indicates that it removed more than 2300 Jesuits from the empire; creoles were 55%, peninsulars, 37%, and foreigners, 8%. The affected creoles included several who devoted the remainder of their lives to writing patriotic histories of their American homelands.

Conflict in the Convents

The Crown expanded its authority over the Church in Spain through a concordat in 1753 that roughly doubled its authority to name clerics there. Using this enhanced patronage, it appointed numerous bishops and archbishops who supported regalism. The prelates, in turn, initiated an effort to return convents to observance of their original rule, thereby removing what they considered excesses. In central Mexico, Francisco Fabián y Fuero, bishop of Puebla, and Francisco Antonio de Lorenzana y Butrón, archbishop of Mexico, vigorously tried to force the communal life (*vida común*) on convents in their sees in the 1760s and early 1770s. Both peninsular prelates served one relatively brief assignment in the Americas and used it for personal advancement. Although up-to-date regalists, they rejected the increasingly widespread view of Spanish intellectuals that women were both rational and equal. Rather they behaved condescendingly toward females in general and probably also shared the popular European belief that creoles unavoidably suffered shortcomings due to their place of birth. While this attitude harmed their cause in Mexico, Lorenzana advanced as Archbishop of Toledo in 1771 and ultimately became a cardinal, while Fabián y Fuero became Archbishop of Valencia in 1773.

Nunneries filled almost exclusively with native daughters and other creole women bore the brunt of the initiatives to replace the *vida particular* or "individual life" with "communal life." While some nuns applauded the proposed reform, daughters of prominent New Spain families generally opposed it. These prestigious and powerful nuns of the black veil had entered a specific nunnery secure in the knowledge that they could continue a comfortable life. Thus, they owned their living quarters (*celda*), had personal servants and slaves, ate the foods they wanted, and oversaw their personal expenditures. Giving up these pleasures for a shared dormitory, poorer meals eaten in common, fewer servants and slaves, and assignments formerly provided by lower class lay sisters (*donadas*) lacked appeal.

The conflict extended beyond the convents and the prelates to successive peninsular viceroys and the Council of the Indies before the issue reached the monarch. In 1774, Charles III gave black veil nuns (Figure 6.1) the opportunity to accept or decline the *vida común*. While those in the city of Guadalajara and a small number of other convents supported the more stringent lifestyle, they were but a minority in New Spain. In the Bishopric of Puebla, a solid majority of 161 nuns rejected the common life; 120 accepted it. The professed nuns in the Archbishopric of Mexico vented their displeasure most emphatically; all 601 voted against the common life.

Division over the *vida común* even afflicted the newly established convent of La Purísima Concepción in San Miguel el Grande, Mexico. Although its native daughter founder approved a constitution that required the nuns to follow the communal life, a faction of native daughters quickly sought to reduce the restrictions. They soon ran afoul of reformist Bishop of Michoacán Pedro Anselmo Sánchez de Tagle who supported the convent's constitution and had a low opinion of women in general. "After all, they are Women, and it is necessary to use some deception from time to time in dealing with them."[1] Considering their failure to obey authority a grave matter that threatened the convent's existence, he asked three clerics to review a thick file on the "rebellious nuns." Certainly two and probably all three of the consultants were Mexican creoles. Individually they offered solutions less extreme than the bishop's desire to remove the faction's leader from her elected position of abbess if not from the convent entirely. Was this division of opinion based on place of birth? Although the evidence gives no explicit reason to believe it was, the

Figure 6.1 Sor Juana Inés de la Cruz. A brilliant native daughter poet of Mexico whose works continue to find readers.
Source: Vicente Riva Palacio, *Mexico a través de los siglos*, Vol. 2. 1888. (Mexico: Ballescá y Compañía, 1887), 744. Reproduced by permission of the Mercantile Library at the University of Missouri-St. Louis.

divergence of opinion between respected creole clerics and the peninsular bishop is suggestive. What is clear is that both supporters and opponents of the "rebellion" were creoles. As in the male orders, factional differences were frequent. Nonetheless, the many native daughters and other creole nuns avoided the imposed rotation in office that characterized provincial elections among the friars.

Native Son Complaints

Mexico City's Council Seeks Native Son Appointments

The strongest late eighteenth-century argument for native son appointments came from New Spain. Issued on behalf of all creoles in North

America, the document came from the city council of Mexico in 1771, the year in which both visitor-general José de Gálvez and Archbishop Antonio de Lorenzana departed for Spain. While allegations of anti-creole policy recommendations determined the timing of Mexico's "Representation," by that date, the Crown's reinvigorated policy of discriminating against native sons had become ever more evident. No native sons were among three creoles named to the *Audiencia* of Mexico in the 1740s. Although one joined the court in the 1750s and another in the 1760s, both had previously served on other *audiencias*. The four new men appointed to the *Audiencia* of Guadalajara after mid-century were peninsulars. When it created the office of a permanent secretary to the viceroy of New Spain in 1742, the Crown sent a peninsular to fill it. Only European Spaniards were named director general and *contador* general of the tobacco monopoly from 1765 to 1771. These provisions offered little encouragement to native sons.

Against this backdrop, the "Representation" defended creoles' honor against allegedly anonymous claims made, in fact, by peninsular Archbishop Lorenzana.[2] After attacking native sons' rationality, ability, and loyalty, he had argued that the Crown should systematically favor European Spaniards for high offices in the Church, military, and civil administration. In response, the city council cautioned that implementing the proposed policy was the way to lose America and ruin the state. Besides this warning, the council's representation reminded Charles III of relevant legislation that supported preference for native sons for high office. Echoing earlier creole apologists, it cited laws that prohibited foreigners from obtaining benefices in Spain. Canon law excluded not only foreigners from such positions, but also men from the same kingdom and province unless they were natives of the diocese. In secular positions, the council asserted, principles favored the "Americans" (the term used in this document as in the earlier one by Ahumada) to the exclusion of all foreigners. Although acknowledging that, as vassals of the same monarch, European Spaniards technically were not foreigners (*extranjeros*) in America, the representation maintained that they held foreign status when it came to the award of offices. After all, men loved only the land where they were born, that is, either America or Spain. The standard peninsular goal of returning to Spain wealthy confirmed their love for their true home.

As in Ahumada's "Representation," the city council used travel expenses as an argument against appointing peninsulars to office. Transportation from Spain to Vera Cruz for Archbishop Lorenzana and his entourage cost 20 000 pesos; his predecessor had spent even more, some 25 000 pesos. Land transportation to the capital added to the bill. Thus, total expenses related to the archbishop's arrival and installation in Mexico City reached 30 000–40 000 pesos. European Spaniards typically arrived in debt to serve positions whose salaries at best could pay only normal daily expenses. To cover their obligations and return wealthy to Spain, they accepted bribes and sold justice. High-ranking officials sought benefits for family members and retainers as well, a practice that worked against native sons who had spent years in study and service.

Birthplace rendered European Spaniards unqualified for offices among the indigenous peoples. Their ignorance of native languages and local law and practice meant that, when assigned to Indian districts, they failed to implement legislation intended to assist and protect their parishioners. This exemplified why the city council argued that the most qualified candidates from the diocese, not the entire empire or Spain, should be named to ecclesiastical positions. Put another way, the king and his representatives should favor native-born candidates even if Europeans arrived with outstanding qualifications. This point was significant, for, as Ahumada had contended earlier, without the incentive of appointments, native sons and other creoles would have no reason to apply themselves, study, and cultivate the sciences. "Shameful ignorance" (*vergonzoso idiotismo*) would prevail and the government of the Indies would fail.

American Spaniards (at least the elite native sons represented by the city council) considered compensated service in the Church and state to be essential to their well-being. They believed "mechanical offices" were incompatible with their "luster of birth" and incapable of providing an acceptable income. Consequently, few creoles regularly applied themselves to commerce. Without salaries from government jobs, their children would descend into the lower ranks of society (*la plebe*) or be forced to embrace celibacy as friars or priests, a result that would reduce the size of the population. Granting married Europeans positions in America, however, adversely affected demographic expansion in Spain as the recipients left their wives behind. In any case, unmarried peninsular males viewed posts in the Indies as disadvantageous because, if they married there, their children would suffer by virtue of American birth. The proposed solution to these concerns? Prohibit all emigration of European Spaniards.

As both Pedro Bolívar y de la Redonda and Ahumada had done much earlier, the council emphasized that American office seekers faced the additional handicaps of distance from Madrid and the related expenses of travel and residence there. Unlike European emigrants who expected to improve their lives in the Indies, Americans remained at home because it offered more advantages than relocation to Spain. The higher cost of living in America, moreover, meant that a creole with a government position in Spain could not afford to send adequate support for a family left behind. The city council's message echoed that of earlier writers: Europeans could enjoy positions in Spain; Americans would happily fill those in the Indies.

Like analogous earlier efforts, the Representation brought no satisfaction. Indeed, a committee of powerful royal advisors convoked by the Count of Aranda, President of the Council of Castile, had already crafted another approach to tighten bonds between Spain and the Indies through appointments. The two influential Crown attorneys on the Council – the future counts of Campomanes and Floridablanca – correctly understood that many in the New World believed that the Crown and its officials only sought to enrich themselves from its resources. Appealing to Americans' interests might stimulate their love of the Crown. Thus, the royal advisors proposed attracting creole youth to Spain for their education, creating for Americans a military regiment stationed in Spain, and "following the policy of always sending Spaniards [peninsulars] to the Indies with the principal offices, bishoprics, and prebends, and placing creoles in these posts in Spain."[3] Their approach, the ministers noted perhaps with a Machiavellian chuckle, had the additional benefit of turning creoles in Spain into hostages to keep America loyal to the king.

José de Gálvez, the former visitor-general and future Marquis of Sonora, shared these sentiments. On February 21, 1776, two days after Charles III named him Minister of the Indies, a royal order stated that "to reward equally the competence, merit, and services of the American Spaniards", the *Cámara* of Castile would consider them for prebends and high *letrado* positions in the tribunals of Spain, and the *Cámara* of the Indies would consider Europeans for comparable posts in the Indies. Always, however, one third of the canonries and prebends of the Indies would be reserved for *españoles indianos*.[4] To drive home the point, another royal order of September 17, 1776, ordered the *Cámara* to recommend European Spaniards for the position of dean of the Cathedral of Mexico and to do the same for other vacancies on the cathedral chapters of the Indies. While the benefits of integrating creoles and peninsulars in ecclesiastical, political, and military institutions made perfect sense to royal ministers, it missed the point of the city council's representation. Native sons wanted to fill *all* positions at home and few wanted a career in Spain.

The city council of Mexico complained about these orders as well, leading to a strong rebuke from Gálvez who pointed out that the *Cámara* had just recommended, and the king had selected, an American for the position of archdeacon of the cathedral chapter. The city council should be grateful, especially given how few European Spaniards were in that body, and cease its "unfounded complaints."[5] The aldermen, of course, knew how many native sons, other creoles, and peninsulars were on the cathedral chapter, the *audiencia*, and every other royal institution in the capital. The king's recent selection had been, in fact, a creole from Panama, not a native son, testimony to Gálvez's influence and ability to put into practice his position from years earlier: while creoles had ample ability, they should not be named to offices in their home regions. But not all disagreements between Crown and creoles were limited to exchanges of correspondence.

The Comunero Rebellion

In New Granada between 1778 and 1781, peninsular visitor-general Juan Francisco Gutiérrez de Piñeres reorganized the tobacco monopoly, worked to raise the yield of sales taxes, and increased the price of tobacco and cane liquor. His efforts disregarded the "unwritten constitution" that employed negotiation between the Bogotá elite and authorities in Spain and thus was a constitutional issue. In addition, the visitor-general's innovations provoked a popular riot in the town of Socorro in March 1781. After two more demonstrations, in mid-April the elite of Socorro joined and assumed leadership of what became known as the *Comunero* Rebellion, a name referring to a rebellion against Charles I in 1520–1521. Some members of Bogotá's elite also were sympathetic. The richest man in New Granada was native son Jorge Miguel Lozano de Peralta, Marquis of San Jorge de Bogotá and brother-in-law of peninsular *oidor* Benito de Casal y Montenegro. A member of Bogotá's city council, Lozano had a history of quarreling in its meetings. At one point an alderman born in Seville, yelled at him: "You bear the stigma of this land, you are an enemy of the chapetones and you are a pagan."[6] While no blood was shed, the marquis responded with a damage suit against his colleague. In 1783, he vented his and other native sons' frustration to Charles III:

> What value do we in this part of the world gain from all the services and merits that we have rendered Your Majesty? What advantage do we derive from the blood our ancestors gloriously shed in the service of God, our Lord, and Your Majesty? . . . . What benefits do we receive from the viceroys here and their retainers who insult, mock, humiliate, and oppress us?[7]

Even before the *Comuneros* marched to the outskirts of Bogotá, a lampoon posted in the capital and sent elsewhere attacked the visitor-general and appealed to anti-*chapetón* sentiment. While the document berated brutal peninsular agents for the royal monopolies and condemned their violation of local women, its ultimate slogan was the traditional, "Long live the king and death to bad government." For the elite in Bogotá, the solution to "bad government" was to have a virtual monopoly of offices. Even more broadly, they wanted to return to the earlier practice of government by negotiation and compromise in which native sons had actively participated. The formal document forced on the archbishop, city fathers and several "captains-general" of the capital outside of Bogotá provided something for all free men in the viceroyalty. Among its terms, the visitor-general would be expelled, the tobacco monopoly abolished, and the increase in price on cane liquor rescinded. One provision laid out the native sons' desire to control offices:

> In governmental positions of primary, secondary, and tertiary rank nationals of this America should be preferred and privileged over Europeans who daily exhibit the disdain they hold for the people from around here [New Granada]. No amount of good will on the part of the Americans can rid them of this notion. In their ignorance they believe that they are the masters and that all Americans without distinction are inferior creatures . . . only in cases of necessity and according to their ability, good intentions, and favorable inclinations may Europeans hold some governmental positions.[8]

In other words, native sons and a few *radicados* should hold office. Although modestly less restricted, the call for local self-rule within the empire was reminiscent of the Mexico City Council's bold but futile call to prohibit Spanish immigration.

Lima's Instructions and Mexico City's Repeated Protest

The municipal council of Lima had its complaints as well. Among them was frustration over appointments made to the capital's *audiencia* since mid-century. Then native sons had dominated the court, but the gradual decline in their numbers was manifest by 1780 when, for the first time since early in the century, peninsulars outnumbered them by more than three ministers. With only two *limeños* on the *audiencia* in the early 1790s, the city council prepared a set of instructions for native son José Baquíjano y Carrillo, its deputy to the court in Madrid. Among them it asked that locally born Spaniards be given one-third of the *audiencia*'s positions, for, just as in Navarre, "it is obvious that no American should have an impediment preventing him from holding a *plaza togada* in his own *patria*."[9] It also sought a rotation between Europeans and creoles in the positions of prior and consul on the merchant guild of Lima.

The limited request for native son positions on the *audiencia* at first glance accords with the royal order of February 1776. But where that document said "Spanish Americans," the councilors wanted it to read "native sons of Peru" if not Lima itself. More than any of its counterparts, Lima's city council knew the difference between the categories as a result of nearly two centuries of experience. While the city's representative secured a rare native son appointment to the *Audiencia* of Lima in 1797, it was to the less prestigious criminal chamber and initially without salary. His pay and advancement to the civil chamber came only later.

Shortly before Lima drafted its instructions, the Mexico City Council resubmitted a close copy of its 1771 protest. With more force than their Peruvian counterparts, the city fathers of Mexico pointed out to Charles IV (Figure 6.2) the relevant legislation supporting native sons for high office and their belief that no more peninsular appointees need be sent to New Spain. With only 1 native son and two other creoles among the 19 ministers on the *Audiencia* of Mexico in 1790, their continued dissatisfaction with appointment policy was grounded in ongoing patent discrimination against Mexican attorneys.

Figure 6.2 Equestrian statue of Charles IV. The ill-fated Bourbon monarch of Spain who abdicated to his son Ferdinand VII in 1808 and subsequently to Napoleon.

Source: Espino Barros, Eugenio, comp. *Album Gráfico de la República Mexicana*, 2nd ed. (Mexico, DF: Gran Establecimiento Tipo-Litográfrico de Müller Hnos., 1910), 35. Reproduced by permission of the Mercantile Library at the University of Missouri-St. Louis.

Social Diversity among Native Sons and Daughters

Magnates

Between the mid-eighteenth century and 1808, most of the 100 or so families worth a million or more pesos in New Spain were able to maintain their wealth and status. Many of these magnate families had one or more members engaged in international commerce, still the best single route to earn great wealth. A quicker route to enviable riches, however, was marriage to a wealthy widow or heiress, a course followed repeatedly from the sixteenth century onward. For example, native daughter Luisa María Sánchez de Tagle was the only child of Mexican creole Damiana Dávila y Rojas and peninsular Luis Sánchez de Tagle y de la Rosa, I Marquis of Altamira, an extraordinarily successful silver merchant and financier. In a typical action for flourishing European merchants, Luis invited his nephew Pedro Sánchez de Tagle from Spain to work with him in Mexico and, after the young man had demonstrated his abilities, Luisa María wed him in 1661. His bride's resources confirmed Pedro in the front rank of Mexico's elite families. Over the years, he entered the Order of Calatrava, enjoyed his wife's title of nobility as consort, served as prior of Mexico City's merchant guild, and became a permanent alderman of the capital. The third and fourth Marquises of Altamira, both Mexican creoles, also married peninsulars. In this manner, wealthy native daughter families incorporated successful Europeans through marriage and remained at the summit of Mexican society.

Another 400 families or so formed the second rung of the capital's elite. Whether headed by a native daughter, native son, or a peninsular, these families invested in land both as part of a diversified portfolio and because it provided collateral for credit. While some widows and daughters were active in business, sons of the magnates were as apt to follow a career in wholesale commerce as to enter a profession. Those who entered the Church or became university-educated lawyers were well positioned to advance within the clergy and serve in royal *letrado* positions. As did high positions in convents for native daughters, the offices the sons obtained offered prestige appropriate for their families' status.

The range of investments and marriages of an elite family in eighteenth- and early-nineteenth-century Lima illustrates again the inclusion of peninsulars into established local families. Juan Bautista Baquíjano entered the City of Kings in the early eighteenth century and promptly contacted a prosperous Basque merchant from a municipality adjacent to his hometown. Extraordinarily successful in commerce, at the age of 47, Juan Bautista married 20-year-old *limeña* María Ignacia Carrillo de Córdoba. She descended on the paternal side from an early immigrant who fought in Chile during the 1570s and, later, against corsairs while a military assistant to his brother-in-law the viceroy of Peru, and descended on the maternal side from an early settler of the 1550s. Her *limeño* father married a first-generation creole in Chile and purchased an appointment as regent of Lima's Tribunal of Accounts, a post he held for over 30 years; his brother was a merchant in Lima's *Consulado*. Her brothers included

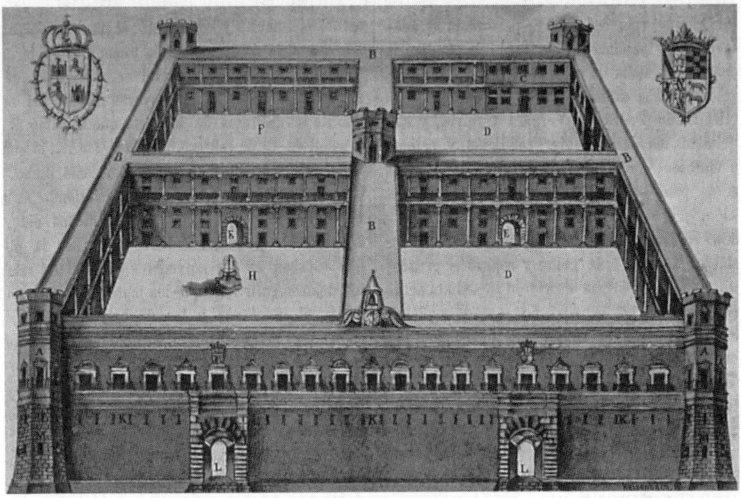

Figure 6.3 Viceregal palace in Mexico City. Interior of the viceregal palace of New Spain in the sixteenth and seventeenth centuries.
Source: Vicente Riva Palacio, *Mexico a través de los siglos*, Vol. 2 (Mexico: Ballescá y Compañía, 1888), 579. Reproduced by permission of the Mercantile Library at the University of Missouri-St. Louis.

a member of the cathedral chapter of Lima and a chaplain in the viceregal palace (Figure 6.3). An older sister married a Panamanian *audiencia* minister whose brother-in-law was later selected as bishop of Cuzco. Thus, the family's ties in the 1740s extended from Lima to Panama, Charcas, and Chile. A few years before his death in 1759, Juan Bautista purchased the title Count of Vistaflorida.

Her husband's passing left the Countess with numerous business responsibilities, two sons, and five daughters. Assisted by a brother and later a son-in-law, she continued the family's success in managing business operations in agriculture, trade, and shipping. The elder son inherited the family title of nobility and ultimately settled in Madrid where he invested in government bonds and lent money to prominent officials. Second son José became a professor (*catedrático*) at the University of San Marcos, a native son *audiencia* minister in Lima, and ultimately was named a councilor of state in Spain. Although neither son wed, the Baquíjano daughters married well. One's husband was a local magistrate of Lima whose aunt was the sister of a long-serving *limeño* minister on the *Audiencia* of Chile. A second wed a *limeño* officer who became one of the few pensioned members of the newly created Order of Charles III in 1774. A third daughter married the second Count of San Xavier y Casa Laredo, whose brother Gaspar served on *audiencias* and ultimately reached the Council of the Indies, and whose sister wed Antonio de Ulloa, a famed scientist, traveler, and administrator. After the Count's premature death, she married the nephew of Viceroy Francisco Gil de Taboada (1790–1796). A fourth daughter wed a Salamanca lawyer whose *audiencia* service in Lima led to his promotion as the first regent of the *Audiencia* of Charcas. The final daughter entered matrimony with a peninsular merchant whose success brought him recognition as an elected official of the Lima merchant guild. In sum, the Baquíjano sisters contracted marriages with both peninsulars and native sons that together created and expanded familial links to the capital's city council, its merchant guild, the militia, the *audiencia*, and the viceroy. When the matriarch died in 1791, she left a fortune worth over a million pesos. As in other parts of the Indies, native daughter marriages to successful peninsulars integrated them into an established and extended elite family.

"Poor Whites"

Impoverished Spaniards inhabited the Indies as they did Spain. In America, however, persons of Spanish descent were supposed to be able to look down on the rest of society as a right that originated with the conquest. When native sons were distant from the top of the social hierarchy, they might become the "social poor." Although not necessarily destitute, they lacked the resources to live in the style considered appropriate for Spaniards. Their poverty thus differed from that of persons they believed should be poor, those at the bottom of the social hierarchy. Blaming bad luck rather than personal failings for their financial adversity, they formally solicited the status of "solemn poor" in order to reduce their legal costs in court. This approach, which the Crown supported, served to maintain the privilege of being Spaniards despite a shortage of funds. Confirming that Quito's economic difficulties in the eighteenth century did not spare Spaniards, the number of petitioners seeking the status of "solemn poor" who used the honorific *don* or *doña* rose dramatically by 1800.

Judged by economic status, however, far more native sons struggled than those identified as "solemn poor." As a group they had a lengthy if not illustrious pedigree. Footloose, homeless Spaniards without discernable legal means of support had caught the attention of clerics and royal administrators soon after conquest. Labeled "vagabonds" in the mid-sixteenth century, they roamed the countryside with *casta* companions, molested the indigenous peoples, and generally made themselves obnoxious. Repeated orders from Madrid to officials in New Spain and Peru to force vagabonds – both peninsulars and creoles – to find employment never solved the problem and their number grew.

As the population of white plebeians grew over the course of Spanish rule, the number of Spanish criminals also increased. Of nearly 1000 prisoners sentenced to serve in a garrison or overseas at the end of the eighteenth century by New Spain's special criminal tribunal known as the *Acordada,* 28% of the men were identified as Spaniards of indeterminate birthplace. Similarly, among persons prosecuted by the criminal chamber of the *Audiencia* of Mexico between 1800 and 1817, Spaniards constituted more than a third.

In the city of Mexico, poor Spaniards joined other *castas* and indigenous people at the outlets for *pulque*, a popular alcoholic beverage made from the fermented liquid of the century plant (*maguey*). To deal with cash flow problems, many native daughters in the city of Mexico, especially those who were widowed heads of households, joined *casta* and indigenous women in pawning items of value for small sums at neighborhood grocery stores and, after its creation in 1775, for larger amounts at a state-operated pawnshop, the *Monte de Piedad.* How many impoverished Spaniards were among the 10 000–15 000 homeless that Humboldt reported on the streets of the city of Mexico in the early nineteenth century is unknown. Clearly, however, native sons throughout the empire spanned the social spectrum from the very wealthy to the homeless.

Creoles by "Quality"

The creole population of the empire had never been exclusively of Spanish ancestry. While elites frequently claimed pure Spanish lineage, some noted with pride that their first ancestor in the Indies had married an indigenous woman of royal or at least noble birth. After the mid-sixteenth century, Spaniards usually married Spaniards, although a few wed indigenous people and *castas*. Particularly in the eighteenth century, however, designation as an American Spaniard became increasingly a matter of "quality" (*calidad*) or presumed ethnicity based on characteristics that included language, dress, lifestyle, and skin color rather than lineage. Demonstrating "pure" lineage in any case was a sometimes-flawed process that relied heavily on parish records of marriage, birth, and death. These documents, in turn, reflected the priest's designation, as a result of either his observation or the person's self-identification, in a book of records for whites or another volume for nonwhite parishioners. An episode from 1699 Mexico City illustrates both the fallibility and mutability of the priest's designation.

Domingo Velásquez sought ordination and went to the cathedral where his baptism was recorded. To the supplicant's chagrin, the priest found the entry in the book for *castas*. Protesting what he considered a grave and inexplicable mistake, Velásquez enlisted three aged neighbors to testify that they knew him and his parents and, of more importance, that all members of his family were "known and taken and commonly reputed" to be Spaniards "without any mixture."[10] To his undoubted relief, the testimony convinced the priest that the original record was erroneously placed and he duly inscribed Velásquez's birth in the ledger for Spaniards.

Individuals also experienced changes in identity outside of Mexico City. In Orizaba, a census of 1777 documented that a third of the men classified as Spaniards had married mestizos and that Spanish women married non-Spanish men over 40% of the time. The 1791 census revealed that more than 20% of Spanish men were married to non-Spaniards and that Spanish women continued to marry non-Spaniards. Strikingly, of more than 1000 nonindigenous people counted in both censuses, 260 listed in the one for 1791 were reported to be of higher *calidad*, for example, Spaniard rather than mestizo, while 70 dropped into a lower category. The latter census also revealed more Spaniards classified as artisans than in any other employment category and that they accounted for almost 35% of men classified as laborers. These figures demonstrate that the category "Spaniard" was mutable both upward and downward in terms of *calidad* and that numerous men accepted as Spaniards were not only artisans but also laborers. Despite creole apologists' focus on native son appointments to the offices of Church and state, the expansion of the white population from the sixteenth century onward progressively resulted in males accepted as Spaniards sharing occupations with men who were not.

Between the mid-eighteenth century and 1808, the Crown systematically favored peninsulars for positions that native sons and other creoles had previously held. Faced with the legacy of selling appointments to treasury, provincial, and *audiencia* positions, it combined this pro-peninsular policy with a careful monitoring of officials' marriages. The creation of pension systems for the widows and orphans of employees strengthened enforcement of long-standing policies to prevent marriages by officials to local women, for participants had to meet age requirements, obtain a license to marry, and register the spouse to make her and their children eligible for benefits.

In order to increase revenues to pay for higher military expenditures after 1763, the Crown replaced tax farmers with government officials. It also created new monopolies and again used its own appointees to oversee them. The expansion of royal offices thus provided the Crown with increased opportunities to name peninsulars, and it did so, especially to high-paying positions. The introduction of the intendant system epitomized this approach. Intendants were almost always peninsulars, although their *letrado* lieutenants were frequently creoles born outside of the intendancy.

The royal effort to integrate the empire more effectively by naming creoles to cathedral chapters and high *letrado* positions in Spain, creating special military units in Spain for them, and establishing a school for American nobles in Granada produced more irritation than tangible benefits among native sons and other creoles. By the 1790s, the brief increase in peninsulars named to cathedral chapters in the 1770s and early 1780s had largely given way to renewed native son and other creole appointments. Nonetheless, the Crown's pro-peninsular appointment policies had stirred the city council of Mexico and later that of Lima to protest threatened and real changes. When the Crown backed off, complaints declined, but discrimination against native sons remained part of the historical record that local creoles were ready to criticize whenever the opportunity should arise.

Appointment practice provided ample evidence of native sons' second-class status, but the Crown also managed to emphasize the second-class status of the Indies as a whole. In order to retire previously issued bonds, in 1804, the Crown forced the Church to demand repayment of its loans and then to exchange the proceeds for new government bonds. The policy threatened economies wherever officials enforced the order as few borrowers could pay off their principal and the application of the order flooded the real estate market and quickly reduced the value of land subject to sale. Especially in New Spain, the largest and richest American kingdom at the time, the forced repayment of more than 10 million pesos of loans alienated debtors regardless of place of birth. Native sons and daughters were correct if they believed the Crown valued the Indies primarily as a source of funds to finance Spain's engagement in European wars and its costly alliance with Napoleonic France. The unanswered question: how long would native sons and daughters, other creoles, and peninsulars in the American kingdoms continue to pay?

7

From Abdications to Independence

Native sons lived in an era of political revolution and independence between 1808 and the mid-1820s. The abdications of Charles IV and Ferdinand VII in 1808 and their retention in France initiated the reordering of mainland Spanish America. By placing their Old and New World kingdoms in the hands of Napoleon Bonaparte, the monarchs provoked both a constitutional crisis throughout their New and Old World realms and a war of independence against French rule in Spain. For six tumultuous years, juntas founded on the principle that sovereignty returned to the people in the absence of a monarch opposed the rule of the French emperor's brother José I, "King of Spain and the Indies." Britain allied with Spain against the French invaders and successive governments of resistance – the Junta Central, Regency, and Cortes of Cádiz – sought from the American realms financial assistance and political support through their elected representatives. A written constitution promulgated in 1812 encapsulated revolutionary changes that, if fully implemented, would have provided substantial regional autonomy in the Indies, although not complete equality, as part of a single "Spanish Nation."

Ferdinand's restoration to the throne, nullification of the Constitution, and decision to send a large military force to the Americas pushed autonomists toward separatism. Although a revolt in Spain in 1820 forced the monarch to accept the Constitution, it became clear in the following year that the reestablished Cortes would not support American self-rule within the empire. By the mid-1820s, separatists joined or at least accepted by autonomists had triumphed. Primarily from their ranks

Spaniards in the Colonial Empire: Creoles vs. Peninsulars?, First Edition. Mark A. Burkholder.

emerged the new countries' rulers. Anti-peninsular sentiment, long muted by marriage, friendship, and shared economic interests, also prevailed. As a result of the European Spaniards' voluntary departure, expulsion, and death, the new states were effectively peninsular-free.

Peninsulars on the Eve of Crisis

Peninsulars in the Indies totaled perhaps 30 000–40 000 at the turn of the nineteenth century. In contrast, native sons across America numbered over 2 million out of a total population of 12–13 million. The expansion of the white population had resulted from modest European immigration, natural reproduction by creoles, and, particularly in the eighteenth century, extensive passing by *castas* accepted as whites by virtue of their "quality" despite mixed ancestry. New Spain's peninsulars probably numbered no more than 15 000 in 1808, half of them in the military and about 1500 in the clergy. Mexico City in 1790 counted only 2359 "Europeans," almost all of them males. In contrast, the capital's native sons and other creoles totaled almost 50 000 with native daughters accounting for nearly 60%. The prosperous mining town of Guanajuato in 1792 had but 314 resident peninsulars out of nearly 7500 whites. In Antequera, Oaxaca, the Europeans, more than 95% of them male, accounted for about 1.5% of the lay population.

Despite their small numbers, European Spaniards retained a prominent presence in key royal institutions and were important in trade and finance. The four viceroys in 1808 were from Europe, as were more than two-thirds of *audiencia* ministers; only a handful of native sons sat on the courts. No native sons and just one creole were among the 27 mainland intendants. Bishops and archbishops included just five native sons and four other creoles. Peninsulars also could be found as prebendaries of cathedral chapters, if rarely in any but wealthy parishes. Also visible in the regular army, they continued to hold most of the highest ranks despite declining numbers. Of more than 450 royal positions in the city of Mexico in 1808, native sons and other creoles held over half of them, dominating those of lower rank. In the private sector, Europeans owned rural property, engaged in commerce, financed miners, and lent money. They retained their leading position as wholesale merchants in the capitals and major ports of the empire even if they were not invariably the richest. Lima's wealthiest merchant, at least in 1819, was Ignacio Santiago y Rotalde, a native son of a European Spaniard and a *limeña*. Marriage between successful peninsulars and elite native daughters continued to be the rule.

Few peninsulars actually had great wealth. Two-thirds or more of those in the city of Mexico, the western hemisphere's richest capital at the turn of the nineteenth century, were of middling status at best and many failed to reach that level. Visible as pawnbrokers and considered usurers by Crown and public alike, immigrants were sufficiently entrenched among storekeepers in the capital that the populace referred pejoratively to all retailers as *gachupines*. European Spaniards also engaged in unskilled labor, served as house servants, and worked in low-prestige artisan positions that identified them economically as plebeians along with many *castas* and indigenous people. In Guanajuato, merchants divided almost equally between peninsulars and a combination of native sons and other creoles. Among dealers or small-scale retailers, the American-born outnumbered immigrants by 15 to 1. Native son and mestizo mineworkers each numbered over 1300 and mulattoes were almost 1900. Only five peninsulars engaged in this physically demanding and dangerous occupation. The primary division between most immigrants and native sons was place of birth rather than type of employment.

Response to the Abdications

As the implications of events in Spain sank in among local elites in America, their initial response was to pledge loyalty to Ferdinand VII. Quickly they divided, however, into "loyalists" and "autonomists," differing over the course to follow until the king returned to the throne. "Loyalists" at first favored recognizing Seville's self-styled Supreme Junta of Spain and the Indies, but soon accepted the more broadly based Junta Central that convened in late September 1808. In contrast, many native sons embraced the patriots' model of local juntas adopted in Spain. Proponents of self-rule *within* the empire, these "autonomists" agreed that, in the absence of the monarch, sovereignty had returned to the people and their representatives should govern until he returned to the throne. Although this endorsement of self-rule followed the same reasoning that had led to provincial juntas in Spain, loyalists in the Indies considered it a treasonous subterfuge for independence.

When viceroy of New Spain José de Iturrigaray appeared to be leaning toward the autonomist position, a loyalist group headed by prominent

European merchants and officials deposed him on September 15, 1808. Without legal authority, the heavily peninsular *Audiencia* of Mexico and the European Archbishop Francisco Javier de Lizana named Iturrigaray's peninsular successor the following day. Arrests of autonomist leaders ensued and some frustrated adherents of self-rule began plotting against what they correctly considered an illegal government in New Spain. In Charcas and Quito, the creation of juntas in 1809 provoked military responses that restored loyalist control.

Elections and American Grievances

Mandated elections created a new arena of competition between native sons and peninsulars. The receipt of patriotic donations and other revenues spurred the Junta Central in January 1809 to seek a representative from each of the Americas' four viceroyalties and five independent captaincies-generals. The directive further declared that Spain's dominions in the Indies "are not properly colonies . . . , but an essential and integral part of the Spanish monarchy."[1] This statement was especially significant to Americans for it not only asserted the equality of the new World realms but also confirmed their centuries-old claim that they lived in kingdoms and thus had a direct relationship with the monarch. Moreover, the Junta Central ordered the capital city of each of the nine jurisdictions to send "instructions," that is, "grievances" with its delegate. In response to these unprecedented developments, chief executives and leading municipalities of the designated divisions initiated the required, cumbersome procedure to select representatives. At least 99 municipal councils from Mexico to Chile participated.

These initial elections quickly dispelled any naïve belief that native sons would dominate them. In New Spain, the peninsular faction responsible for overthrowing Viceroy Iturrigaray limited the participating cities to 14. These elected eight peninsulars and six Americans as the pool from which the representative would be selected by lot. The outcome led native sons to protest the Europeans' eligibility and they secured a revision limiting it to native sons of the electoral district in the next set of elections. The successful candidate, Miguel de Lardizábal, was a native son who had sailed to Spain in his teens and lived there for nearly 50 years. In Venezuela, the candidate chosen was an eminent creole from Popayán, but protests that he was neither worthy nor a native son prodded the

Council of the Indies to nullify the election. Revised electoral guidelines clarified that the person selected had to be an American and preferably a native son or at least a citizen (*vecino*) closely tied to the province he would represent, that is, a *radicado*. Persistence had produced a victory, but all native sons recognized their woeful underrepresentation compared to the 36 Junta members sent by the Spanish provinces. The point had to be fought at a later date, for the body's short life allowed only one New World delegate to assume his place.

As directed by the Junta Central, municipal councils in the Indies discussed concerns to include in their representative's instructions. Developing these statements increased political awareness, honed native sons' sense of grievance, and both stimulated expectations that redress would follow and documented Americans' recognition of their inequitable representation. Among other matters, native sons wanted full equality with peninsulars, and their grievances predictably included the discrimination against them in appointments to office. Although the complaint was long-standing, their frustration had intensified as appointments since 1750 reversed many earlier successes and as the Crown selected peninsulars to inaugurate new positions.

Native sons found peninsulars' attitude of superiority particularly objectionable. A newspaper article published in September 1810 revealed the anger toward *chapetones* of an autonomist who soon supported independence:

> The European Spaniard who set foot in these lands became noble as soon as he arrived, and was rich within a few years, master of all employment and thereby all powerful over subordinates, with the arrogance typical of those who are in command far from home. . . . [He] bawled at them [creoles] with contempt: "Americans, keep your distance, you are not our equals, spare us that degradation for nature has created you to vegetate in obscurity and dejection."[2]

Resentment over peninsulars' attitudes, of course, was neither unique nor of recent vintage.

The Cortes of Cádiz

In February 1810, the recently installed Regency ordered a new round of elections for deputies to the forthcoming General and Extraordinary

Cortes. In response to earlier complaints, the electoral guidelines stipulated that only native sons (36 in number) could represent their provinces as proprietary deputies. This time peninsulars protested. Although the four peninsulars and one Mexican who comprised the Regency issued a modification to the guidelines declaring their eligibility if residents and living in the jurisdiction, it reached New Spain too late to do them any good. This clarification of August 20, 1810, also extended suffrage and eligibility to serve as deputies to indigenous and mestizo males. In New Spain, elections held during the summer of 1810 for proprietary deputies to the Cortes led to victorious native son autonomists throughout the viceroyalty. Elections elsewhere produced proprietary native son deputies from the major subdivisions of the Kingdom of Guatemala, Panama, Peru, Montevideo, Maracaibo province in Venezuela, Cuba, Puerto Rico, and Santo Domingo. The Cortes opened on August 24, 1810, before many elected deputies arrived as a result of distance from Spain, slow communication, and a complicated electoral procedure. Anticipating the problem, the Regency set up a system under which Americans present in Cádiz could elect 30 substitute deputies or *suplentes* to serve until the proprietary deputies were present. When the Cortes opened, 27 of the 28 American deputies in attendance were substitutes, a number of them representing provinces affected by insurgency, that is, Chile, Paraguay, Charcas, Buenos Aires, Bogotá, and Quito. The presence of 74 European deputies highlighted the extent of American underrepresentation if based on total population.

No issue created more trouble for the Cortes than American representation. Deputies believed erroneously that the America's population was 16.5 million while Spain's was only some 10.5 million. Using these figures as the basis for allocating deputies would give the Indies more than a 3:2 advantage, an intolerable result for most peninsular representatives. Rancorous discussion began the day after the Cortes opened as American deputies immediately tried to link representation to total population and to force new elections for an increased number of deputies. On October 15, 1810, however, a majority supported using only persons of European and New World origins as the basis for representation in the future. The exclusion of an estimated 5.5–6 million *castas* from citizenship left Spain and America with what the deputies believed was approximately the same number of citizens and equal representation. Americans had lost one of the most fundamental issues the Cortes would face. The decision had immediate relevance. With war against the

French going badly, peninsular deputies refused to support immediate, new elections based on the October 15 formula. Already selected representatives would write a constitution.

The lack of equal representation based on population continued to rankle American deputies and enjoyed pride of place on a list of "propositions" they submitted to the Cortes on December 16, 1810. Three other grievances dealt directly with long-standing creole complaints concerning appointments to government, ecclesiastical, and military positions. One called for equality in employment for Spaniards and Native Americans for all posts. A second proposed that native sons should receive half of all posts in each American kingdom. A third asked for the creation of an advisory committee in each province to recommend candidates for its posts. The requested equality in employment passed, but since creoles considered native son appointments most important, they gained little.

The Cortes also approved a new institution, the "provincial deputation," for Spain and the Americas. The 18 deputations authorized in America included 6 in New Spain, 2 in the Kingdom of Guatemala, 2 in the Caribbean, and 1 in each *audiencia* district in South America. Composed of two *ex officio* appointees and seven elected members, the body was to oversee, among other responsibilities, tax assessment in the province and public expenditures by municipalities. It was also to create municipal councils in all communities with 1000 or more inhabitants; in New Spain. this resulted in an increase of nearly 900 councils by 1814. These additional municipalities provided thousands of new opportunities for political involvement by native sons, even though hereditary positions in existing cities and towns would be eliminated.

Constitution of 1812

The great triumph of the Cortes was to write and approve the "Political Constitution of the Spanish Monarchy," a document better known as "the Constitution of 1812." Authored by native sons of Spain and the Indies, this charter specifically assigned sovereignty to the "Spanish nation," that is, "all Spaniards" in Europe and the Americas, rather than to a monarch. As earlier, it defined citizens (*ciudadanos*) to include Spaniards, indigenous people, and any racial combination of the two, but not African slaves, freedmen, or *castas* save in special cases. Citizenship bestowed the right to hold municipal posts and to vote for other officials, notably deputies to the Cortes. It also established a constitutional, limited monarchy, an independent judiciary, and a strong elected legislative body that was to meet each year in Madrid. Significant freedom of the press received constitutional sanction, and the Catholic Church retained its unchallenged status as the religion of state. Finally, uniformity replaced the hodgepodge jurisdictions and geographic variations in law and authority. In short, this revolutionary document envisioned a single, uniformly administered "national" entity quite unlike Spain and its overseas realms in 1808. American deputies were proud of their accomplishment. They could point to numerous ways in which the Constitution served their interests better than the monarchy of the past. But the charter failed to address equality of representation in a way that most Americans considered fair. The equality promised by the governments of resistance, including the Cortes, was a chimera. Peninsulars remained more equal than native sons.

Peninsulars Use the Press

In Cádiz the *Diario de Sesiones de las Cortes Generales y Extraordinarias* and other publications reported in detail on speeches delivered in the Cortes and actions taken. The news accompanied the next ship sailing to America. Fanned by open discussion of key issues, a war of words between peninsulars and native sons quickly escalated. Exacerbated acrimony accompanied the reading of the *Consulado* of Mexico's lengthy comments and gratuitous insults on May 27, 1811. Published during the debate over American representation, the remarks demonstrated European deprecation of the entire American population. Systematically, the peninsular author denigrated New Spain's three million indigenous as stupid, lazy, lascivious, and prone to drunkenness; in short, they were incapable of self-government. The two million *castas* were no better. As for the "whites" or "American Spaniards," their dispositions were not significantly different as evidenced by the large number who were plebeians. Their poor judgment extended to squandering their patrimonies without regard for the future while their laziness exceeded their ability. They gambled, drank, and generally wasted their time in unproductive activities. Out of a million or more "indigenous whites," no more than 15 000 were "active citizens" and few of them qualified as "true citizens." Although the author noted that European Spaniards degenerated from their association with the "indigenous whites," the former were responsible for creating patrimonies for sons who were "ungrateful, squanderers, and their enemies." Scandalized by the insults, livid American deputies tried to leave the Cortes, but guards restrained them.[3]

300 Years of Infamy

Unanimous opposition to Napoleon and enthusiasm for Ferdinand VII in 1808 soon gave way to increased interest in autonomy within "the Spanish Nation." In some locations, native sons' critique of Spanish rule and its peninsular agents became shrill. Freedom of the press on political issues stimulated criticism voiced within the Cortes and throughout the empire. Venezuela's declaration of independence in early July 1811 promised to "generously forget the long series of ills, injuries, and privations which the sad right of conquest has indistinctly caused to all descendants of the Discoverers, Conquerors, and Settlers" throughout America. In sum, it railed against "three hundred years of Spanish dominion."[4] A Chilean newspaper commented in 1813, "There is always a natural clash of interests between a Metropolis and its colonies." Other writers referred to Spanish rule as "three centuries of shackles" and "centuries of infamy and lamentation!"[5] Antipathy at the individual level between American and European Spaniards and long-standing native son complaints about the Crown's general, although not consistently enforced, policy of excluding them from office expanded into a wholesale condemnation of the colonial enterprise from the time of conquest.

One of the most cited native son publications appeared in 1811. Its author, lawyer and priest José Guridi y Alcocer, the deputy for Tlaxcala, Mexico, to the Cortes, provided quantitative data on creoles named to various positions in America and thereby provided unequivocal proof of discrimination to both contemporaries and later historians. Only 4 Americans, but 166 peninsulars, had been viceroys; just 14 creoles but 588 European Spaniards had been captains-general, governors, and presidents; no more than 278 Americans had been bishops and archbishops in contrast to 700 born in Spain. These numbers proved magnetic for writers focused on Spain's ill treatment of creoles. In *An Exposé of the Dissentions of Spanish America*, English writer William Walton drew upon them to assert that out of the 754 executives, only 18 were creoles. Focusing on Bourbon rule, he concluded: "Thus, from the time of Philip

V, does it appear, that rapacious, and often immoral Peninsulars, held every office of profit and distinction, and little else was left to the excluded natives [native sons], but ill treatment, continued insults and outrages. . . ."[6] He failed to mention, if he knew, the extent to which native sons and other creoles secured offices during the reign of Philip V and early years of Ferdinand VI. In this way the reiterated and exaggerated allegation of creoles' virtual exclusion from office became central among claimed "causes" of independence.

Creole Appointments to Royal and Church Offices, 1808–1814

Between 1808 and 1814, native sons and other creoles obtained more appointments to the *audiencias* and other high offices than at any time since the Crown stopped selling appointments in the mid-eighteenth century. A combination of 4 native sons (8%) and 23 other creoles (43%) received just over half (51%) of new *audiencia* appointments. The American percentages were impressive gains over the years 1751–1808 when the Crown named only 7 native sons (3%) and 57 other creoles (22%) or 1 American for every 3 peninsulars. The number of creoles named intendant, a peninsular stronghold since its introduction in 1764, also increased with three native sons and five other Americans named for a combined 31%. Although only five new bishops were named between 1808 and Ferdinand's return, one was a native son. In sum, both native sons and other creoles showed tangible gains in high-ranking appointments during Spain's War of Independence. Even this improvement, however, was far from the level of native son participation in high office proposed in the "propositions" made to the Cortes in 1810.

The Return of Ferdinand VII

The defeat of the French and subsequent return of "The Beloved Ferdinand" to Spain in spring 1814 ended the conditions that had led to the Constitution. The personal links between monarch and separate kingdoms had been restored and what Ferdinand considered a treasonous substitution of popular for royal sovereignty had been ended. By then, however, the idea of popular sovereignty, electoral experience, unprecedented freedom of the press, the formal presentation of grievances, a written constitution, a powerful legislature, restrictions on the monarch, and expectations of change within "The Spanish Nation" had fomented a political revolution in America. Political life would never be the same. Indeed in some regions, unambiguous movements for independence generally led by native sons and other creoles had already overtaken the autonomist position of greater self-rule within the empire and resulted in protracted insurgencies and civil war.

Ferdinand's return profoundly altered the imperfect but potentially improved relationship within a constitutional Spanish Nation located on both sides of the Atlantic. Even before reaching Madrid, the monarch closed the Cortes, abrogated the Constitution, and jailed its leading supporters whether of Spanish or American birth. Before the reaction abated, as many as 12 000 liberals were in jail or exile. The king also proceeded to reimpose insofar as possible the pre-1808 institutions and practices on his many realms in Spain and the Americas. It became clear almost immediately that he had learned nothing while living in a French chateau. "Compromise" was absent from his vocabulary. Instead he determined to reestablish royal authority in the Indies by force, sending an army of more than 10 000 men to Venezuela and New Granada. This decision brought further rebel persecution of the peninsulars he ostensibly supported. In Spain, disillusioned liberals turned to conspiracy as a means to reestablish constitutional rule.

American Panorama, 1808–1814

During Spain's War of Independence, the political stability that had generally characterized almost 300 years of Spanish rule in mainland America faltered. While local elites had always sought advantageous policies for themselves and wanted native son officials who would provide more responsiveness to their concerns, it took the abdications of 1808 to galvanize politically active supporters of self-rule within the empire. After initial, almost frenzied protests of loyalty to Ferdinand, in much of the Indies, identifiable factions of "autonomists" that included both males and females were soon participating in discussions about possible alternative forms of rule in the monarch's absence. In general, native sons supported the creation of local juntas to rule in Ferdinand's name during his absence. Peninsulars, in contrast, preferred continued rule by

Europeans in America and to recognize a government of resistance in Spain, a course of action made easier by the fall of 1808 with the creation of the Junta Central. As the war in Spain dragged on, a Regency replaced the Junta Central, and a French victory seemed almost inevitable when, in February 1810, the invaders began a siege of Cádiz. The autonomist position appeared as a way to preserve the Americas for Ferdinand VII even if Spain were lost. Where separatists gained the upper hand, civil war often ensued.

Fearing a French triumph, some peninsular officials in the Americas joined native sons in creating juntas that often grew out of municipal councils. Despite short-lived efforts in Quito, Chuquisaca, and La Paz in 1809, more juntas were formed in 1810; 16 appeared in New Granada alone. Although Spaniards from both sides of the Atlantic supported or at least acquiesced in the formation of juntas in Caracas, Buenos Aires, Bogotá, and Santiago, the new governments soon pruned Europeans from their ranks, leaving native sons in control. Division among locally born Spaniards, however, became apparent. While many desired home rule within the empire, a revolutionary idea in its own right, a small but increasing number of separatists sought complete political independence and utilized the free press to promote their case. In 1811, independence was declared in Paraguay, Caracas, Quito, Bogotá, and some other locations in New Granada. Only Paraguay was able to retain its independence without an intervening restoration of Spanish authority by force of arms.

Under a strong peninsular viceroy until 1816, Peru remained under Spain's control despite a rebellion in Cuzco in 1814–1815 and without a strong autonomist faction of native sons in Lima. Indeed it was able to reattach Charcas after defeating its autonomists. Santiago, Chile followed a careful path that led the Regency to recognize its legitimacy in 1811, the only such body to obtain this confirmation. Peru's Viceroy José Fernando Abascal was skeptical, however, and sent an army in 1813 that reestablished royalist rule.

The richest American viceroyalty in 1808 remained New Spain. There, a move for home rule in 1808 provoked a peninsular coup that displaced the viceroy, imprisoned the most vocal autonomists, and stimulated conspiracies, one of which flowered into a destructive rural rebellion in 1810 led by the native son priest Miguel Hidalgo (Figure 7.1). The rebellion failed and its leader was captured, defrocked, and executed in 1811. Despite native son leaders, the multitude of indigenous and mestizo rebels demonstrated their disinterest in distinguishing native sons from

Figure 7.1 Miguel Hidalgo. A native son cleric who initiated a rebellion against peninsulars in Mexico in 1810.
Source: Francisco García Calderón, *Latin America: Its Rise and Progress*, trans. Bernard Miall (London: T. Fisher Unwin, 1913; 1919 printing), 28. Reproduced by permission of the Mercantile Library at the University of Missouri-St. Louis.

peninsulars. The massacre of whites regardless of birthplace at Guanajuato led most Spaniards to band together regardless of birthplace. Although mestizo priest José María Morelos inherited Hidalgo's mantle, gained some underground native son support in Mexico City, and proved able to gain temporary control of significant territory in southern Mexico, his revolt also failed.

After the peninsular coup of 1808, Mexico's autonomists devoted their attention to achieving home rule via the governments of resistance in Spain. Thus, they took elections seriously and prevailed in limiting New Spain's representatives to native sons. Their delegation to the Cortes of Cádiz was the largest from the Americas and included able participants. Although they lost on the issue of equal representative based on total population, the proposal by one of their number to create provincial deputations was successful. Nineteen New Spain deputies signed the Constitution of 1812.

From August to October 1812, government officials in loyalist locations in the Americas read the Constitution aloud to civil, military, and ecclesiastical officials, as well as to the general public. Formal observances followed, for example, ringing church bells and masses. Expanded legal political activity ensued, especially in the new constitutional municipalities where voters selected parish electors for the provincial elections as well as aldermen, magistrates, and other local officials. In aggregate, elections occurred in regions that were home to more than three-quarters of Spanish America' population. Autonomists in New Spain organized themselves to triumph in the first popular elections held at the municipal, provincial, and Cortes levels. The results swept native sons into office, leading peninsulars to complain that local creoles hated them "simply for having been born in Spain."[7]

Anti-Peninsular Policies

Fed by rumor and exaggeration, the insecurity and upheaval that characterized the civil wars of the 1810s and early 1820s stimulated virulent anti-peninsular sentiment. Birth in Spain became the single criterion that justified confiscating peninsulars' property, countless deaths, and thousands of exiles. Most native sons almost automatically equated peninsulars with loyalists. Despite cases in which successful peninsulars' marriages to elite creole women could mitigate birth in Spain, the few efforts to alleviate Europeans' suffering were largely unsuccessful.

The creation of a provincial junta in the Indies inexorably brought the expulsion of peninsular officials starting with those in the highest ranks. The Junta of Caracas formed in April 1810 immediately expelled Venezuela's captain-general and its *audiencia* ministers, except for a creole from Havana who had joined the rebellion. Similarly in Buenos Aires, the junta installed in May1810 promptly arrested and banished the viceroy and imprisoned and deported most of the *audiencia* ministers. Soon afterward, it exiled or executed any peninsulars considered opponents.

A precocious declaration of independence in Caracas in 1811 led to a short-lived federal republic. After a short civil war in which native sons

Figure 7.2 Simón Bolívar. A native son of Venezuela, "The Liberator" declared "war to the death" against peninsulars who refused to actively embrace the cause of independence.
Source: Francisco García Calderón, *Latin America: Its Rise and Progress*, trans. Bernard Miall, (London: T. Fisher Unwin, 1913; 1919 printing), 70. Reproduced by permission of the Mercantile Library at the University of Missouri-St. Louis.

fought on both sides, the loyalists restored royal authority. The leader of the surviving republicans was Simón Bolívar (Figure 7.2), son of an elite Venezuelan family. At first he rejected a proposal to kill all European Spaniards, limiting his assent to those with weapons in hand. Subsequently, both insurgents and counterinsurgents slaughtered civilians, plundered property, raped, committed other horrendous cruelties. In response, on June 15, 1813, Bolívar ordered war to the death in a decree that forced European Spaniards to choose sides: "Spaniards and Canarians, even if you profess neutrality, know that you will die unless you work actively to bring about the freedom of America. Americans, know that you will live, even if you are guilty."[8] His anti-peninsular commitment even appeared in the date of subsequent decrees, for example, in "Valencia on September 30, 1813, third year of our independence and first of the war to the death." Reacting to one defeat, he ordered an officer "to shoot all Europeans and Canarians."[9] Successful in creating the Second Republic, in reality a military dictatorship, "The Liberator," as Bolívar was now known, ordered over 1000 captured European Spaniards executed in February 1814. No other leader exceeded his ferocious policy.

In Buenos Aires in 1808, initial cooperation took place between native sons and peninsulars even though militia units were organized on the basis of birthplace and ethnicity, for example, regiments of Basques, Catalans, native sons of Buenos Aires (the "Patriots"), slaves, and free blacks. A failed attempt by counterrevolutionaries to take over the municipal council on New Year's Day 1809 resulted in their wealthy European leader, merchant Martín de Alzaga, and his coconspirators receiving sentences of exile in Patagonia and the peninsular militia units being disbanded. Although they had earlier orchestrated the defeat of British forces that had invaded the city, Alzaga and his lieutenants suffered execution following their return to the capital. The native sons in charge readily employed military force against opponents at home or located outside the capital in regions previously part of the viceroyalty of Río de la Plata.

In August 1820, José de San Martín, the visionary creole officer who masterminded the campaign that gave Chile independence, sailed to Peru with a foreign army composed of Argentines and Chileans. When he finally entered Lima the following July, he expected enthusiastic support, but found instead that he had to apply intense pressure on native sons and peninsulars to sign a Declaration of Independence. Given the option either to endorse or to flee, many loyalists in Lima's elite chose the latter regardless of birthplace. Soon afterward, "The Protector," as he was now known, allowed defense minister Bernardo Monteagudo to initiate a program to rid Peru of its peninsulars, despite its unpopularity among *limeños*. Monteagudo described his system in 1823:

> I employed all the means in my power to inflame hatred against the Spaniards [peninsulars]: I prompted measures of severity, and I was always ready to support those who wanted to reduce their number and weaken

their public and private influence. This was my system, and it was not simply prejudice.[10]

Peninsulars who remained in the capital suffered persecution: a 6:00 p.m. curfew, forced monetary donations to the new government, and attacks in the press. In 1822, unwed peninsular males who had failed to obtain citizenship were forced to leave half of their possessions to the state and depart Peru. The 600 or so Europeans remaining in Lima were awakened at 3:00 a.m. on May 2, 1822, forced to walk if able and carried if not to Callao from which they were soon deported to Chile. A foreign witness attested that "the ruin of the old Spaniards was complete" by mid-1822.[11] The fortresses at the capital's port of Callao served as the grave for many loyalist peninsulars and native sons in Lima's elite. Several thousand civilians and over 2000 soldiers perished of starvation, scurvy, and typhus before the forts' surrender in January 1826. As for the unpopular Monteagudo, native son Marquis of Torre Tagle, to whom San Martín had delegated his authority while meeting with Simón Bolívar at Guayaquil in July 1822, removed him from office and the capital. The former minister foolishly returned to Lima and was assassinated in 1825.

From Viceregal New Spain to Independent Mexico

Absolutists were delighted and autonomists in New Spain remained loyal to Ferdinand VII upon his restoration despite his enthusiastic reversal of the work of the governments of resistance and especially the political revolution embedded in the Constitution of 1812. After the viceregal government defeated the Morelos rebellion in 1815, the distinction between banditry and insurgency largely disappeared. At the same time, ongoing taxation to support municipal defenses exhausted villagers' capacity to pay, and amnesties fostered movement of armed men back and forth from insurgency to counterinsurgency. In this bleak environment, the possibility of self-rule within the empire, still the choice of the majority of politically active New Spaniards, unexpectedly appeared once more.

On January 1, 1820, a revolt calling for the restoration of the Constitution of 1812 began in the army gathered near Cádiz for embarkation to the Indies. In early March, liberals ousted by Ferdinand in 1814 and a growing number of radicals forced the monarch to swear allegiance to the charter. Of immediate importance, loyalist armies in America would receive no reinforcements. Already Paraguay, future Argentina, Chile, and parts of New Granada were independent. Bolívar recently had been victorious over royalist forces at Boyacá, New Granada, and was returning to Venezuela. San Martín was preparing to sail to Peru. The rest of Spain's empire in South America would be independent within five years. Yet New Spain, as in 1808, remained the most important realm in the Indies, the home of the most native sons and a strong group of peninsulars. Insurgents and counterinsurgents alike were worn down by a decade of struggle, but viceregal rule remained in place.

When unofficial word started to reach American regions with loyalist governments in April 1820, popular pressure forced officials to swear allegiance to the Constitution. In the same month, a Provisional Junta, composed of liberals advising Ferdinand until the Cortes could meet, notified the remaining royal executives in the Americas that constitutional rule had been restored in the Spanish Nation. Thus, they were to reestablish provincial deputations and constitutional city councils and schedule new elections to choose deputies for the Cortes. As in the earlier Cortes of Cádiz, substitutes chosen from among Americans in Spain would serve until the proprietary deputies arrived. Also as before, the authorization of only 30 substitutes to represent them prompted native son protests.

New Spain and the Kingdom of Guatemala were among the few administrative units that had participated in all elections during Ferdinand's confinement. In 1820, officials quickly restored their constitutional municipal governments and eight provincial deputations. In New Spain, elections were held in fall 1820 for representatives on its provincial deputations, and deputies for the Cortes scheduled to meet in 1821–1822. In December, a new set of elections occurred for municipal officials and representatives to the 1822–1823 Cortes. With neither literacy nor property qualifications, participation by adult males was widespread.

When the Cortes opened in Madrid in the summer of 1820, the substitute American deputies quickly turned to the issue of unequal representation, but without success. Elected proprietary deputies, a majority from New Spain, participated in the session from February to June, but again failed to gain an expansion of their number. Even before the proprietary New Spain deputies arrived, however, the substitutes had crafted a plan for American autonomy within the framework of constitutional government. In May 1821, the expanded native son representatives secured an increase in the number of provincial deputations, obtaining one for every intendancy. With expectations rising, a high-level group of officials agreed to present a proposal to the Cortes for the creation of three regencies in the Indies. If adopted, it would provide the self-rule that native sons still sought.

American lobbying against "brutal anti-American" and "anticonstitutional" officials produced the appointment in January 1821 of liberal General Juan O'Donojú, a Mason sympathetic to the autonomists' objectives, as New Spain's captain-general and superior political chief (the office of "viceroy" had again disappeared with the return to constitutional government). He sailed to Vera Cruz intending to strengthen the constitutional system in New Spain and expecting he would be asked to implement the regency for New Spain and Guatemala that was under discussion. After O'Donojú's departure, however, Ferdinand rejected the plan for regencies as an effort to "drive him to the guillotine."[12] News of a rebellion in favor of independence in New Spain ended any chance of autonomy within the Spanish Nation. Antagonism between peninsular and native son deputies in the Cortes reached new heights and, with no satisfactory concessions in sight, the American deputies began to depart for their homelands. Spain's empire in mainland North America was history.

The Plan of Iguala

The denouement in New Spain unfolded in 1821 as a logical consequence of experience with constitutional government and the autonomists' discussion of a regency for New Spain and Guatemala. Native son colonel Agustín de Iturbide, once a scourge of the insurgents but more recently unemployed and out of favor as a result of charges of corruption and abuse of authority, joined other guests in the fashionable Mexico City salon of prominent elite native daughter María Ignacia Rodríguez de Velasco, also known as Güera Rodríguez. There he, the host, and others discussed political affairs and possibilities for autonomy. Returned to a command in November 1820 by former viceroy and constitutional Superior Political Chief and Captain General Juan Ruiz de Apodaca, Iturbide proved unable to defeat the insurgents and thereby resuscitate his career and fortune. Adopting Güera Rodríguez's ideas for attracting peninsulars and native sons of varied political leanings and occupations, Iturbide sounded out and courted suggestions from clerics and military officers among others. On February 24, 1821, he issued the resulting Plan of Iguala.[13]

The Plan offered a compromise to achieve complete independence based on representative constitutional monarchy (as in the earlier proposal for a regency) and potentially an agreement with Spain. Significantly, the Plan protected the Church, the military, and the peninsulars. All officeholders supporting independence would continue at their posts regardless of birthplace; those who opposed it were to leave "the empire" with their families. Unlike the Constitution of 1812, the Plan granted citizenship to all inhabitants, abolishing the category of *castas*. An Army of the Three Guarantees formed of officers and troops of the old royalist army as well as "old partisans of independence" would insure the conservation of the Church, political independence, and the "intimate union of Americans and Europeans." The emperor would be Ferdinand VII, but if he failed to arrive in Mexico within the time prescribed, the throne would be offered to his brothers in turn, the Archduke Charles (grandson of Charles III), or another candidate if necessary.

Ruiz de Apodaca and other high-ranking officials, clerics, and officers initially declined to support the Plan, but Vicente Guerrero, the most prominent insurgent leader, gave it his backing on March 9. By the time O'Donojú reached Vera Cruz in late July, the Plan had numerous adherents, although a military coup in Mexico City temporarily kept the capital under loyalist control. On August 24, the peninsular superior political chief and Iturbide signed the Treaty of Córdoba which, like the Plan of Iguala it was based on, resembled very closely the proposal for regencies in the Cortes that O'Donojú incorrectly anticipated would gain approval. The two leaders soon agreed on a transitional government. By the time they reached Mexico City, the leader of the coup had backed down and the capital supported the Plan. On September 28, 1821, the provisional governing junta signed the Declaration of Independence and selected a five-member Council of Regency composed of Iturbide, O'Donojú, another native son, a *radicado* peninsular, and a *radicado* creole from Venezuela. The Constitution of 1812, written by peninsular and native son deputies, became a basis for legal precedents and, with modification in 1824 for a republican and federal state in which all free inhabitants were citizens, the template for Mexico's Constitution of 1824.

The Plan of Iguala's specific protection of Europeans who supported Mexican independence and the inclusion of peninsulars on both the Council of Regency and the provisional governing junta reflected Iturbide and his initial collaborators' vision of creating a stable government. Following his brief rule as emperor of Mexico, however, the anti-peninsular sentiment that had persisted among insurgents and some autonomists throughout the 1810s moved to the fore. Most republicans were anti-European although at first monarchists were not.

Spain's rejection of the Treaty of Córdoba left peninsulars unprotected. Divided by the Constitution of 1812 into liberals and conservatives (*serviles*), affluent Europeans found themselves subjected to forced loans in a difficult economy that highlighted their continued presence as merchants. The fall of Iturbide in March 1823 meant the end of the Third Guarantee of the Plan of Iguala – peninsulars' legal protection also incorporated in the Treaty of Córdoba. When a constituent congress adopted the Constitution of 1824, the document eliminated Europeans' security by omitting reference to the validity of either the Treaty or the preceding Plan. A revolt in 1825, although unsuccessful, showed popular support for removing the Spaniards from all military, ecclesiastical, and civil posts; small wonder that between 1821 and 1827, European emigration totaled perhaps 3000–4000, a number that included prosperous merchants as well as 6 peninsular ministers of the *Audiencia* of Mexico.

In May 1827, Congress approved the replacement of all Europeans employed by the federal government in public, civil, military, and ecclesiastical positions – other than bishops – until Spain recognized Mexican independence. Some states also started to restrict and fire peninsular employees as well. An expulsion law adopted by the state of Jalisco in late August 1827 provided a model other states followed. In December, Congress adopted an expulsion law that allowed a few exceptions, for example, for old age and demonstrated service in the cause of Mexican independence. Nearly 2000 Europeans were expelled; exceptions totaled over 4500, but many of them would face expulsion later as a result of subsequent legislation into the mid-1830s.

Independence in Brazil

The French invasion of Portugal provoked a very different response than it did in Spain. With the enemy nearing Lisbon, Prince Regent John, his wife, and the queen sailed with some 10 000 courtiers, bureaucrats, and their families to Brazil. As John recreated the institutions of state in Rio de Janeiro, it became immediately clear that Brazilians held no offices in them. To the annoyance of native sons (*brasileiros* or *americanos*), Portuguese immigrants (*reinois*) were the recipients of posts and other favors. Although Brazil was elevated to a kingdom ostensibly equal to Portugal in 1815 and served as the center of the empire, John returned to Portugal in 1821 to make Lisbon the capital once more. He left his son Pedro behind as Prince Regent. When the Cortes ordered Pedro to Portugal, he refused and in December 1822 was crowned a constitutional emperor of an independent Brazil. In this way the former colony achieved independence without the lengthy wars that wracked Spanish realms in America. As occurred with peninsulars in Spanish America, *reinois* had to choose between loyalty to Brazil or Portugal. Ten days after his coronation, Pedro I ordered the sequestration of their property.

The alternatives of self-rule within the empire or independence outside of it became possible only as a result of a complex and interrelated chain of events that fostered a political revolution: the French invasion of Spain; the abdications of Charles IV and Ferdinand VII, the formation of juntas in Spain, and confident belief among autonomists in the Indies that American realms had the right to do the same; the Junta Central's declaration of American equality and call for elected deputies from the Indies to join it; the preparation of grievances for the deputies, the call for election of deputies to the Cortes, and a second preparation of grievances; the refusal of a majority in the Cortes to grant equality of representation based on total population to America; and the return of Ferdinand VII to the throne, his refusal to compromise, and his decision to employ force against all who refused to accept his effort to return to pre-1808 institutions and form of rule.

But the genie was out of the bottle. The rhetoric of Spanish liberalism voiced at the Cortes at Cádiz, the experience of elections with broad male suffrage, the politicization that resulted from compiling lists of grievances, and, especially in peripheral regions that had emerged on the basis of exportable crops in the eighteenth century, the desire for free trade made self-rule attractive to those who chose to blame "300 years of Spanish domination" for their *patrias*' problems.

Between 1808 and 1826, all of mainland Latin America gained independence. By the latter date, republics had replaced monarchy everywhere but Brazil. The freedom to trade without restrictions imposed from Europe was generally in place, although the importance of its taxation would increase substantially. Black slavery remained and, despite constitutional definitions that described all free inhabitants as citizens (using *ciudadanos* rather than the older term of *vecinos*), informal social hierarchies based on "quality" rather than purity of ancestry produced stratification in which skin color continued to wield great influence.

Independence and its aftermath virtually eliminated the 30 000–40 000 peninsulars present in mainland Spanish America in 1808. No explicit agenda in that year proposed the death and voluntary or forced exile of Europeans that followed. For more than three centuries, young peninsular males had sought better lives in the Indies than they could expect in Spain. Enough of them, especially those engaged in wholesale trade, labored sufficiently hard to create a stereotype of peninsulars' behavior noted by travelers and native sons and daughters alike. The Europeans, of course, formed their own stereotypical view of native sons as lazy, spendthrift whiners. Many, indeed probably most, peninsulars who worked their way to financial success married native daughters. As the Crown knew well, the mutual advantages of pooling business, social, and political ties often proved irresistible, turning outsiders into *radicados* and integrating them into a local elite.

Exiles from mainland America selected Cuba and Puerto Rico as favorite havens. Others journeyed to Spain and a few went to France. Foreigners would replace peninsular merchants, but only rarely did outsiders replace the new countries' locally born creoles in office. For good or ill, native sons at last formally dominated their *patrias*.

Glossary

Acordada A special criminal tribunal and rural law enforcement agency in eighteenth-century New Spain.

Adelantado Frontier governor. Title sometimes given to the leader of an expedition of conquest.

Advenedizos Newcomers. A term applied to recently arrived peninsular Spaniards.

Aguardiente Distilled spirits, often from sugar cane.

Alcabala A sales tax.

Alcalde del crimen A judge of the criminal chamber in the *audiencias* of Mexico and Lima.

Alcalde mayor A magistrate or official of a district or province known as an *alcaldía mayor*.

Alcalde, alcalde ordinario A local magistrate and member of a municipal council that elected him to office.

Alcaldía mayor The jurisdiction of an *alcalde mayor*; term generally used in the Viceroyalty of New Spain.

Alguacil Sheriff or constable.

Americano Español Spaniard born in America; a creole.

Americanos Term applied to indigenous population, but later used for and by creoles. Also Portuguese born in Brazil.

Archdeacon The second highest dignitary in a cathedral chapter.

Audiencia Territorial jurisdiction of a regional court and advisory body to its chief executive; also the name of this high court and advisory body.

Spaniards in the Colonial Empire: Creoles vs. Peninsulars?, First Edition. Mark A. Burkholder.

Beneficio Clerical benefice or income.

Beneméritos Descendants of conquistadors and early settlers. Creoles and often native sons.

Bozal Imported slave from Africa.

Brasileiros Portuguese born in Brazil

Caballero Knight of a military or civil order; term applied to well-to-do hidalgos, particularly in major municipalities.

Calidad Quality. Used to indicate a position in what was nominally a racial hierarchy on the basis of appearance, occupation, economic status, and family connections, rather than documentable ancestry. Thus, a person could be identified as a "creole" because of "*calidad*" when lacking undiluted Spanish ancestry.

***Cámara* of the Council of the Indies** Small upper chamber of the Council of the Indies whose duties included recommending candidates for usually high-ranking positions in Church and royal administration to the monarch.

Casta A person in the Indies of mixed racial background whose ancestry included one or more African or was suspected of such ancestry because of illegitimate birth.

Castile The crown of Castile, composed of different kingdoms and provinces.

Catedrático Holder of an academic chair or professorship.

Cathedral chapter *Cabildo eclesiástico.* A body composed of five dignitaries (dean, archdeacon, *chantre*, *maestrescuela*, and treasurer) and other prebendaries who administered the sacraments within the cathedral, oversaw the collection of the tithe and other fiscal duties, and governed the diocese in the absence of the chapter.

Chantre Choirmaster of a cathedral. One of five dignitaries in the cathedral chapter (q.v.).

Chapetón Term applied, particularly in Peru, to a newly arrived peninsular.

City of Kings Lima, Peru

Ciudadano Citizen, *vecino*.

Cochineal A red dye made from an insect of the same name.

Colegial Student enrolled in a *colegio* (q.v.).

Colegio College. A secondary school.

Colegio mayor A residential college for postbaccalaureate students.

Conde/sa Count, countess.

Consulado Merchant guild.

Contador, contador general Accountant or auditor in an official agency.

Conversos "New Christians"; applied to converted Jews and Muslims.

Corregidor/corregidor de indios A magistrate and chief administrative officer for a district or province known as a *corregimiento* (q.v.)

Corregimiento Administrative province or district; analogous to an *alcaldía mayor*.

Council of the Indies Supreme administrative and judicial body in Spain for affairs in and concerning the Indies.

Criolla/o Creole; person of Spanish ancestry who is born in the Americas. Also applied to descendant of Africans who is born in the Americas.

Dean Dean. The highest-ranking dignitary in a cathedral chapter (q.v.).

Dignidades Dignitaries. The five highest-ranking members of a cathedral chapter (q.v.).

Diocesan clergy See secular clergy.

Doctrina An Indian parish.

Domiciliarios Peninsulars who entered the priesthood in the Indies.

Don/doña Lord/Lady; a little-used title during the conquest, but increasingly employed by subsequent generations.

Encomendero Holder of an *encomienda* (q.v.).

Encomienda A grant of authority over a group of indigenous. It carried the obligation to Christianize and protect them in exchange for labor services and/or tribute.

Escribano Notary, scribe.

Español A Spaniard (q.v.) born in the Old World or the New.

Español americano American Spaniard; synonym for creole.

Español europeo European Spaniard; synonym for peninsular.

Español indiano Spaniard of the Indies; used as a synonym for creole.

Europeo European; Spaniard born in Spain. Synonym for peninsular.

Europeus European; Portuguese born in Portugal.

Extranjero Foreigner.

Fijo Fixed battalions. Applied to permanently stationed military units.

Fiscal Crown attorney on an audiencia or council.

Forastero A foreigner or outsider; person residing in a community other than that of birth without establishing citizenship.

Fuero Special judicial privileges enjoyed by a particular group, for example, ecclesiastical *fuero* or military *fuero*.

Futura The right in order of seniority to enter the first available position in an office or tribunal, for example, treasury office or *audiencia.*

Gachupín Derogatory term for peninsular Spaniard; used primarily in New Spain.

Hacendado Owner of rural property known as an *hacienda*; frequently a large estate devoted to livestock raising or agricultural activities.

Hidalgo An untitled noble; the lowest rank of nobility.

Hidalguía Castilian aristocratic ideal of nobility.

Hijos de la tierra Sons of the land; creoles.

Hijos de provincia See *domiciliarios.*

Hijos patrimoniales Priests native to a bishopric.

Indiano Creole. Also a peninsular that returned to Spain with wealth from the Indies (q.v.).

Indies (*Indias*) Term Spain used for its realms in the Americas.

Junta A committee, board, council.

Lanzas A tax paid by titled nobles upon accession to the title; originally, in lieu of fighting men supplied to the crown.

Letrado University-trained lawyer or holder of a law degree.

Limeña/o Person born in Lima, Peru.

Limpieza de sangre "Purity of blood"; without Jewish or Muslim ancestry.

Madrileña/o Person born in Madrid, Spain.

Maestrescuela The fourth of five dignitaries in a cathedral chapter. He had responsibilities as schoolmaster, teacher, and chancellor in a university.

Marqués/a Marquis; marquise or marchioness.

Mayorazgo Entail.

Media anata A tax collected from certain government officials equal to a half-year salary.

Merced Royal gift or grant, for example, of an office or income, to an individual.

Mestizo Offspring of a union between a Spaniard and an Indian.

Montañes Person from "the Mountains" of Burgos or Santander.

Mulatto/oes Offspring of a Spaniard and a person of African ancestry.

Native son, native daughter Male or female creole living in or aspiring to return to his or her region of birth, for example, a Peruvian creole in Peru.

Natural de Native of; born in [a location].

Obrajes Textile manufactories.

Oficios mecánicos Manual arts or trades.

Oidor Judge on an *audiencia*; a civil judge on the *audiencias* of Lima and Mexico.

Oposiciones Formal competition for certain positions in the secular clergy.

Paisano Compatriot.

Pardo Person with some, but not all, African ancestry; often interchangeable with mulatto.

Patria/Patria chica Homeland, country, nation/more specific homeland or place of birth, for example, village, town, city.

Patronato Real Royal Patronage. The Crown's authority over the Church.

Pecho Direct taxation in Spain paid only by commoners.

Peninsular Spaniard born in Spain; used for Spaniards in the Indies starting in the early nineteenth century.

Peso A coin and monetary unit. Most commonly a silver coin of 8 silver *reales* or 272 *maravadises.*

Plazas togadas Positions primarily in audiencias and councils filled by magistrates authorized to wear the judicial robes (togas) of office.

Pobladores Settlers.

Prebendary Cleric with a benefice in a cathedral chapter.

Pretendiente Person seeking office.

Procurador/Procurador general Representative of a municipality or other body with the special charge to defend or advance local rights and interests before royal courts and councils.

Pulque Alcoholic beverage made from the sap of the *maguey* or agave.

Radicado Person rooted in a community other than the one of birth, usually through marital and economic ties.

Regidor Alderman of a municipal council.

Regnícola Native of a realm.

Regulars or regular clergy Members of religious orders, for example, Franciscans.

Reinois Portuguese born in Portugal.

Relator Court reporter who summarized the arguments of opposing sides.

Repartimiento The allocation of an indigenous chieftain and his people to a Spaniard to provide labor; a forced labor draft. Also a cash advance to natives by a Spanish official.

Repartimiento de mercancías Also *repartimiento de bienes*. Forced sale of merchandise to indigenous by Spanish officials.

Secular clergy Diocesan clergy. Clerics in the Church's hierarchy from parish priest to archbishop.

Señor/a Sir or mister/madam or mistress.

Señorío Seigneurial jurisdiction.

Sevillana/o Person born in Seville, Spain.

Spaniard A person of Spanish ancestry born in the Old World or the New; both peninsulars and creoles were Spaniards, although term is often used to identify peninsulars only when in opposition to creoles.

Supernumerary Position and person filling it beyond the authorized number of "regular" positions in a tribunal or agency.

Suplente Substitute.

Teniente Lieutenant, assistant.

Vecino Citizen of a municipality with all of its rights and responsibilities.

Visita An official inspection into the conduct of government officials, usually unscheduled.

Visitador One who conducts a *visita*.

Visitador-general One who conducts an inspection with a broad range of responsibilities and considerable authority.

Zambo Offspring of an indigenous and a black (referred to as mulatto in New Spain).

Notes

Preface

1 This use of *vecino* as citizen diverges from current usage (*ciudadano*) that attaches the term to a national state, but contemporaries fully appreciated the difference between a municipality's citizens and its temporary and even other permanent residents.

Chapter 1: Spain and Its Early Empire in America

1 Angus MacKay, *Spain in the Middle Ages: From Frontier to Empire, 1000–1500* (Macmillan, 1977), 39.
2 J. H. Elliott, "The Spanish Conquest and Settlement of America," in Leslie Bethell, ed., *The Cambridge History of Latin America,* vol. I: *Colonial Latin America* (Cambridge, UK: Cambridge University Press, 1984), 149.
3 Bernal Díaz del Castillo quoted in J. H. Parry, *The Age of Reconnaissance: Discovery, Exploration and Settlement, 1450–1650* (Cleveland, OH: The World Publishing Company, 1963), 19.
4 Alonso de Aguilar quoted in Peggy K. Liss, *Mexico under Spain 1521–1556: Society and the Origins of Nationality* (University of Chicago Press, 1975), 95.
5 Luis Martín, *Daughters of the Conquistadores: Women of the Viceroyalty of Peru* (Albuquerque, NM: University of New Mexico Press, 1983), 14–15.
6 Articles 37, 46, and 47 of the New Laws. Lesley Byrd Simpson, *The Encomienda in New Spain: The Beginning of Spanish Mexico* (Berkeley and Los Angeles, CA: University of California Press, 1966), 131.
7 Bernal Díaz del Castillo, *The Discovery and Conquest of Mexico 1517–1521,* trans. A. P. Maudslay (New York: Ferrar, Straus and Cudahy, 1956), 313, 317.

Spaniards in the Colonial Empire: Creoles vs. Peninsulars?, First Edition. Mark A. Burkholder.

The author did admit that some of the original men with Cortés had also taken some gold and that he had taken "some small boxes" and four precious stones.

Chapter 2: Native Sons and Daughters in the Church

1 Francisco Morales, O. F. M., *Ethnic and Social Background of the Franciscan Friars in Seventeenth Century Mexico* (Washington, DC: Academy of American Franciscan History, 1973), 16.
2 Ibid., 56.
3 Antonio de Remesal quoted in Adriaan C. van Oss, *Catholic Colonialism: A Parish History of Guatemala 1524–1821* (Cambridge University Press, 1986), 158.
4 Ángel Martínez Cuesta, "Las monjas en la América colonial 1530–1824," *Thesaurus* 50, nos. 1–3 (1995): 581.
5 W. Eugene Shiels, S. J., *King and Church: The Rise and Fall of the Patronato Real* (Chicago, IL: Loyola University Press, 1961), 123–124.
6 Kenneth J. Andrien, *Crisis and Decline: The Viceroyalty of Peru in the Seventeenth Century* (Albuquerque, NM: University of New Mexico Press, 1985), 105.
7 José Antonio Mazzotti, "El Dorado, Paradise, and Supreme Sanctity in Seventeenth-Century Peru: A Creole Agenda," in Ralph Bauer and José Antonio Mazzotti, eds, *Creole Subjects in the Colonial Americas: Empires, Texts, Identities* (Chapel Hill, NC: University of North Carolina Press, 2009), 390–391.

Chapter 3: Native Sons in Office

1 J. H. Elliott, *Empires of the Atlantic World: Britain and Spain in America, 1492–1830* (New Haven, CT: Yale University Press, 2006), 120.
2 J. I. Israel, *Race, Class and Politics in Colonial Mexico 1610–1670* (Oxford, UK: Oxford University Press, 1975), 82.
3 Alejandro Cañeque, *The King's Living Image: The Culture and Politics of Viceregal Power in Colonial Mexico* (New York: Routledge, 2004), 166.
4 *Recopilación de leyes de los reynos de las Indias,* law xiiii, title II, book III (Madrid, 1681; reprint 1973), 4.
5 John H. Parry and Robert G. Keith, eds., *New Iberian World: A Documentary History of the Discovery and Settlement of Latin America to the Early 17th Century,* vol. I: *The Conquerors and the Conquered* (New York: Times Books), 354.
6 Ibid., 357.

7 D. A. Brading, *The First America: The Spanish Monarchy, Creole Patriots, and the Liberal State 1492–1867* (Cambridge, UK: Cambridge University Press, 1991), 294.
8 Anthony Pagden, "Identity Formation in Spanish America," in Nicholas Canny and Anthony Pagden, eds, *Colonial Identity in the Atlantic World, 1500–1800* (Princeton, NJ: Princeton University Press, 1987), 61.
9 Alonso de Solórzano y Velasco, *Discurso legal e información en derecho en favor de los nacidos en los Reynos del Perú, y conveniencias para que en él sin el óbice de aver nacido allí, puedan obtener Plazas de Oydor y demás que les están prohibidos* (Sevilla, 1652).
10 Title page of Pedro de Bolívar y de la Redonda, *Memorial informe y discurso legal, histórico y politico . . .* (Madrid, 1667).

Chapter 4: The Heyday of Native Sons and Daughters, circa 1630–1750

1 Jorge Juan and Antonio de Ulloa, *Discourse and Political Reflections on the Kingdoms of Peru*, ed. John J. TePaske, trans. John J. TePaske and Besse A. Clement (Norman, OK: University of Oklahoma Press, 1978), 224.
2 L. P. Wright, "The Military Orders in Sixteenth and Seventeenth Century Spanish Society. The Institutional Embodiment of a Historical Tradition," *Past and Present* 43 (May 1969): 55.
3 Charles F. *Walker, Shaky Colonialism: The 1746 Earthquake-Tsunami in Lima, Peru, and its Long Aftermath* (Durham, NC: Duke University Press, 2008), 143.
4 Rebecca Earle, " "Two Pairs of Pink Satin Shoes!!" Race, Clothing, and Identity in America (17th–19th Centuries)," *History Workshop Journal* 52 (Autumn, 2001): 188.
5 Juan Antonio de Ahumada, *Representación politico-legal* (reprint, Mexico City: 1820).

Chapter 5: Reforms, Commentaries, and Officials, 1750–1808

1 John J. TePaske, *A New World of Gold and Silver*, ed. Kendall W. Brown (Boston: Brill, 2010), 112.
2 Patricia Seed, "Social Dimensions of Race: Mexico City, 1753," *Hispanic American Historical Review* 62, no. 4 (November, 1982): 576
3 Antonello Gerbi, *The Dispute of the New World: The History of a Polemic, 1750–1900*, revised and enlarged edition translated by Jeremy Moyle (Pittsburgh, PA: University of Pittsburgh Press, 1973), 6.
4 Ibid., 54, 58.

5 John D. Browning, "Cornelius de Pauw and Exiled Jesuits: The Development of Nationalism in Spanish America," *Eighteenth-Century Studies* 11, no. 3 (Spring, 1978): 293.

6 Benjamin Keen, *The Aztec Image in Western Thought* (New Brunswick, NJ: Rutgers University Press, 1971), 261.

7 William Guthrie, edited and enlarged by James Ferguson, *A New Geographical, Historical, and Commercial Grammar and Present State of the Several Kingdoms of the World* (Dublin, Ireland: James Williams and John Exshaw, 1780), 704, 711.

8 Gerbi, *Dispute*, 160; William Robertson, *The History of America*, third edition, vol. III (London, UK: W. Strahan, T. Cadell, J. Balfour, 1780), 318–319.

9 Jorge Cañizares-Esguerra, *How to Write the History of the New World: Histories, Epistemologies, and Identities in the Eighteenth-Century Atlantic World* (Stanford University Press, 2001), 181.

10 Gerbi, *Dispute*, 298.

11 Irving A. Leonard, ed., *Colonial Travelers in Latin America* (New York: Alfred A. Knopf, 1972), 163–164.

12 Jorge Juan and Antonio de Ulloa, *Discourse and Political Reflections on the Kingdoms of Peru*, ed. John J. TePaske, trans. by John J. TePaske and Besse A. Clement (Norman, OK: University of Oklahoma Press, 1978), Chapter VII for what follows.

13 Alexander von Humboldt, *Political Essay on the Kingdom of New Spain*, ed. Mary Maples Dunn, trans. John Black (New York: Alfred A. Knopf, 1972), 71–72.

14 Anthony McFarlane, "The Rebellion of the *Barrios*: Urban Insurrection in Bourbon Quito," in John R. Fisher, Allan J. Kuethe, and Anthony McFarlane, eds, *Reform and Insurrection in Bourbon New Granada and Peru* (Baton Rouge, LA: Louisiana State University Press, 1990), 202.

15 C. E. Castañeda, "The Corregidor in Spanish Colonial Administration," *Hispanic American Historical Review* 9, no. 4 (November, 1929): 447.

16 J. R. Fisher, *Government and Society in Colonial Peru: The Intendant System 1784–1814* (London, UK: The Athlone Press, 1970), 87.

17 John Lynch, *Spanish Colonial Administration, 1782–1810: The Intendant System in the Viceroyalty of the Río de la Plata* (New York: Greenwood Press, 1969; reprint of 1958 edition by Athlone Press), 79.

Chapter 6: The Church, Complaints, and Social Change, 1750–1808

1 Margaret Chowning, *Rebellious Nuns: The Troubled History of a Mexican Convent, 1752–1863* (New York: Oxford University Press, 2006), 91.

2 The "Representation" is available in Juan E. Hernández y Dávalos, *Colección de documentos para la historia de la Guerra de independencia de México*, ed. Virginia Guedea and Alfredo Ávila (Mexico: Universidad Nacional Autónoma de México, 2007), Document 195. http://es.scribd.com/librosmex/d/65594778-HYDI195 (accessed February 1, 2012).
3 Jaime Eyzaguirre, *Ideario y ruta de la emancipación chilena* (Santiago, Chile: Editorial Universitario, 1957), 53.
4 Richard Konetzke, ed., *Colección de documentos para la historia de la formación social de Hispanoamérica 1493–1810, vol. III, primer tomo (1691–1779)* (Madrid, Spain: Consejo Superior de Investigaciones Científicos, 1962), 405–406.
5 Ibid., 434–435.
6 John Leddy Phelan, *The People and the King: The Comunero Revolution in Colombia, 1781* (Madison, WI: University of Wisconsin Press, 1978), 72–73.
7 Ibid., 72–73.
8 Ibid., 179–180.
9 John Preston Moore, *The Cabildo in Peru under the Bourbons: A Study in the Decline and Resurgence of Local Government in the Audiencia of Lima 1700–1824* (Durham, NC: Duke University Press, 1966), 181.
10 R. Douglas Cope, *The Limits of Racial Domination: Plebeian Society in Colonial Mexico City, 1660–1720* (Madison, WI: University of Wisconsin Press, 1994), 68.

Chapter 7: From Abdications to Independence

1 Royal Decree by the Junta Central, January 22, 1809.
2 *Gaceta de Buenos Aires* of September 25, 1810. Quoted in John Lynch, *San Martín: Argentine Soldier, American Hero* (New Haven, CT: Yale University Press, 2009), 31.
3 Jaime E. Rodríguez O., *The Independence of Spanish America* (New York: Cambridge University Press, 1998), 85.
4 *Interesting Official Documents Relating to the United Provinces of Venezuela* (London, UK: Longman and Co., 1812), 5.
5 Simon Collier, *Ideas and Politics of Chilean Independence 1808–1833* (Cambridge University Press, 1967), 192, 194–195.
6 William Walton, *An Exposé of the Dissentions of Spanish America* (London, 1814), 47–48.
7 Rodríguez O., *Independence*, 97.
8 David Bushnell, ed., *El Libertador: Writings of Simón Bolívar*, trans. Frederick H. Fornoff (New York: Oxford University Press, 2003), 116.

9 Salvador de Madariaga, *Bolívar* (New York: Schocken Books, 1969), 219–220.

10 John Lynch, *San Martín: Argentine Soldier, American Hero* (New Haven, CT: Yale University Press, 2009), 140.

11 Timothy E. Anna, *The Fall of Royal Government in Peru* (Lincoln, NE: University of Nebraska Press, 1979), 184.

12 Rodríguez O., *Independence*, 201–202.

13 Gilbert M. Joseph and Timothy J. Henderson, eds, *The Mexico Reader: History, Culture, Politics* (Durham, NC: Duke University Press, 2002), 192–195.

Suggestions for Further Reading

The following titles in English are readily accessible and their bibliographies offer additional titles for investigating the topics introduced in this book. Among textbooks are: Mark A. Burkholder and Lyman L. Johnson, *Colonial Latin America* (8th ed., Oxford University Press, 2012); Jonathan C. Brown, *Latin America: A Social History of the Colonial Period* (2nd ed., Wadsworth Publishing, 2004); Peter Bakewell and Jacqueline Holler, *A History of Latin America to 1825* (3rd ed., Wiley-Blackwell, 2009); and Cheryl E. Martin and Mark Wasserman, *Latin America and Its People*, vol. I (3rd ed., Prentice Hall, 2011). Leslie Bethell, ed., *The Cambridge History of Latin America*, vols. 1–3 (Cambridge University Press, 1984–1985), provides a detailed examination by multiple authorities. An outstanding comparative history is J. H. Elliott, *Empires of the Atlantic World: Britain and Spain in America, 1492–1830* (Yale University Press, 2006). An even broader approach is Thomas Benjamin, *The Atlantic World: Europeans, Africans, Indians and Their Shared History, 1400–1900* (Cambridge University Press, 2009).

The best introduction to the emergence and development of "creole patriotism" is D. A. Brading's rich study, *The First America: The Spanish Monarchy, Creole Patriots, and the Liberal State 1492–1867* (Cambridge University Press, 1991). Anthony Pagden's thoughtful essay "Identity Formation in Spanish America," is one of several valuable contributions on colonial identity throughout the Americas in Nicholas Canny and Anthony Pagden, eds. *Colonial Identity in the Atlantic World, 1500–1800* (Princeton University Press, 1987). Ralph Bauer and José Antonio Mazzotti, *Creole Subjects in the Colonial Americas: Empires, Texts, Identities*

(The Omohundro Institute of Early American History and Culture and University of North Carolina Press, 2009) provide an erudite introduction to 17 essays by literary scholars of the Americas. Jorge Cañizares-Esguerra offers a fascinating intellectual history in *How to Write the History of the New World: Histories, Epistemologies, and Identities in the Eighteenth-Century Atlantic World* (Stanford University Press, 2001). J. I. Israel, *Race, Class and Politics in Colonial Mexico 1610–1670* (Oxford, UK: Oxford University Press, 1975) examines peninsulars and native sons in mid-seventeenth century Mexico. A useful monographic study is Marvyn Helen Bacigalupo, *A Changing Perspective: Attitudes Toward Creole Society in New Spain (1521–1610)* (London, UK: Tamesis Books Limited, 1981).

Repeatedly native sons developed and appropriated religious symbols unique to the Americas. Three works focused on Our Lady of Guadalupe are: Stafford Poole, C. M., *Our Lady of Guadalupe: The Origins and Sources of a Mexican National Symbol, 1531–1797* (Tucson, AZ: University of Arizona Press, 1995), D. A. Brading, *Mexican Phoenix Our Lady of Guadalupe: Image and Tradition Across Five Centuries* (Cambridge, UK: Cambridge University Press, 2001), and Jacques Lafaye, *Quetzalcóatl and Guadalupe: The Formation of Mexican National Consciousness 1531–1813*, trans. Benjamin Keen (Chicago, IL: University of Chicago Press, 1976).

Travelers' accounts provide first-hand observations on society and material culture. The following have been translated into English. J. Eric and S. Thompson, ed., *Thomas Gage's Travels in the New World* (Norman, OK: University of Oklahoma Press, 1958); Josephe and Francisco Mugaburu, *Chronicle of Colonial Lima: The Diary of Josephe and Francisco Mugaburu, 1640–1697*, trans. and ed. Robert Ryal Miller (Norman, OK: University of Oklahoma Press, 1975); Jorge Juan and Antonio de Ulloa, *Discourse and Political Reflections on the Kingdoms of Peru*. ed. John J. Tepaske, trans. John J. TePaske and Besse A. Clement (Norman, OK: University of Oklahoma Press, 1978); Jorge Juan and Antonio de Ulloa, *A Voyage to South America*, The John Adams Translation, abridged (New York: Alfred A. Knopf, 1964); Robert Ryal Miller and William J. Orr, eds., *Daily Life in Colonial Mexico: The Journey of Friar Ilarione da Bergamo, 1761–1768*, trans. William J. Orr (Norman, OK: University of Oklahoma Press, 2000); Alexander von Humboldt, *Political Essay on the Kingdom of New Spain*, The John Black Translation, abridged; ed. Mary Maples Dunn (New York: Alfred A. Knopf, 1972); Irving A. Leonard, ed., *Colonial Travelers in Latin America* (New York: Alfred

A. Knopf, 1972); and Concolorcorvo, *El Lazarillo: A Guide for Inexperienced Travelers between Buenos Aires and Lima, 1773*, trans. Walter D. Kline (Bloomington, IN: Indiana University Press, 1965). Ruth Hill, *Hierarchy, Commerce, and Fraud in Bourbon Spanish America: A Postal Inspector's Exposé* (Nashville, TN: Vanderbilt University Press, 2005) sheds fascinating insights into Concolorcorvo and his travels. On material culture in colonial Latin America, see Arnold J. Bauer, *Goods, Power, History: Latin America's Material Culture* (Cambridge, UK: Cambridge University Press, 2001).

The Spanish background to empire can be found in Angus MacKay, *Spain in the Middle Ages: From Frontier to Empire, 1000–1500* (London, UK: Macmillan Press, 1977); John Edwards, *The Spain of the Catholic Monarchs 1474–1520* (Oxford, UK: Blackwell Publishers, 2000); J. H. Elliott, *Imperial Spain 1469–1716* (New York: St. Martin's Press, 1964); John Lynch, *Spain 1516–1598: From Nation State to World Empire* (Oxford, UK: Basil Blackwell, 1991); Henry Kamen, *Spain 1469–1714: A Society of Conflict*, 3rd ed. (Harlow, UK: Pearson, Longman, 2005); and, most recently, William D. Phillips, Jr. and Carla Rahn Phillips, *A Concise History of Spain* (Cambridge, UK: Cambridge University Press, 2010). Two more focused studies are Helen Nader, *Liberty in Absolutist Spain: The Habsburg Sale of Towns, 1516–1700* (Baltimore, MD: The Johns Hopkins University Press, 1990) and Pablo E. Pérez-Mallaína, *Spain's Men of the Sea: Daily Life on the Indies Fleets in the Sixteenth Century*, trans. Carla Rahn Phillips (Baltimore, MD: The Johns Hopkins University Press, 1998). Ida Altman and James Horn, eds., *"To Make America": European Emigration in the Early Modern Period* (Berkeley and Los Angeles, CA: University of California Press, 1992); Ida Altman, *Emigrants and Society: Extremadura and Spanish America in the Sixteenth Century* (Berkeley and Los Angeles, CA: University of California Press, 1989); Ida Altman, *Transatlantic Ties in the Spanish Empire: Brihuega, Spain and Puebla, Mexico 1560–1620* (Stanford, CA: Stanford University Press, 2000); and Juan Javier Pescador, *The New World Inside a Basque Village: The Oiartzun Valley and Its Atlantic Emigrants, 1550–1800* (Reno and Las Vegas, NV: University of Nevada Press, 2004) provide an introduction to Spaniards emigrating to the Indies.

Information on conquistadors and *encomenderos* is available in James Lockhart, *The Men of Cajamarca: A Social and Biographical Study of the First Conquerors of Peru* (Austin, TX: Institute of Latin American Studies at the University of Texas, 1972); Robert Himmerich y Valencia, *The*

Encomenderos of New Spain, 1521–1555 (Austin, TX: University of Texas Press, 1991); José Ignacio Avellaneda, *The Conquerors of the New Kingdom of Granada* (Albuquerque, NM: University of New Mexico Press, 1995); and Hugh Thomas, *Who's Who of the Conquistadors* (London, UK: Cassell, 2000). On early colonial society in Peru and New Spain, see James Lockhart, *Spanish Peru, 1532–1560: A Colonial Society* (Madison, WI: University of Wisconsin Press, 1968) and Peggy K. Liss, *Mexico Under Spain 1521–1556: Society and the Origins of Nationality* (Chicago, IL: University of Chicago Press, 1975).

An excellent survey of women is Susan Migden Socolow, *The Women of Colonial Latin America* (New York: Cambridge University Press, 2000). Among the many contributions by Asunción Lavrin are her edited volume *Sexuality and Marriage in Colonial Latin America* (Lincoln, NE: University of Nebraska Press, 1989) and her remarkable *Brides of Christ: Conventual Life in Colonial Mexico* (Stanford, CA: Stanford University Press, 2008). See also Margaret Chowning, *Rebellious Nuns: The Troubled History of a Mexican Convent, 1752–1863* (New York: Oxford University Press, 2006); and Kathryn Burns, *Colonial Habits: Convents and Spiritual Economy of Cuzco, Peru* (Durham, NC: Duke University Press, 1999).

A helpful introduction to life in rural areas is Louisa Schell Hoberman and Susan Migden Socolow, eds., *The Countryside in Colonial Latin America* (Albuquerque, NM: University of New Mexico Press, 1996).

Additional material on land and labor can be found in Susan E. Ramírez, *Provincial Patriarchs: Land Tenure and the Economics of Power in Colonial Peru* (Albuquerque, NM: University of New Mexico Press, 1986); Noble David Cook with Alexandra Parma Cook, *People of the Volcano: Andean Counterpoint in the Colca Valley of Peru* (Durham, NC: Duke University Press, 2007); Cheryl English Martin, *Rural Society in Colonial Morelos* (Albuquerque, NM: University of New Mexico Press, 1985); Lesley Byrd Simpson, *The Encomienda in New Spain: The Beginning of Spanish Mexico* (Berkeley and Los Angeles, CA: University of California Press, 1966); and Herman W. Konrad, *A Jesuit Hacienda in Colonial Mexico: Santa Lucía, 1576–1767* (Stanford, CA: Stanford University Press, 1980).

Hoberman and Socolow have also edited a fine introduction to urban life, *Cities & Society in Colonial Latin America* (Albuquerque, NM: University of New Mexico Press, 1986). Additional material on urban conditions, society, and government is in Jay Kinsbruner, *The Colonial Spanish-American City: Urban Life in the Age of Atlantic Capitalism*

(Austin, TX: University of Texas Press, 2005); Peter Marzahl, *Town in the Empire: Government, Politics, and Society in Seventeenth-Century Popayán* (Austin, TX: Institute of Latin American Studies, University of Texas, 1978); and two older works, John Preston Moore, *The Cabildo in Peru under the Bourbons: A Study in the Decline and Resurgence of Local Government in the Audiencia of Lima 1700–1824* (Durham, NC: Duke University Press, 1966) and his earlier work, *The Cabildo in Peru Under the Hapsburgs: A Study in the Origins and Powers of the Town Council in the Viceroyalty of Peru, 1530–1700* (Durham, NC: Duke University Press, 1954).

Scholarship on the Church is extensive, but relatively few works in English offer detail on the social background of clerics. Helpful are the following: John Frederick Schwaller, *The Church and Clergy in Sixteenth-Century Mexico* (Albuquerque, NM: University of New Mexico Press, 1987); Adriaan C. van Oss, *Catholic Colonialism: A Parish History of Guatemala, 1524–1821* (Cambridge, UK: Cambridge University Press, 1986); Francisco Morales, O. F. M., *Ethnic and Social Background of the Franciscan Friars in Seventeenth Century Mexico* (Washington, DC: Academy of American Franciscan History, 1973); Antonine Tibesar, O. F. M., *Franciscan Beginnings in Colonial Peru* (Washington, DC: Academy of American Franciscan History, 1953); John J. Clune Jr., *Cuban Convents in the Age of Enlightened Reform, 1761–1807* (Gainesville, FL: University Press of Florida, 2008); and the very recent Karen Melvin, *Building Colonial Cities of God: Mendicant Orders and Urban Culture in New Spain* (Stanford, CA: Stanford University Press, 2012). Details about one prominent Jesuit school can be found in Luis Martín, *The Intellectual Conquest of Peru: The Jesuit College of San Pablo 1568–1767* (New York: Fordham University Press, 1968). Material on colonial saints is available in Allan Greer and Jodi Bilinkoff, eds., *Colonial Saints: Discovering the Holy in the Americas* (New York: Routledge, 2003) and Ronald J. Morgan, *Spanish American Saints and the Rhetoric of Identity 1600–1810* (Tucson, AZ: University of Arizona Press, 2002)

The following studies examine various offices and officeholders in the sixteenth and seventeenth centuries: Alejandro Cañeque, *The King's Living Image: The Culture and Politics of Viceregal Power in Colonial Mexico* (New York: Routledge, 2004); Ethelia Ruiz Medrano, *Reshaping New Spain: Government and Private Interests in the Colonial Bureaucracy, 1531–1550* (Boulder, CO: University Press of Colorado, 2006); John Leddy Phelan, *The Kingdom of Quito in the Seventeenth Century: Bureau-*

cratic Politics in the Spanish Empire (Madison, WI: University of Wisconsin Press, 1967); Kenneth J. Andrien, *Crisis and Decline: The Viceroyalty of Peru in the Seventeenth Century* (Albuquerque, NM: University of New Mexico Press, 1985); J. H. Parry, *The Sale of Public Office in the Spanish Indies Under the Hapsburgs* (Berkeley and Los Angeles, CA: University of California Press, 1953); and Louisa Schell Hoberman, *Mexico's Merchant Elite, 1590–1660: Silver, State, and Society* (Durham, NC: Duke University Press, 1991). Richard L. Kagan, *Students and Society in Early Modern Spain* (Baltimore, MD: The Johns Hopkins University Press, 1974) outlines the emergence and success of the post-baccalaureate residential *colegios mayores* in Spain in placing alumni in *letrado* positions.

Spain's circumstances in the late seventeenth and early eighteenth centuries are outlined in Henry Kamen, *Spain in the Later Seventeenth Century 1665–1700* (New York: Longman, 1980) and John Lynch, *Bourbon Spain 1700–1808* (Oxford, UK: Basil Blackwell, 1989). Native sons and other creoles in the *audiencias* are treated in Mark A. Burkholder and D. S. Chandler, *From Impotence to Authority: The Spanish Crown and the American Audiencias, 1687–1808* (Columbia, MO: University of Missouri Press, 1977) and Mark A. Burkholder and D. S. Chandler, *Biographical Dictionary of Audiencia Ministers in the Americas, 1687–1821* (Westport, CT: Greenwood Press, 1982). Patronage in early eighteenth-century Mexico is treated in Christoph Rosenmüller, *Patrons, Partisans, and Palace Intrigues: The Court Society of Colonial Mexico, 1702–1710* (Calgary, AB: University of Calgary Press, 2008). A detailed study for Quito is Tamar Herzog, *Upholding Justice: Society, State, and the Penal System in Quito (1650–1750)* (Ann Arbor, MI: University of Michigan Press, 2004). A unique perspective is available in Charles F. Walker, *Shaky Colonialism: The 1746 Earthquake-Tsunami in Lima, Peru, and its Long Aftermath* (Durham, NC: Duke University Press, 2006).

Numerous historians have worked on the second half of the eighteenth century. Valuable studies on New Spain include D. A. Brading, *Miners and Merchants in Bourbon Mexico 1763–1810* (Cambridge, UK: Cambridge University Press, 1971); Christon I. Archer, *The Army in Bourbon Mexico, 1760–1810* (Albuquerque, NM: University of New Mexico Press, 1977); John E. Kicza, *Colonial Entrepreneurs: Families and Business in Bourbon Mexico City* (Albuquerque, NM: University of New Mexico Press, 1983); Doris M. Ladd, *The Mexico Nobility at Independence 1780–1826* (Austin, TX: Institute of Latin American Studies at the University of Texas, 1976); Stanley J. Stein and Barbara H. Stein, *Apogee of*

Empire: Spain and New Spain in the Age of Charles III, 1759–1789 (Baltimore, MD: The Johns Hopkins University Press, 2003); Barbara H. Stein and Stanley J. Stein, *Edge of Crisis: War and Trade in the Spanish Atlantic, 1789–1808* (Baltimore, MD: The Johns Hopkins University Press, 2009); Susan Deans-Smith, *Bureaucrats, Planters, and Workers: The Making of the Tobacco Monopoly in Bourbon Mexico* (Austin, TX: University of Texas Press, 1992); D. S. Chandler, *Social Assistance and Bureaucratic Politics: The Montepíos of Colonial Mexico, 1767–1821* (Albuquerque, NM: University of New Mexico Press, 1991); Linda Arnold, *Bureaucracy and Bureaucrats in Mexico City 1742–1835* (Tucson, AZ: University of Arizona Press, 1988); Linda A. Curcio-Nagy, *The Great Festivals of Colonial Mexico City: Performing Power and Identity* (Albuquerque, NM: University of New Mexico Press, 2004); Juan Pedro Viqueira Albán, *Propriety and Permissiveness in Bourbon Mexico*, trans. Sonya Lipsett-Rivera and Sergio Rivera Ayala (Wilmington, DE: Scholarly Resources, 1999); and Gabriel Haslip-Viera, *Crime and Punishment in Late Colonial Mexico City 1692–1810* (Albuquerque, NM: University of New Mexico Press, 1999).

Studies on other parts of the empire from roughly 1750 to 1808 include for Peru: John R. Fisher, *Bourbon Peru 1750–1824* (Liverpool, UK: Liverpool University Press, 2003); Kendall W. Brown, *Bourbons and Brandy: Imperial Reform in Eighteenth-Century Arequipa* (Albuquerque, NM: University of New Mexico Press, 1985); J. R. Fisher, *Government and Society in Colonial Peru: The Intendant System 1784–1814* (London, UK: The Athlone Press, 1970), and Mark A. Burkholder, *Politics of a Colonial Career: José Baquíjano and the Audiencia of Lima* (Albuquerque, NM: University of New Mexico Press, 1980). For the Río de la Plata, see John Lynch, *Spanish Colonial Administration, 1782–1810: The Intendant System in the Viceroyalty of the Río de la Plata* (London, UK: The Athlone Press, 1958, reprinted Greenwood Press, 1969); and Susan Migden Socolow, *The Bureaucrats of Buenos Aires, 1769–1810: Amor al Real Servicio* (Durham, NC: Duke University Press, 1987). For New Granada, see Allan J. Kuethe, *Military Reform and Society in New Granada, 1773–1808* (Gainesville, FL: The University Presses of Florida, 1978); Ann Twinam, *Miners, Merchants, and Farmers in Colonial Colombia* (Austin, TX: University of Texas Press, 1982); John Leddy Phelan, *The People and the King: The Comunero Revolution in Colombia, 1781* (Madison, WI: University of Wisconsin Press, 1978); John R. Fisher, Allan J. Kuethe, and Anthony McFarlane, eds., *Reform and Insurrection in Bourbon New Granada and Peru* (Baton Rouge,

LA: Louisiana State University Press, 1990); Anthony McFarlane, *Colombia before Independence: Economy, Society, and Politics under Bourbon Rule* (Cambridge, UK: Cambridge University Press, 1993); Victor M. Uribe-Uran, *Honorable Lives: Lawyers, Family, and Politics in Colombia, 1780–1850* (Pittsburgh, PA: University of Pittsburgh Press, 2000). Two useful works on Venezuela are Robert J. Ferry, *The Colonial Elite of Early Caracas: Formation & Crisis, 1567–1767* (Berkeley and Los Angeles, CA: University of California Press, 1989) and P. Michael McKinley, *Pre-Revolutionary Caracas: Politics, Economy, and Society 1777–1811* (Cambridge, UK: Cambridge University Press, 1985). Material on other regions can be found in Allan J. Kuethe, *Cuba, 1753–1815: Crown, Military, and Society* (Knoxville, TN: University of Tennessee Press, 1986); Jacques A. Barbier, *Reform and Politics in Bourbon Chile 1755–1796* (Ottawa, Canada: University of Ottawa Press, 1980); Kenneth J. Andrien, *The Kingdom of Quito, 1690–1830* (Cambridge, UK: Cambridge University Press, 1995); and Cynthia E. Milton, *The Many Meanings of Poverty: Colonialism, Social Compacts, and Assistance in Eighteenth-Century Ecuador* (Stanford, CA: Stanford University Press, 2007). A remarkable study that crosses numerous administrative boundaries is Ann Twinam, *Public Lives, Private Secrets: Gender, Honor, Sexuality, and Illegitimacy in Colonial Spanish America* (Stanford, CA: Stanford University Press, 1999).

The final years of Spanish rule on the American mainland are treated broadly in: Jaime E. Rodríguez O., *The Independence of Spanish America* (Cambridge, UK: Cambridge University Press, 1998); John Lynch, *The Spanish American Revolutions 1808–1826*, 2nd ed. (New York: W. W. Norton, 1986); Christon I. Archer, ed., *The Wars of Independence in Spanish America* (Wilmington, DE: Scholarly Resources, 2000); Jeremy Adelman, *Sovereignty and Revolution in the Iberian Atlantic* (Princeton, NJ: Princeton University Press, 2006); and Timothy E. Anna, *Spain & the Loss of America* (Lincoln, NE: University of Nebraska Press, 1983). More regional examinations include Timothy Hawkins, *José de Bustamante and Central American Independence* (Tuscaloosa, AL, 2004); Jordana Dym, *From Sovereign Villages to National States: City, State, and Federation in Central America, 1759–1839* (Albuquerque, NM: University of New Mexico Press, 2006); Patricia H. Marks, *Deconstructing Legitimacy: Viceroys, Merchants, and the Military in Late Colonial Peru* (University Park, PA: Pennsylvania State University Press, 2007); Timothy E. Anna, *The Fall of the Royal Government in Peru* (Lincoln, NE: University of Nebraska Press, 1979); Christon I. Archer, *The Birth of Modern Mexico 1780–1824*

(Wilmington, DE: Scholarly Resources, 2003); Eric Van Young, *The Other Rebellion: Popular Violence, Ideology, and the Mexican Struggle for Independence, 1810–1821* (Stanford, CA: Stanford University Press, 2002); Hugh M. Hamill, Jr. *The Hidalgo Revolt: Prelude to Mexican Independence* (Gainesville, FL: University of Florida Press, 1966); Lyman L. Johnson, *Workshop of Revolution: Plebeian Buenos Aires and the Atlantic World, 1776–1810* (Durham, NC: Duke University Press, 2011); Simon Collier, *Ideas and Politics of Chilean Independence 1808–1833* (Cambridge, UK: Cambridge University Press, 1967) and Rebecca A. Earle, *Spain and the Independence of Colombia 1810–1825* (Exeter, UK: University of Exeter Press, 2000). Three biographies are Karen Racine, *Francisco de Miranda: A Transatlantic Life in the Age of Revolution* (Wilmington, DE: Scholarly Resources, 2003); John Lynch, *Simón Bolívar: A Life* (New Haven, CT: Yale University Press, 2006); and John Lynch, *San Martín: Argentine Soldier, American Hero* (New Haven, CT: Yale University Press, 2009). Harold Dana Sims has examined the postindependence expulsion of peninsulars in *The Expulsion of Mexico's Spaniards 1821–1836* (Pittsburgh, PA: University of Pittsburgh Press, 1990).

Index

Spaniards in the Colonial Empire: Creoles vs. Peninsulars?, First Edition. Mark A. Burkholder.